Fogelson, Robert M.
Violence as protest

Violence as Protest

Violence as Protest
A STUDY OF RIOTS
AND GHETTOS

Robert M. Fogelson

1971
DOUBLEDAY & COMPANY, INC.
GARDEN CITY, NEW YORK

"Violence as Protest" reprinted with permission from *Urban Riots: Violence and Social Change*, Proceedings of the Academy of Political Science, Vol. 82 (July 1968), 25–41.

"From Resentment to Confrontation" reprinted with permission from the *Journal of Social Issues*, XXVI, No. 1 (May 1970).

"White on Black" reprinted with permission from the *Political Science Quarterly*, Vol. 83 (September 1967), 337–67.

FOR
David and Paulann Caplovitz
AND
Allan and Catherine Silver

Men who engage in dangerous and desperate behavior . . . have a certain claim to have taken seriously the meanings which they see in their own acts, and wish others to see in them.

ALLAN SILVER

Contents

Preface

Early in August 1966 I received a call from Martin Timin, a staff member of the President's Commission on Law Enforcement and Administration of Justice (otherwise known as the President's Crime Commission). Timin told me that Professor Lloyd Ohlin, a commission task force head then at the Columbia School of Social Work, was looking for someone to study the 1960s riots and that Professor Allan Silver of Columbia's Sociology Department had mentioned my name. Would I be interested, Timin asked? I answered that I might, provided that the commission and I could reach agreement on an approach to the subject. A few weeks later I met with Ohlin and Timin at the commission's office in Washington; and after arriving at an understanding we joined James Vorenberg, a Harvard Law School professor serving as Executive Director of the commission. Vorenberg was, to say the least, unenthusiastic: the project did not impress him, and neither, it seemed, did I; and I was about ready to abandon the whole thing. But Ohlin and Timin argued persuasively and eventually prevailed upon Vorenberg to permit, though not to finance, the study. Ohlin then convinced the New World Foundation and the Stern Family Fund to underwrite the costs; and by the end of August I started work.

During the next six weeks I gathered information about riots, read books and reports about ghettos, spoke with businessmen in New York's Harlem, rode in patrol cars around Chicago's West Side, and talked with teen-agers in south-central Los Angeles. I also discussed my ideas with Professor Nat Cohen of U.C.L.A., who was supervising a survey of the Los Angeles riots sponsored by the U. S. Office of

xi

Economic Opportunity, and scholars analyzing other riots. It was an illuminating, if exhausting, experience. In the meantime Timin and his associates collected official reports, arrest statistics, and other documents from Rochester, Dayton, and other cities that I did not have time to visit. They also provided access to files of the Attorney General's Office, the Vice-President's Commission on Youth Opportunities, and other government agencies which would not otherwise have been open to me. Under the intense pressure which is apparently normal for presidential commissions I spent another six weeks analyzing the material and writing the report. And late in November I submitted a first draft running slightly over a hundred pages entitled "The 1960s Riots: Interpretations and Recommendations."

Put briefly, the report argued that the riots, far from being meaningless outbursts by black riffraff, were articulate protests by ordinary blacks. Accordingly it focused on two distinct, but closely related, questions: what were the blacks protesting against? and why were they protesting violently? To answer the first question I examined the triggering incidents and subsequent violence, particularly the looting, arson, and assault, and then connected them to police malpractice, racial discrimination, economic deprivation, consumer exploitation, and involuntary residential segregation. To answer the second question I studied why the customary restraints on rioting were not very effective in the black ghettos and why the moderate black leaders were unable to confine their people's protest to nonviolent channels and to restrain the rioters once the riots were under way. Underlying my analysis was the assumption that, as Allan Silver has observed, "men who engage in dangerous and desperate behavior . . . have a certain claim to have taken seriously the meanings which they see in their acts, and wish others to see in them." The report then offered recommendations to alleviate the ghetto's grievances, strengthen the society's restraints, and thereby restore public order and enhance social justice in America.

A few weeks later I received word that Vorenberg strongly objected to the report. And though I never learned why, I heard several plausible reasons. Apparently he believed that the commission had little to gain (and much to lose) by speaking out on so controversial and complicated an issue, especially on the basis of one short study. A critical response might have undermined credibility in the commission's reports on law enforcement and criminal justice, which were its principal responsibilities. Apparently he also found the report too radical, and not only for himself, but also for the commissioners, who were, with exceptions, a rather conservative bunch. In all likelihood, California Attorney General Thomas C. Lynch and a few others subscribed to many of the notions about riots which were sharply criticized in the report. And apparently Vorenberg thought little of the report anyway. In the face of these objections, Timin made a valiant attempt to salvage the major points of the report by toning down my criticism of public officials and indictment of ghetto conditions. But to little avail. For though a few of these points were included in the commission's brief statement on the riots, the report itself was shelved.

This left me in a quandary. I was too deeply involved, intellectually and emotionally, in the study to accept this situation; but I was also quite aware that the report was too long for an article (and too rough for publication). David Caplovitz, then with Columbia's Bureau of Applied Social Research, and other friends and colleagues who liked the report encouraged me to develop it into a full-length book. But to do so meant not only to postpone (and, as it turned out, to drop) plans to write a book on Harlem, but also to petition the Social Science Research Council and the Columbia University Council on Research in the Social Sciences, which had given me grants to study Harlem, to allow me to analyze the riots instead. After a while I persuaded myself that I could learn as much, if not more, about the ghettos by analyzing the riots as by studying Harlem; and both councils, exhibiting commendable flexibility, approved the change. So late in the spring, a few months before the summer's riots erupted in Newark, Detroit, Milwaukee, and scores of other cities, I started working on this book. And along with teaching at Columbia and M.I.T. I have been at it since.

The book then is about the 1960s riots. In it I have analyzed not only the Los Angeles, Newark, and Detroit riots but also the hundreds of less severe riots which have broken out in the black ghettos over the past six years. By so doing I have doubtless overlooked subtle differences among the riots. But I am more impressed by their essential similarities; and I am satisfied that it is in the similarities, if anywhere, that the meaning of the riots is to be found. I have also concentrated on the conditions underlying the riots instead of on the tactics employed to suppress them, that is, the maneuvers of the police and the deployment of the National Guard. This subject is neither unimportant nor uninteresting. But, in view of my conviction that the riots were essentially a manifestation of the conditions of ghetto life and not of the irresponsibility of black riffraff or outside agitators, it is somewhat peripheral. Underlying this analysis is the assumption that the riots were protests, or, as I have described them at the beginning of the study, articulate protests against genuine grievances in the black ghettos. And from this assumption I have drawn the conclusion that only by examining what the rioters did and said is it possible to discover what they were protesting against and why they were protesting violently.

The book is about the black ghettos, too. In it I have identified the conditions common to south-central Los Angeles, Newark's Central Ward, Detroit's West Side, and the other ghettos which were manifested in the riots. In the process I have no doubt blurred many differences among the ghettos. But once again I am more impressed by their fundamental similarities; and I am convinced that the similarities explain why the riots have erupted in virtually every ghetto in the United States. Lest there be any misunderstanding, I have not presented a balanced portrait of the ghettos. I have ignored the residents as they raise their families, visit their relatives, enjoy their friends, and otherwise establish and maintain the personal and social ties which help them survive subordination and segregation. Rather I have focused on them as they are subjected to police malpractice, racial discrimination, economic deprivation, consumer exploitation, residential segregation, and the other indignities of ghetto life. In other words, I have attempted to illuminate the riots by analyzing the ghettos and to illuminate the ghettos by analyzing the riots; and what has been lost in balance has, I trust, been gained in relevance.

The book is also about white society. For as the National Advisory Commission on Civil Disorders—otherwise known, after its chairman Otto Kerner, former Governor of Illinois, as the Kerner Commission—observed in a memorable passage: "What white Americans have never fully understood—but what the Negro can never forget—is that white society is deeply implicated in the ghetto. White institutions created it, white institutions maintain it, and white society condones it." I have not presented a balanced portrait of white society either. I have focused on whites and white institutions at their worst: on patrolmen as they harass blacks not as they protect them, on employers as they turn away blacks not as they hire them, and on merchants as they exploit blacks not as they serve them. I have also focused on white landlords and realtors not as they house blacks but as they exclude them and on white politicians and bureaucrats not as they support moderate black leaders but as they undermine their influence. This is a distorted picture, but not a misleading one. Most whites and white institutions act at their worst in the ghetto, and thus it is at their worst that most blacks perceive them; and this combination of white actions and black perceptions ultimately accounts for the 1960s riots.

The book is not about public policy per se. I have not written a white paper; nor have I compiled long lists of recommendations, followed by longer scenarios of prospects and options. I have not noticed a shortage of lists and scenarios in recent years; nor have I gained much expertise in solving problems and drafting legislation. The book is not, however, without policy implications. Here and there I have mentioned where existing programs are irrelevant or detrimental and where drastic changes are imperative. Implicit in this analysis is the conviction that American society has so far failed to redress the ghetto's grievances mainly for political reasons. I have also criticized the classic conservative statement on the riots, the report of the Governor's Commission on the Los Angeles Riots (otherwise known, after its chairman John A. McCone, former head of the C.I.A., as the McCone Commission). This critique, which reflects many of my early ideas about riots and ghettos, was first published in 1967 and is here reprinted, with minor revisions, as an appendix. I have also analyzed the classic liberal statement on the riots, the Kerner Commission Report. And this analysis suggests that the racial problem cannot be resolved without radical changes in the institutions which administer everyday life in the black ghettos.

I have tried to be reasonably objective, but it has not been easy. The riots are events which polarize opinion: sympathetic observers see in them the ghetto's grievances, and unsympathetic observers see in them the black's irresponsibility. And I count myself among the former. I do not believe that the blacks prefer disorder or that they gain much by rioting. To the contrary, they have suffered most of the personal casualties; and, if recent polls and elections are indicative, the riots have aroused a good deal of latent hostility in the white community. But neither do I believe that the rioting was entirely unjustified. If ghetto conditions are as bad as many blacks contend, it may well be better that they protest them violently than accept them with resignation. It might be better if they protest nonviolently, but they have long done so, and to little avail. Whether the blacks will resort to rioting or other forms of violence in the years ahead is impossible to say; but surely it will depend in large part on whether American society moves to redress the ghetto's grievances. This is a difficult, but hardly insuperable, task; and if it is put off much longer, it will make a sham of American democracy and may even destroy American society.

I incurred many obligations while writing this book. Besides the New World Foundation, Stern Family Fund, Social Science Research

Council, and Columbia University Council on Research in the Social Sciences, the RAND Corporation, Kerner Commission, and N.I.M.H. helped support my activities. I am particularly grateful to Robert Shellow, formerly with the Kerner Commission, and to Edward Flynn and Steve Baratz, of the Applied Research Division and the Metro Center, respectively, of the N.I.M.H., for backing the analysis of riot participation first published by the commission and reprinted here, with minor revisions, as Chapter 2. This analysis was made jointly with Robert Hill under the auspices of the Bureau of Applied Social Research; and Dr. Hill deserves much of the credit for it. I am also particularly thankful to the Boston, Chicago, Omaha, Rochester, and a score of other police departments which supplied the arrest sheets on which this analysis was based. The cooperation of Nat Cohen and his colleagues at U.C.L.A.'s Institute of Government and Public Affairs, who shared ideas on the Los Angeles riots with me, was exemplary. So was the cooperation of the Academy of Political Science, the *Political Science Quarterly*, the *Journal of Social Issues*, and the *American Political Science Review*, which permitted me to reprint material originally published in their pages.

Wendy Bush, Howard Gardner, John Hallowell, Peter Seidman, and Naomi Shapiro worked as research assistants. Sam Coleman, Robert Cross, Walter Gellhorn, Charles Halpern, Robert Hill, Oscar Handlin, Michael Lipsky, Gary Marx, Lloyd Ohlin, Chester Rapkin, Frank and Jinx Roosevelt, David and Sheila Rothman, Martin Timin, Immanuel Wallerstein, and Lloyd Weinreb read and criticized sections of the study. Sigmund Diamond, then managing editor of the *Political Science Quarterly*, suggested valuable revisions of Chapter 3 and the Appendix, which initially appeared in his journal. And my cousin Nancy Kirk criticized and edited the entire manuscript, eliminating verbiage, clarifying ambiguities, and otherwise improving the text. To all of them I am deeply indebted. I also owe special thanks to David Caplovitz and Allan Silver, good friends and former colleagues, who not only encouraged me to pursue the study of riots and ghettos but also introduced me to many of the ideas and approaches which underlie this work. Without their moral and intellectual support I would probably not have written this book. For this reason, and for many others which need not be elaborated on here, I have dedicated this book to them (and to their wives, Paulann and Catherine).

Robert M. Fogelson

Cambridge, Massachusetts
December 1969

Violence as Protest

1: Violence as Protest

On July 16, 1964, two weeks after Congress passed President Lyndon B. Johnson's civil rights bill, a white policeman shot and killed a black youngster in New York City. Two days later, following a rally protesting police brutality, a crowd marched through Harlem and demonstrated before the 28th precinct headquarters. The police tried to disperse the demonstrators but succeeded only in arousing them, and that evening the first full-scale riots in two decades erupted in Harlem. From July 18 to July 20 blacks not only defied and attacked the police, but also assaulted white passers-by and looted and burned neighborhood stores. Moderate black leaders, including such national figures as James Farmer and Bayard Rustin, pleaded with the rioters to return to their homes, but to little avail. In the meantime the police department ordered all available personnel into Harlem to quell the rioting, and on July 21 order was restored. By then, however, the riots had spread to Bedford-Stuyvesant, the vast black ghetto in Brooklyn. And not until July 23—with one dead, over one hundred injured, nearly five hundred arrested, hundreds of buildings damaged, and millions of dollars of property destroyed—were both communities under control.[1]

A day later riots broke out in Rochester after the police arrested a black teen-ager outside a neighborhood dance. A crowd tried to free the prisoner, stoned the chief of police, and then rampaged through the ghetto, looting and burning, for two days. The rioting in this normally peaceful city was so widespread that Governor Nelson Rockefeller mobilized a thousand National Guardsmen.[2] Except for relatively minor disturbances in Jersey City the following weekend

1

and in Elizabeth and Paterson, New Jersey, and Dixmoor, Illinois, a week later, the next month passed without serious incident. Then on August 28, when it seemed as if the worst were over, riots erupted in Philadelphia after two patrolmen arrested a black woman for blocking traffic at a busy intersection. Intoxicated and apparently angry at her husband, she resisted; and they dragged her out of the car. A crowd quickly gathered; it shouted abuse at the policemen, tossed stones and bricks at their reinforcements, and looted and burned nearby stores. Despite the efforts of the Philadelphia police and the appeals of moderate black leaders, the rioting continued for two more nights and finally subsided on August 31.[3] Leaving two dead, over three hundred injured, and another three hundred arrested, the Philadelphia riots climaxed the nation's most turbulent summer in twenty years.

Except for unreconstructed southerners and northern reactionaries who found reason for their racism that summer, most whites, and especially white liberals, were appalled and perplexed by the riots. Appalled because the conservatives were exploiting the rioting to discredit the civil rights movement and to bolster Barry Goldwater's presidential candidacy, and perplexed because the blacks had probably made more progress in the two decades preceding the riots than at any time since emancipation. The reasons for this progress—the Supreme Court's decisions outlawing segregation, the nation's sustained postwar economic boom, and the black migration from the rural South to the urban North—need not be considered at this point. Suffice it to say, most blacks shared in the nation's wealth and influenced its decisions more in the 1960s than ever before.[4] And though these advances were long overdue and imperfectly realized, at no other time (and in no other administration) was there so strong a commitment to eradicate racial subordination and segregation.

Most whites were also bewildered because blacks were disavowing the principles and tactics of nonviolent protest applied so successfully in the South in the late 1950s and early 1960s. For blacks, after all, civil rights were battles to be won and not gifts to be taken. And to win them they had produced skillful, inspired leadership, maintained rigorous discipline and boundless patience, and abided by strict nonviolence.[5] By 1964, largely as a result of these efforts, most whites were convinced that subordination and segregation were wrong. Hence they found it hard to believe that, as the 1964 riots revealed, many blacks were unhappy with the pace of progress, black leadership, discipline, and patience were at the breaking point, and nonviolence was only one form of social protest. By themselves, however, the 1964 riots showed no clear pattern. And though Attorney General Robert Kennedy and others were aware of incidents in Cleveland, New York, and other cities which had foreshadowed the 1964 riots, it was still conceivable as late as mid-1965 that these disorders were just one summer's deviation from the mainstream of the civil rights movement.

The Los Angeles riots of August 1965, which devastated the Pacific coast's largest black ghetto, proved that this was not the case. These riots closely resembled the 1964 riots. In Los Angeles, as in Rochester, an ordinary arrest triggered the rioting; there, too, the rioters looted and burned stores and assaulted policemen and passers-by, the moderate black leaders failed to restrain the rioters, and the local police and National Guard eventually quelled the rioting. The Los Angeles riots were, however, the country's worst racial disorder since the East St. Louis massacre of 1917. By the time order was restored, thirty-four were dead, over a thousand injured, nearly four thousand arrested, hundreds of buildings damaged, and tens of millions of dollars of property destroyed.[6] Notwithstanding other disturbances in Chicago and San Diego, the summer of 1965 was less tumultuous than the summer of 1964. But so vast, so awesome, so devastating, and so widely reported were the Los Angeles riots—for a full week they received front-page coverage nationally and internationally—that henceforth there could be no doubt that a distinct pattern of summer violence was emerging in the black ghettos.

For this reason various governmental authorities took precautionary measures to head off rioting in 1966. The Justice Department instructed its Assistant United States Attorneys to report on conditions in a score of inflammable communities, and the Vice-President's Task Force on Youth Opportunity authorized its field representatives to investigate potential trouble-spots. Meanwhile, city officials devised emergency programs to employ and entertain black youths and otherwise keep them off the streets, and local and state police departments, aided by the F.B.I., prepared riot-control plans.[7] But these measures were not designed to alleviate ghetto conditions, only to prevent severe disorders; and so it was with mounting apprehension that local and federal officials awaited the summer. They did not have to wait long. Rioting erupted in Los Angeles, Chicago, and Cleveland in June, and, to list only a few of more than two dozen other places, in Omaha, Dayton, San Francisco, and Atlanta in July and August.[8] It battered cities previously stricken and cities hitherto spared, cities believed to be tense and cities thought to be quiet. None of these riots matched the Los Angeles riots in magnitude or intensity, but taken together they marked the summer of 1966 as the most violent yet.

By June 1967 other riots had erupted in Nashville, Cleveland, and Boston, and most Americans, white and black, expected another turbulent summer.[9] Stokely Carmichael and Martin Luther King, Jr., charging that the federal authorities had done little to alleviate ghetto conditions, predicted more riots. So did Senator Robert F. Kennedy of New York State, Mayor John V. Lindsay of New York City, Mayor Samuel W. Yorty of Los Angeles, and other national and local figures of various political persuasions.[10] Yet the riots which erupted that summer in Cincinnati, Buffalo, Newark, Detroit, and Milwaukee, to list only a few of the scores of stricken cities, far exceeded their worst expectations. Indeed, the Detroit riots, which left forty-three dead, over a thousand injured, over seven thousand arrested, and at least fifty million dollars of property destroyed, were the worst riots since the New York City draft riots a century ago.[11] By the end of the summer city officials, federal administrators, editors, politicians, and state and national commissions were all trying to explain why. Yet wherever criticism was directed and however blame was apportioned, one conclusion was clear: the Los Angeles,

Newark, and Detroit riots had assumed a place in the history of American race relations no less important, if not more so, than the East St. Louis, Chicago, and Washington riots a generation ago.

This was made even clearer in April 1968 when the assassination of Martin Luther King, Jr., triggered major riots in Washington, Baltimore, and Chicago and minor riots in more than a hundred other cities. These riots, which closely resembled the previous riots, had a tremendous impact. For a full week the nation, which was already numbed by the assassination, reeled under the rioting; and not until National Guardsmen (and, in Washington, federal soldiers) were summoned was order restored in urban America.[12] The summer of 1968 was relatively peaceful, and so was the summer of 1969; but what future summers hold remains to be seen, and in any event the country has not yet worn off the shock of six years of rioting. Even now there is no agreement among whites and blacks or liberals and conservatives about where responsibility for the riots lies; nor is there agreement among the individuals in these groups. There is, however, substantial agreement that the 1960s riots confronted America with the greatest threat to public order since the dreadful industrial disputes of the late nineteenth and early twentieth centuries. And for this reason, if for no other, a scholarly attempt to interpret these riots is very much in order.

Some observers, including journalists who have written full-length accounts of the Harlem, Bedford-Stuyvesant, and Los Angeles disorders, have implied that the 1960s riots were the latest in a long series of American race riots.[13] There is indeed a tradition of interracial rioting in the United States. To mention only a few examples, race riots erupted in Cincinnati and Philadelphia during the antebellum period and in New York City and Detroit during the Civil War. They broke out immediately after the war in New Orleans and Memphis and around the turn of the century in Wilmington, North Carolina, New York City, Atlanta, Georgia, and Springfield, Illinois. They reached one peak around World War I in East St. Louis, Wash-

5

ington, and Chicago and another during World War II in Detroit and Los Angeles, only to subside later in the 1940s.[14] At a quick glance, moreover, the race riots resemble the 1960s riots: blacks played a prominent role in both types of disorders; so did excitement, rumor, violence, death, and destruction. Nevertheless, a closer examination of the race riots, and especially the 1917, 1919, and 1943 riots, reveals that the 1960s riots were not extensions of this tradition.

Unlike the recent riots, which were as a rule precipitated by routine police actions, the earlier riots were in the main triggered by black challenges to the racial status quo. The outbreak of the Chicago riots of 1919 was a case in point.[15] At a time of tension generated by black migration and white racism a black youth swam from a beach set aside by tacit understanding for blacks to a nearby beach reserved for whites. At the same time several blacks who had been forced to leave this beach earlier in the day returned determined to stay. Whites and blacks started brawling and throwing stones. The black swimmer, rocks falling around him, remained in the water, clinging to a railroad tie; but when a white youth swam toward him, he abandoned the tie, took a few strokes, and then drowned. The police made no arrests, infuriating the blacks, who retaliated by mobbing a patrolman. When gangs of whites counterattacked that evening, the worst interracial riots in the city's history were under way. Hence rioting was precipitated in Chicago in 1919 by the blacks' refusal to accept, and the whites' determination to maintain, segregated recreational facilities and not by routine police actions.

By contrast with the black rioters, who looted and burned stores and only incidentally assaulted passers-by, the white rioters vented their hostility for the most part against people, not property. The violence of the East St. Louis riots of 1917 was characteristic.[16] Angered by the employment of black immigrants as strikebreakers, white mobs attacked blacks in downtown East St. Louis. The rioters dragged their victims out of streetcars, stoning, clubbing, kicking, and afterwards shooting and lynching them. They also burned houses and, with a deliberation which shocked reporters, shot black residents as they fled the flames. They killed them as they begged for mercy and even refused to allow them to brush away flies as they lay dying. The blacks, disarmed by the police and the militia after an earlier riot and defenseless in their wooden shanties, offered little resistance. And by the time the East St. Louis massacre was over the rioters had murdered at least thirty-nine blacks, wounded hundreds more, and, in pursuit of their victims, damaged hundreds of buildings and destroyed about a million dollars of property.

The government authorities, and especially the local police, did not attempt to restore law and order in the race riots with the firmness they exhibited in the 1960s riots. This was certainly true in their response to the Washington riots of 1919.[17] When several hundred sailors (and a few civilians), out to avenge an alleged insult to a mate's wife, rampaged through southwest Washington attacking blacks, the district and military police arrested only two whites (and eight blacks). And when the sailors, joined by soldiers, resumed their assaults the next evening, the police with a handful of reinforcements provided scant protection for the terrified blacks. Law enforcement in the capital broke down not just because the police were outnumbered but also because the policemen as individuals sympathized with the rioters. Not until the police lost control and the blacks armed themselves did the District Commissioners request the cooperation of the military authorities and restore order. Hence the whites rioted in Washington in 1919 with an impunity which was in marked contrast to the danger faced by the blacks a generation later.

Lastly, few responsible white leaders labored so valiantly, if vainly, to prevent the riots and restrain the rioters in 1917, 1919, and 1943 as the moderate black leaders (or at any rate the so-called black leaders) did in the 1960s. This was clearly the case in Detroit in 1943.[18] A host of fascist spokesmen, including Father Charles E. Coughlin and the Reverend Gerald L. K. Smith, and racist organizations, including the Ku Klux Klan and the Black Legion, had long fomented racial animosity there. And though Detroit's civic leaders did not support these agitators, they did not forthrightly oppose them or otherwise deal with the community's racial problems. Once the rioting was under way, Detroit's elected leaders responded am-

7

bivalently. Not that they sanctioned the violence; on the contrary, they deplored it, though always from a distance. But they so feared for their political futures and their city's reputation that they did not call for the National Guard until the rioting threatened the whole community and not just the black residents. Whether Detroit's white leaders could have intervened more effectively in 1943 than Los Angeles' black leaders did in 1965 is a moot question because with the exception of a few courageous ministers they did not try.

The distinctive character of the race riots emerges from these brief descriptions. The riots were interracial, violent, reactionary, and ultimately unsuccessful attempts to maintain the racial status quo at times of rapid social change. They were interracial because whites, first- and second-generation European immigrants in Chicago and uprooted southerners in Detroit, were the aggressors, and blacks, newcomers themselves, the victims. They were violent because the whites did not know how to achieve their goals—how to force the blacks to leave East St. Louis and how to keep them in their place in Washington—through legitimate means. They were reactionary because the whites hoped to deprive the blacks of freedom of movement, equal access to public accommodations, and other rights which inhere in Americans whatever their color.[19] And however effective in the short run, they were unsuccessful in the long run. And not simply because the means and ends were at odds with American ideology but also because the economic, social, and political changes underlying the migration of southern blacks and the militancy of northern blacks were too powerful.

The differences between the race riots and the 1960s riots are so marked that it is only necessary now to note a few reasons why the tradition of interracial rioting has waned since World War II. First, the racial status quo has changed so much that the issues which precipitated the race riots are no longer at stake; also, the tremendous expansion of white suburbs and black ghettos has insulated the protagonists from one another. Second, many children of the first- and second-generation immigrants who rioted in 1917, 1919, and 1943 are now middle-class Americans who do not have to rely on violence

8

to uphold their racial privileges. Third, the governmental authorities, and especially the local police, are so determined to maintain public order that except in the rural South few groups, white or black, can riot with impunity anymore.[20] And fourth, again except in the deep South, white leaders are so committed to orderly social change they cannot sanction rioting even on behalf of causes to which they are otherwise sympathetic.

These changes can be exaggerated. The American tradition of interracial violence is waning; but, as intermittent rioting—primarily, though not exclusively, in the South—in the 1950s and 1960s revealed, it is not yet moribund. On several occasions mobs of middle-class whites have forcibly resisted the movement of middle-class blacks into residential suburbs of Philadelphia, Chicago, and other northern metropolises.[21] And gangs of working-class whites, themselves bypassed in the suburban exodus, have violently protested the influx of working-class blacks into East New York and other ethnic communities.[22] Nevertheless, the authorities have restored order so swiftly and thoroughly in these disorders that few people have been injured and few buildings damaged. By such measurements as actual outbreaks, lives lost, arrests booked, and property destroyed, these disturbances are much less serious than the riots under consideration here. There are of course no assurances that whites will restrain themselves in the suburbs or that blacks will confine their violence to the ghettos in the future. But until then interracial rioting must be considered a vestige of a waning American tradition.

Other observers, including left-wing radicals and, more recently, black militants, have insisted that the riots, far from being traditional race riots, were incipient colonial rebellions.[23] By this they mean two things. First, that the riots were manifestations of a world-wide struggle against colonialism, the determined attempt of colored peoples everywhere to overthrow their white masters. The situation of black people in the United States, the radicals assume, is essentially the same as the situation of colored people in Africa and Asia; the blacks are a colonial people, the whites a colonial oppressor, and the ghettos colonies. Second, that the riots were expressions of a widespread struggle against capitalism, the proletariat's historic effort to regain its manhood, dignity, and freedom through socialism. The blacks resorted to violence, the radicals presume, because they have no hope whatever to achieve meaningful equality under the existing economic and political system. This interpretation is certainly as much a vision as a definition. But it deserves careful consideration, particularly for its implication that the riots are political actions (and revolutionary ones at that).

There are, as the radicals argue, similarities between the 1960s riots and colonial uprisings. In Chicago, Cleveland, and Los Angeles as well as in Nigeria, Uganda, and Nyasaland somewhat earlier, colored people resorted to violence in order to force social change.[24] Afro-Americans and Africans alike rioted in protest against genuine grievances and treated the customary restraints on rioting with indifference and even outright contempt. There are also similarities between the racial problem and the colonial situation. In both cases white people have subordinated and segregated colored people and then justified their exploitation and victimization on the grounds of innate racial inferiority.[25] What is more, many blacks who have recently overcome the long-standing antipathy toward their color, ignorance of their origins, and shame about their race have responded by identifying closely with the world's colored people. Their racial pride enhanced by the emergence of independent African nations after World War II, these blacks are now convinced that their future in the United States is inextricably linked with the destiny of colored people everywhere.[26]

There are, however, profound differences between the 1960s riots and colonial uprisings. The differences between the recent rioting and terrorist activity against the British in Kenya, guerrilla warfare against the French in Madagascar, and abortive invasions of Portuguese Angola are obvious.[27] Less obvious but no less noteworthy are the differences between the 1960s riots and the colonial uprisings in Nigeria, Uganda, Nyasaland, and other places which took the

form of riotous protests. The 1960s riots were spontaneous and unorganized, opposed by the moderate black leaders, confined almost
entirely to the ghettos, and quelled with vigor but not without
restraint by the authorities. The colonial uprisings, by contrast, developed out of nonviolent demonstrations against colonial exploitation; the African leaders led the demonstrations and then directed
the uprisings. The rioters rampaged outside the native districts, attacking government buildings as well as private holdings; and the
authorities, relying largely on the military, responded relentlessly and
ruthlessly.[28] Hence the 1960s riots were more restrained than the
colonial uprisings, a pattern which suggests that the stakes were
higher and the frustrations deeper in Africa than in America.

The differences between the 1960s riots and the colonial struggle
reflect the differences between the racial problem and the colonial
situation. The blacks have greater opportunities to enter the middle
class and exert political power than colonial people do. But, by the
same token, the blacks are much more limited than colonial people
in their ultimate aspirations; a minority, they can belong to the nation but cannot take it over. Also, for all their prejudice, white Americans, and especially their leaders, have a more ambivalent attitude
towards colored people than European colonialists do. They subor-
dinate and segregate blacks unevenly, as much by omission as by
commission, and often against their own law and ideology.[29] Lastly,
the ghetto is not a colony—unless by a colony is meant nothing more
than a dependent neighborhood, a definition which would include
most parts of the modern metropolis. The ghetto is exploited, but
not so much by the whole society as by fragments of it, and not
so much to oppress its inhabitants as to avoid them. These differences do not mean that the racial problem is less serious than the
colonial situation, only that it is very different.[30]

There are also, as the radicals claim, analogies between the 1960s
riots and socialist struggles. Although the blacks have traditionally
based their pleas for social justice on the sanctity of the law and
consistently honored the commitment to orderly social change,[31]
they are still the nearest group to an American proletariat nowadays.

By rioting for six summers now they have not only broken the law and ignored this commitment, but, by looting and burning stores, disobeying the police, and attacking patrolmen, they have also destroyed private property and challenged public authority. There are also many black militants who have lost all hope of achieving meaningful equality under the existing system—and not only the members of the Revolutionary Action Movement and other fringe groups. Before his assassination Malcolm X (whose ideas on these and other matters were in flux at the time) concluded that racism and capitalism were so intertwined that the one could not be abolished without eliminating the other. And, more recently, Eldridge Cleaver (and, by implication, the members of the Black Panthers) insisted that the blacks cannot expect social justice under the prevailing economic and political conditions.[32]

The analogies between the 1960s riots and the socialist struggle do not withstand careful scrutiny, however. No doubt the rioters rejected a long-standing strategy by resorting to violence. But there is no necessary connection between violence and socialism, certainly not in the United States; the race riots of 1917, 1919, and 1943 are all cases in point. Accordingly the test of the analogy lies, if anywhere, in the purposes of the riots, that is, were they directed against private property and public authority? It would appear that they were not. The blacks looted to acquire goods enjoyed by most Americans and burned to even the score with white merchants; they did not attempt to undermine property rights in general. They assaulted patrolmen to express specific grievances against the local police and not, as the blacks' attitude toward the National Guard indicated, overall disaffection with public authority. Perhaps even more pertinent, the rioting was confined to the ghettos; the rioters did not destroy private property elsewhere, nor did they attack schools, hospitals, or other government buildings.[33] If anything, these patterns reveal that the violence was directed against the system's abuses and not the system itself.

Hence the 1960s riots were attempts to alert America, not overturn it, to denounce its practices, not renounce its principles. They were not insurrections, and not because blacks lacked the numbers, power, and leaders but rather because they wanted a change in norms not in values. These conclusions are consistent with the most recent surveys of black opinion[34] and with the ideology of all but a small (though increasing) fraction of the black nationalist organizations. The Black Muslims, the largest of these groups, have no fundamental disagreement with capitalist America, only with white America; their utopia is strict, separate, and black, but otherwise quite familiar. And most Black Power advocates are more concerned with procedures than substance; that they insist on self-determination is clear enough, but whether for capitalism, socialism, or something else is not. Indeed, even Malcolm X's tremendous appeal rested as much on his eloquence, courage, and blunt defiance of white society as on any particular ideology, anti-colonialist or anti-capitalist.[35] For the great majority of blacks, the American dream, tarnished though it has been for centuries, is still the ultimate aspiration.

To argue that the 1960s riots were not colonial rebellions is not to imply what future riots will be like. The situation is anything but promising. Black moderates are convinced, and rightly so, that current federal, state, and city programs will not materially improve the ghettos. Black extremists are prepared to intensify their opposition to the system; and rumors about terrorism and guerrilla warfare are spreading through many cities.[36] The riots have greatly stirred the black community too; so has the realization that rioting is a sure way to attract attention. Hence it is impossible to say what the future holds. But there is no certainty that the United States will not experience organized and premeditated violence, and not only inside the black ghettos. Nor is there any certainty that blacks will not direct their hostility against the system itself instead of its abuses. In other words, the 1960s riots, revolutionary in their means, may develop into colonial rebellions, revolutionary in their ends. For the time being, however, it can safely be concluded that these riots were not colonial rebellions.

Still other observers, including the mayors (or acting mayors) of New York, Los Angeles, and many other cities, have insisted that the riots were meaningless outbursts and not rebellions, colonial or otherwise.[37] They have, in effect, denied that the riots were political expressions, no matter how broadly defined. For these officials this interpretation is highly reassuring; it precludes attempts to blame them for the rioting and also relieves pressures to alleviate long-standing problems in the ghettos. Most of these officials are sincere in their convictions; and so are most of their constituents, who also consider the riots meaningless outbursts. Nevertheless, this interpretation is untenable, and for reasons other than the obvious one that no social phenomenon is meaningless; and a brief analysis of these reasons should help clarify the meaning of the riots.

The conception of the riots as meaningless outbursts is intimately related to the absence of a *tradition* of violent protest in America. Not that the United States has been a peaceful country. Quite the contrary: for three and a half centuries Americans have resorted to violence in order to reach goals otherwise unattainable. The whites who assaulted blacks in Washington and Chicago in 1919 were a case in point. So, to list only a few notorious examples, were the Protestants who attacked Catholics in Boston in 1834, the vigilantes who lynched lawbreakers in San Francisco in 1856, and the citizens who massacred the "Wobblies" in Centralia, Washington, in 1919.[38] Indeed, it is hardly an exaggeration to say that the native white majority has rioted in some way and at some time against nearly every minority group in America. And yet most Americans regard rioting not only as illegitimate but, even more significant, as aberrant.[39] From their perspective, which reflects a boundless confidence in orderly social change, riots, no matter how frequently they erupt, are necessarily unique and wholly unrelated.

Under ordinary circumstances the absence of a tradition of violent protest makes it difficult for Americans to perceive the riots as anything but meaningless outbursts. And circumstances today are far from ordinary. The demand for public order and the opposition to

14

rioting and violence are now greater than ever in the United States. This situation, as Allan Silver has perceptively pointed out,[40] reflects not only the spreading consensus that disorder does irreparable and intolerable damage to modern political and economic mechanisms. It also reflects the growing awareness of the spatial interdependence of American cities, the realization that the outbreak of rioting in one neighborhood threatens the security of all the others. It reflects, too, the increasing confidence in the ability of the governmental authorities, and especially the police, to maintain public order in the face of any challenge. And the demand for public order, which has intensified the middle classes' fear of the lower and working classes (and, above all, lower- and working-class blacks), has made it even harder for most Americans to regard the riots as anything but meaningless outbursts (or left-wing conspiracies).

The absence of a tradition of violent protest makes it just as hard for lower- and working-class blacks to express the meaning of the riots. Except in Harlem and Boston, where the rioting erupted after organized demonstrations against police brutality and welfare abuses respectively, nowhere did the rioters prepare a formal statement of grievances. And whatever the meaning of "Burn, Baby, Burn!" the slogan of the Los Angeles riots, surely no one can argue that it is readily understood. Moreover, the racial problem, complex enough to begin with, is obscured because the nation is committed in principle to equality and, save in the rural South, white attitudes toward black people are marked as much by indifference as by hostility. For these reasons it was no mean task for blacks to explain the rioting. What is more, this situation was aggravated because almost without exception the moderate black leaders disapproved of the riots. No one spoke for the rioters as Martin Luther King, Jr., and the Montgomery Improvement Association spoke for the Montgomery bus boycotters.[41] Whatever the meaning of the riots, then, it has to be sought in the rioting itself, and even sympathetic observers might well have trouble finding it there.

The meaning is there, but only if the riots are viewed as violent protests. That they are violent is obvious. But it is not so obvious that they, like the Montgomery bus boycott and other civil rights demonstrations, are also protests, because most Americans regard a violent protest as a contradiction in terms. There is, however, a long, if declining, *history* of violent protest in western society, a history exemplified by the pre-industrial urban mob in eighteenth-century Europe.[42] The mob, which was composed mainly of common people, as opposed to the riffraff, communicated popular dissatisfaction to the authorities; it protested by rioting and otherwise resorting to violence and not by adopting radical ideologies. It also expected a response, and a favorable one, too, from the authorities. To list only a few examples from London: the mob rioting against the Excise Bill in 1733, the employment of Irish labor in 1736, the expulsion of John Wilkes in 1768, and the Catholic Emancipation Bill in 1780.[43] These riots were articulate not so much because the elites understood them as because, in view of the mob's potential for disorder, the violence was restrained and selective.

Ignoring profound differences in grievances and responses, it is fair to say that the 1960s riots were articulate protests in the same sense. On the basis of the available statistical data, it is evident that the black rioters were not primarily the unemployed, ill-educated, uprooted, and criminal. They were rather a substantial and representative minority of the young adults which was widely supported in the ghettos.[44] Also, far from rejecting the prevailing ideology, the rioters demanded that all citizens honor it; they insisted on changes in practices not principles. They made it extremely clear that most blacks do not want to overthrow American society, but simply to belong to it as equals. Moreover, the rioters indicated to reporters during the riots and to interviewers afterwards that they expected the rioting to improve their position by arousing white concern.[45] They could not know then (and indeed they may not know now) that though some whites are more concerned many are more intransigent. Put bluntly, the blacks delivered a protest, but most whites did not receive it.

Also, viewed from a distance, the riots seem unrestrained and indiscriminate, which is what observers probably mean by meaningless;

the mob is overwhelming, the confusion complete. But at closer observation, where individuals are visible and patterns discernible, the opposite appears to be true. Although the rioters vented their rage on patrolmen and passers-by and showed little remorse after the attacks, they killed only a handful of the thousands of whites caught in the rioting and even released unharmed several reporters similarly trapped. This restraint was repeated too often to be considered exceptional.[46] Again, though the rioters damaged hundreds of buildings, destroyed millions of dollars of property, and devastated whole sections of the ghettos, they burned mainly stores that charged excessive prices or sold inferior goods (or did both) and left homes, schools, and churches unharmed. This selectivity was noted by more than one witness, too.[47] Indeed, restraint and selectivity were among the most crucial features of the riots. And it is in these features that the meaning of the disorders is to be found.

Now not all the rioters were restrained and selective. A few, especially the handful of snipers, intended to provoke confrontation, not to arouse concern. Nor were the rioters restrained and selective all the time. The looters did not always choose the merchandise with care, and the arsonists did not always pick the buildings with precision. Nonetheless, most of the rioters were restrained and selective most of the time. What is more, the overwhelming majority of blacks viewed the riots as protests. According to a nation-wide survey conducted for the Kerner Commission, 86 per cent of black men and 84 per cent of black women considered the riots at least in part protests against unfair conditions.[48] And in many cases the rioters' actions confirm these conclusions. During the Harlem riots they surrounded white reporters and instead of beating them told them to write the full story; and after the Los Angeles riots they boasted that they had finally brought the south-central ghetto to the attention of the authorities.[49] All things considered, it is fair to conclude that the riots were protests and, like the civil rights demonstrations of the previous decade, articulate protests, too.

It now remains to discuss what the blacks were protesting against and why they were protesting violently. To this end it is instructive to consider the 1960s riots in connection with two earlier disorders which were their direct precursors, namely, the Harlem riots of 1935 and 1943. Given the circumstances, no two riots should have had less in common. The Great Depression was in its fifth year in the spring of 1935; its economic and political repercussions were evident everywhere, and nowhere more so than in Harlem. Fully half the residents were unemployed and on relief; many were standing in long soup lines, and a few were actually starving. Meanwhile, various left-wing groups—so vividly describd by Ralph Ellison in *The Invisible Man*—were busily planning for a socialist or communist takeover.[50] How different everything was in the summer of 1943 when World War II was reaching its peak and most Americans, black and white, were mobilized. The nation's economy, stimulated by wartime production, was enjoying full employment and even facing manpower shortages. And the country's radicals were silent because of the emotional demands of wartime patriotism and the Nazi invasion of Soviet Russia.[51] These circumstances notwithstanding, the Harlem riots of 1935 and 1943 had a great deal in common.

Contemporaries were hard pressed to explain what it was, however. Most of them, including Mayor Fiorello La Guardia, black author Claude McKay, and the New York *Times*, realized that the Harlem riots were not, strictly speaking, race riots.[52] Quite correctly and not without pride, they cited the absence of interracial violence in 1935 and again in 1943, the year of the Detroit race riots. If they did not blame the Communists, they claimed that though there was no justification for the Harlem riots there were grounds for the blacks' complaints, particularly the suffering of ordinary blacks during the depression and the attacks on black soldiers during the war. Nevertheless, they did not define the Harlem riots more precisely. Rather, they seconded La Guardia's statements that the riots were criminal and thoughtless acts by hoodlums and other irresponsible people who were a minute fraction of New York's overwhelmingly law-abiding black community.[53] La Guardia, who was at his best quelling the rioting and at his worst analyzing it, exhibited the traditional American misconception of violent protest. But he did not have the benefit of the perspective provided by the 1960s riots, a perspective which highlights the common and distinctive features of the Harlem riots.

The Harlem riots, like the 1960s riots, were spontaneous, unorganized, and precipitated by police actions. The 1935 riots began in a Harlem department store when a youth was caught shoplifting and forcibly subdued by the employees. He was then taken to a back room and after a while set free by the police. The shoppers believed that the police were beating the boy, however, and their fears were confirmed by the arrival of an ambulance called by an employee bitten in the scuffle. A crowd quickly gathered and—when, by a remarkable coincidence, the brother-in-law of another employee parked his hearse nearby—concluded that the police had killed the youth. Nothing the police said or did could persuade the blacks otherwise, and the rumor swiftly spread throughout Harlem, setting off the 1935 riots.[54] The 1943 riots, which erupted in a more credible but basically similar way, started in a Harlem hotel when a white patrolman attempted to arrest a boisterous black woman for disorderly conduct. A black soldier intervened, grabbing the patrolman's nightstick and striking him with it, and then turned to leave. The patrolman ordered him to halt and, when he refused, shot him in the shoulder. A crowd soon formed in front of the hospital to which the soldier was taken and, though the wound was not serious, the word that a white policeman had killed a black soldier rapidly passed through the ghetto, triggering the 1943 riots.[55]

Once the rioting was under way, the Harlem rioters directed most of their aggression against property rather than people. Several thousand strong in 1935, the rioters first threw bricks and bottles at the department store windows and the policemen patrolling nearby. Later they roamed the streets, attacking white passers-by and looting and burning neighborhood stores, especially white-owned stores. By the next morning one was dead, over one hundred injured, another one hundred arrested, and several hundred buildings damaged.[56] The violence was worse in 1943, but the pattern was much the same.

Once again the rioters, numbering many thousands, assaulted white passers-by, overturned parked automobiles, and tossed bricks and bottles at policemen. They also looted and burned food and liquor shops, haberdasheries, pawn and jewelry shops, and, again, mainly white-owned shops. By the following day six were dead, over five hundred injured, more than one hundred jailed, and a few million dollars of property destroyed.[57] Like the New York riots of 1964, the Harlem riots of 1935 and 1943 were so completely confined to the ghetto that life was normal for whites and blacks elsewhere in the city.

The official response was about as vigorous in the Harlem riots as in the 1960s riots, too. Early in the 1935 riots Police Commissioner Lewis J. Valentine sent policemen organized in special squadrons and armed with special guns to reinforce the mounted and foot patrolmen and radio-car crews at the department store. And later on, while the police, fully armed and often firing, struggled with the rioters, Mayor La Guardia prepared and distributed a circular calling on law-abiding blacks to cooperate with the authorities.[58] This response, however vigorous, was dwarfed by the response to the 1943 riots. The police department's afternoon shift was kept on duty, freeing the night shift for riot control; and by morning fully five thousand policemen, supported by military police and regular troops, were patrolling Harlem. Another five thousand New York State Guards and fifteen hundred black volunteers were standing by. In the meantime La Guardia closed streets and diverted traffic around Harlem, concentrated subway patrolmen on the Harlem lines, issued a declaration denouncing the rioting, and, accompanied by two well-known moderate black leaders, toured the ghetto appealing for restraint.[59] By dint of the police department's tactics and the Mayor's virtuoso performance, order was restored the following day.

The moderate blacks disapproved of the Harlem riots almost, but not quite, as strongly as they disapproved of the 1960s riots. Few attempted to restrain the rioters in 1935; more grasped the opportunity to denounce racial discrimination. This reaction was not surprising: rioting lasted only one night, discrimination had gone on for several centuries. What was surprising was that none of these leaders, no matter how firmly committed to civil rights, sanctioned the rioting.[60] The moderate black leaders reacted far more forcefully in 1943. A few accompanied La Guardia on his tour of the ghetto, others advised him about riot-control strategies, and still others manned voluntary patrols. Even more impressive, many broadcast from sound trucks, denying the rumor that the white policeman had killed the black youth and urging the rioters to clear the streets.[61] And as the rioting was more violent and the nation more united in 1943 than in 1935, even the leaders who used the occasion to condemn racial segregation did so circumspectly. Nonetheless, these efforts (and the riots themselves) highlighted the inability of the moderate black leaders to channel rank-and-file discontent into legitimate channels and when necessary to restrain the rioters.

Even this short discussion of the Harlem riots and the 1960s riots reveals their striking similarities and essential characteristics. These riots were spontaneous and unorganized, triggered by police actions, and distinguished by looting and burning of neighborhood stores and assaults on patrolmen and white passers-by. In all of them, the governmental authorities responded vigorously to increase the risks in participating, and, save in 1935, the moderate black leaders labored valiantly, if vainly, to restrain the rioters. Hence the essence of the Harlem riots and the 1960s riots is an intense resentment of the police, an intolerable accumulation of grievances, the ineffectiveness of the customary restraints on rioting, and the weakness of moderate black leadership. It is against police malpractice and other grievances, especially economic deprivation, consumer exploitation, and racial discrimination, that the blacks were protesting; and it is because of the ineffectiveness of the customary restraints on rioting and the weakness of moderate black leadership that they were protesting violently. Needless to say, these conditions are among the fundamental features of life in the black ghetto.

Accordingly it is not surprising that these riots first erupted in Harlem rather than in Chicago or the other sites of the twentieth-century race riots. Harlem was the first black ghetto. Developed as a middle-class community around the turn of the century, it was promptly caught in a severe real estate crash; and instead of being quickly settled by whites, it was slowly filled by blacks. Rioting did not break out there during the turbulent postwar years, however. Rather than fight the black influx, as the working-class first- and second-generation European immigrants did in Chicago, the middle-class native Americans in New York quietly moved elsewhere,[62] leaving a black Harlem in their wake. It was during the 1910s and the 1920s, fully a generation before the massive migration from the South after World War II transformed urban America, that Harlem emerged as the nation's first black ghetto. It was in these decades that as the headquarters of the black renaissance it fascinated white Americans in their misguided quest for the exotic and the primitive.[63] And it was in these decades that the conditions developed which led the blacks in Harlem to protest, and to protest violently, in 1935 and 1943.

What emerges from this deliberately circuitous approach is a rather straightforward interpretation: the 1960s riots were articulate protests against genuine grievances in the black ghettos. The riots were protests because they were attempts to call the attention of white society to the blacks' widespread dissatisfaction with racial subordination and segregation. The riots were also articulate because they were restrained, selective, and, no less important, directed at the sources of the blacks' most immediate and profound grievances. What is more, the grievances are genuine because by the standards of the greater society the conditions of black life, physically, economically, educationally, socially, and otherwise, are deplorable. And nowhere in urban America are these conditions—economic deprivation, consumer exploitation, inferior education, racial discrimination, and so forth—more deplorable than in the black ghettos. Having offered this interpretation, which I intend to document in more detail later on, I would like to conclude by considering two closely related questions:

namely, why did the 1960s riots erupt when they did and where they did?

The timing of the riots is baffling. The blacks' grievances were not developments of the 1960s, nor, for that matter, were the burdens of subordination and segregation. If anything, these grievances were probably less serious and these burdens less severe then than at any time in American history. Since World War II large numbers of blacks moved into highly skilled and well-paying jobs and gained positions of political influence. At the same time a large majority of whites grew fairly reluctant to measure a man strictly by the color of his skin. To add to this, a battery of Supreme Court decisions made it much harder for Americans, individuals and authorities alike, to practice racial discrimination.[64] Thus, for all the inequities and prejudices remaining, most blacks were probably better off in the 1960s than in any decade in the recent past. And yet it was in the 1960s—not in the 1940s when the armed forces were segregated, nor in the 1950s when a civil rights act was an occasion—that blacks rioted.

At the heart of this paradox was the unprecedented rise in the blacks' expectations. This rise began with the great migration north in the 1910s and 1920s, gathered momentum during World War II, and accelerated during the late 1950s and early 1960s. It accelerated not only because the nation as a whole enjoyed remarkable prosperity but also because some blacks fully shared in it and a few attained standards long reserved for whites only. It accelerated, too, because civil rights programs made progress, white attitudes about race changed for the better, and, even more important, black pride flourished as it had not since the Garvey Movement of the 1920s.[65] The results were momentous. Blacks were more conscious of their deprivations—indeed, deprivation had a whole new meaning for them; they were dissatisfied with conditions that their fathers and grandfathers would have found tolerable (or at any rate inevitable). The blacks were also less concerned about social constraints, more militant and aggressive, at the least impatient and, when frustrated time and again, dangerously desperate. This rise in expectations was self-

23

perpetuating, too; each new gain generated a new goal, and by the 1960s the blacks would settle for nothing less than a complete equality.

What rendered these expectations so explosive in the 1960s were the dreadful conditions of ghetto life. And not only in Harlem. Although the working-class, first- and second-generation European immigrants in Chicago, Detroit, and other cities resisted the black influx in 1919 and 1943, they eventually conceded the issue. Like the middle-class native Americans in New York, they or their children fled before the massive black migration after World War II, leaving behind them the swelling black ghettos.[66] By the 1960s these ghettos were a full generation old, about as old as Harlem was in the 1930s and 1940s; and, in view of the blacks' expectations, conditions there, no matter how much improved, were intolerable. What is more, the blacks realized that these conditions could be readily remedied. Nor, by virtue of their color, could they easily escape to the suburbs like white immigrants before them. A state of permanent subordination and segregation loomed as a distinct possibility.[67] And thus, as ghetto life intensified the group's grievances and undermined the society's restraints, the blacks rioted to protest their plight.

The location of the 1960s riots is baffling, too. With a few exceptions—notably the Atlanta (1966), Nashville (1966), Tampa (1967), and Miami (1968) riots—they have occurred less in the South, where by any objective consideration the blacks have more reason for rioting, than in the North.[68] This paradox cannot be resolved by the explanation (which is true so far as it goes) that the riots are urban phenomena and that the South is the least urbanized region in the nation. Atlanta, Nashville, Tampa, and Miami are not the only southern cities, and among the others Birmingham, Charleston, Little Rock, New Orleans, and Jackson have thus far been spared rioting. Again, with a few exceptions the riots have occurred almost everywhere in the North, a pattern which is particularly perplexing for most Americans. It is one thing for blacks to riot in New York, Chicago, Philadelphia, Cleveland, Detroit, and Los Angeles, the nation's largest metropolitan centers. Of them Americans expect almost anything, especially in the sweltering summer months. But it is another thing for blacks to riot in Rochester, Dayton, Omaha, and Lansing, and many other normally peaceful, presumably content medium-sized cities. From them Americans expect an occasional scandal, but nothing as serious as full-scale rioting.

There are explanations for these paradoxes, however. The South has suffered fewer riots than the North not simply because southern blacks have lower expectations than northern blacks and southern policemen fewer inhibitions than northern policemen. The South, which has about as many blacks as the North, has far fewer ghettos. Blacks have traditionally been more heavily concentrated in northern cities than in southern cities, where the differences between white and black were so well defined that there was little reason for rigorous residential segregation.[69] Only recently, as the racial status quo has been vigorously challenged in the South, have southern whites, like northern whites before them, retreated to segregated suburbs and left black ghettos behind. Where this has happened, as in Atlanta and Miami, southern blacks, like northern blacks, are most resentful of their grievances and less concerned about society's restraints, more conscious of their strength and less reluctant to test it. This pattern now prevails only in Atlanta and a handful of other southern cities;[70] but the same nation-wide forces transforming the North are emerging in the South, and so the probability of further rioting there may well increase in the future.

This explanation applies to the North as well as to the South. Small cities as well as large metropolises have been devastated by riots largely because northern blacks are everywhere confined to ghettos. And for all the differences between Harlem and Chicago's West Side, Rochester's seventh ward and Cleveland's Hough district, Boston's Roxbury and Brooklyn's Bedford-Stuyvesant, and south-central Los Angeles and all the others, life varies little from one ghetto to the next. In each there are an intense resentment of the police, high unemployment rates, exploitative mercantile practices, excessive levels of violence, widespread residential segregation, and, among other things, ineffective moderate leadership. And in the end the blacks' grievances are no more tolerable in Omaha, Dayton, Lansing, and Rochester than in Chicago, Philadelphia, Newark, and Cleveland. All of which is perhaps another way of saying that the blacks' frustration, resentment, and aggression are a function not of the size of the white communities but of the conditions in the black ghettos.

The interpretation of the 1960s riots as articulate protests against genuine grievances in the black ghettos helps explain why the riots erupted when and where they did. But it does not help explain why they erupted first in Philadelphia, Los Angeles, and Cleveland, later in Buffalo, Newark, and Detroit, and only recently in Washington and Baltimore. A few offhand explanations have been offered, but an extended examination of these explanations is beyond the scope of this introduction; and it would probably not be worth while anyway. For there is no convincing evidence that the blacks' conditions are materially worse in Philadelphia, Los Angeles, and Cleveland than in Buffalo, Newark, and Detroit, or Washington and Baltimore. Indeed, it is probably only a coincidence that the riots erupted in some cities before others (and not at all in still others, such as Oakland, whose turn will doubtless come). And if the interpretation of the 1960s riots offered here is correct, it indicates why they have broken out in nearly every American metropolis except some in the deep South, where the black ghettos are little developed, and others in the Pacific Northwest, where the black population is extremely small.

2: Who Riots?

A great many public figures have already given their views on the 1960s riots. This was their privilege and responsibility. That they have disagreed sharply on the degree of organization and advanced planning, the amount of violence and destruction, the conditions in the black ghettos, and the implications for public policy is not surprising. The differences between California Governor Ronald Reagan and New Jersey Governor Richard J. Hughes and between Acting Mayor of New York Paul R. Screvane and Minneapolis Mayor Arthur Naftalin were marked. So were the differences between the Los Angeles (1965), Newark (1967), Detroit (1967), and Washington, D.C., (1968) riots, on the one hand, and the Rochester (1964), Chicago (1965), San Francisco (1966), and Boston (1967) riots, on the other. What is surprising is that most of these public figures[1] (and, as the public opinion surveys reveal, most of their constituents) have agreed substantially on probably the most perplexing question raised by the riots: that is, who riots?

A few examples illustrate this point. Acting Mayor of New York Paul R. Screvane attributed the Harlem riots of 1964 to "fringe groups, including the Communist Party"; Brooklyn Borough President Abe Stark blamed the Bedford-Stuyvesant riots of 1965 on "small bands of rowdies and hoodlums." And Mayor Frank Sedata of Buffalo insisted that the 1967 riots were instigated by "out-of-towners." Governor Nelson Rockefeller of New York called the Rochester riots of 1964 an act of "lawlessness, hoodlumism, and extremism"; Governor Richard J. Hughes of New Jersey deemed the Newark riots of 1967 "a criminal insurrection." And Governor Ron-

27

ald Reagan of California castigated the rioters as "lawbreakers and mad dogs." Only 1 per cent of the blacks joined in the rioting, according to Mayor Naftalin, about 2 per cent according to Governor Reagan, and roughly 3 per cent according to Governor Hughes. The Governor's Commission on the Los Angeles Riots (otherwise known as the McCone Commission) settled on 2 per cent. Most officials, from President Lyndon Johnson on down to New York's World's Fair President Robert Moses, also agreed that a minority of young troublemakers acted against the will of the majority of responsible blacks. And most moderate black leaders adopted this position too.[2]

These statements make up the "riffraff theory" of riot participation.[3] At the core of this theory are three distinct, though closely related, themes. First, that only an infinitesimal fraction of the black population (2 per cent according to some, and 1 per cent according to others) actively participated in the riots. Second, that the rioters, far from being representative of the black community, were mainly the riffraff—the young, unattached, unskilled, unemployed, uprooted, and criminal—and outside agitators. Indeed, many public figures have insisted that outside agitators, in particular left-wing radicals and black nationalists, incited the riffraff and thereby provoked the rioting. And third, that the overwhelming majority of the black population—the law-abiding and respectable 98 or 99 per cent who did not join in the rioting—unequivocally opposed the riots.[4]

For most whites the riffraff theory is highly reassuring. If the rioters were a tiny fraction of the black population, composed of the riffraff and outside agitators and opposed by a large majority of the ghetto residents, the riots were less ominous than would otherwise be the case. They were also a function of poverty, which is alterable, rather than race, which is immutable; in which case they were peripheral to the issue of white-black relations in the United States. Again, if the riffraff theory is correct, the riots were a reflection less of the social problems of ghettos than of the personal disabilities of newcomers. And the violent acts, the looting, arson, and assault, were not articulate protests, but rather, in the words of the McCone Commission, "formless, quite senseless," and, by implication, "meaning-less" outbursts.[5] Lastly, if the prevailing view of riot participation is accurate, future riots can be prevented merely by elevating the riffraff and muzzling outside agitators without transforming the black ghettos. Without, in other words, radically changing the American metropolis, thoroughly overhauling its basic institutions, or seriously inconveniencing its white majority.

In view of the profound implications of the riffraff theory, it is disconcerting that its adherents have not offered solid supporting evidence. Their estimates of participation were based largely on im-pressions of subordinates, who had good reason to play down the rioting, and not on interviews with lower- and working-class blacks. Their descriptions of the rioters were drawn primarily from personal observations and, in some cases, casual and often poorly informed glances at arrest statistics. Their opinions about ghetto attitudes were formed mainly from cursory soundings of moderate blacks, who opposed the rioting, and not of militant blacks.[6] The adherents of the riffraff theory also overlooked a good deal of evidence which sharply questions and sometimes contradicts their position. The sheer number of arrests indicates that unless the police caught most of the rioters, which is highly unlikely, more than 1 or 2 per cent of the ghetto residents participated. The written and graphic descrip-tions of the riots also reveal that many working- and middle-class blacks joined in the rioting, looting, and assault. And the remarks of blacks during and after the rioting suggest that many who did not themselves participate tacitly supported the rioters.[7]

Why, then, has the riffraff theory been so widely adopted to explain the 1960s riots? Why was it adopted to explain the Harlem riots of 1935 and 1943 and many other American riots as well? The answer can, I believe, be traced to the conviction that no matter how grave the grievances there are no legitimate grounds for violent protest, a conviction shared by most Americans which reflects the nation's traditional confidence in orderly social change. To have accepted the possibility that a substantial and representative segment of the black population participated in or supported the riots would have forced most Americans to draw one of two conclusions. Either that the long-term deterioration of the black ghetto has destroyed the prospect for gradual improvement and provided the justification for violent protest, or that even if conditions are not so desperate many blacks believe otherwise. Neither could have been reconciled with the commitment to orderly social change; either would have compelled most Americans to re-examine the ideology of their race, class, and country. And this they were not inclined to do.[8]

It was not until 1966, when the U.C.L.A. Institute of Government and Public Affairs released a survey of participation in the Los Angeles riots and the California Department of Justice issued a report on the persons arrested there, that the riffraff theory was questioned. And it was not until 1968, when the University of Michigan's Survey Research Center, the Governor of New Jersey's Select Commission on Civil Disorder, and the U. S. Department of Labor completed similar studies of the Newark and Detroit riots, that the theory was seriously challenged.[9] Although these studies did not employ precisely the same methods or arrive at exactly the same findings, they did reach certain conclusions which contradict one or more of the central points of the riffraff theory. First, that a substantial minority of the ghetto population, ranging from roughly 10 to 20 per cent, actively participated in the riots. Second, that the rioters, far from being primarily the riffraff and outside agitators, were fairly representative of the ghetto residents. And third, that a sizable minority (or, in some cases, a majority) of blacks who did not riot sympathized with the rioters.[10]

These conclusions have very different implications than the riffraff theory. If the rioters were a substantial and representative segment of the black population, widely supported in the ghettos, the riots were every bit as ominous as they seemed. They were also a manifestation of race more than poverty. Indeed, there is considerable evidence that working- and middle-class blacks resent the indignities of ghetto life as much as, if not more than, lower-class blacks do.[11] And thus they were central to the relationship of whites and blacks in America. If these conclusions are warranted, the riots were a reflection of social problems endemic to the ghettos and not personal disabilities peculiar to the newcomers. And the violent acts were articulate protests against ghetto conditions. Finally, if the revisionist view of riot participation is valid, future riots can only be prevented by transforming the black ghetto and, by implication, the white metropolis. If for no other reason than to test the riffraff theory, then, an investigation of riot participation is very much in order.

To analyze participation in peaceful protests is hard enough; to analyze participation in riots is immeasurably harder. For riot participation, by its very nature, defies meticulous analysis; and the 1960s riots were not exceptions to this rule. Unlike the August 1963 March on Washington, the June 1968 Solidarity Day March of the Poor People's Campaign, the April 1969 Mobilization Peace Rally,[12] the riots were not orderly gatherings that proceeded during the daytime along fixed and highly visible routes selected well in advance. On the contrary, they were without leaders and outside the laws. The rioters did not march past a single spot or assemble in a special place; nor did they identify themselves to newsmen or sign their names on public statements; and, unlike counter-demonstrators, the non-rioters had little opportunity to make known their opinions. For these reasons even the reporters who covered the riots firsthand found it virtually impossible to estimate the number of rioters with accuracy, determine their character with precision, or gauge community sentiment with confidence.[13]

The journalists have therefore yielded to the social scientists, the most active of whom have been David O. Sears of U.C.L.A.'s Institute of Government and Public Affairs and Nathan S. Caplan, assisted by Jeffery M. Paige, of the University of Michigan's Survey Research Center. Applying the standard techniques of survey research, Sears interviewed 600 blacks from Los Angeles, and Caplan interviewed 393 blacks fifteen years and older from Detroit and 233 black males between the ages of fifteen and thirty-five from Newark.[14] Sears asked his interviewees whether they had been very active, somewhat active, or not at all active in the riots; Caplan asked them first whether or not they had participated, either as rioters or counter-rioters, and then in what ways they had participated. Both Sears and Caplan also posed a number of questions about the desirability, efficacy, and inevitability of riots which were designed to reveal the black community's overall attitude towards rioting. They then analyzed the responses for the samples as a whole and for selected demographic categories.[15]

These studies suffer from severe methodological problems. Some are common to almost all kinds of survey research: are the samples random or biased? are the respondents honest or lying? Others are peculiar to survey research about deviant behavior.[16] After all, rioting is against the law; and many rioters were probably reluctant to admit their involvement. In all likelihood, the blacks' strong suspicion of curious strangers who might be from the welfare bureau, the housing authority, or even the police department reinforced this reluctance. What is more, the Los Angeles and, to a lesser degree, the Newark and Detroit surveys defined participation so vaguely that it was susceptible to different interpretations by the respondents. To be very active or somewhat active (indeed, even to riot or to loot) might have meant one thing to an employed, middle-aged family man and quite another to an unemployed teen-ager or young adult. Lastly, the riots and the official responses changed so markedly from one day to the next that it would not be surprising if the non-rioters (and, for that matter, even the rioters) held one attitude toward the rioting while it was under way and a different one once it was over.[17]

These methodological problems have certain substantive implications. To begin with, the surveys were made so soon after the riots, when many of the respondents feared arrest, that they probably underestimated participation. Conversely, if other surveys are made later on, when the rioting is embedded in the folk history of the ghettos, the interviewees will probably overestimate participation.[18] Also, the surveys may have exaggerated the extent of participation among the riffraff, who were probably more prone than better-off blacks to admit involvement. By the same token, the surveys very likely downplayed the role of outside agitators, who, as outsiders, would have been unavailable and, as agitators, would have been unreliable. Whether the timing of the surveys tended to increase or reduce the reported degree of community support for the riots is less clear. It depends on whether the respondents were at the time more impressed by the deaths, injuries, and destruction or by the widespread public attention. Later, as the blacks forget the losses and the whites forget the ghettos, critics and enthusiasts alike will presumably soften their positions. Hence the Sears and Caplan surveys, while valuable sources of information on riot participation, are, if anything, biased in favor of the riffraff theory.

Surveys are not the only sources. No less valuable, though much less well known, are the official reports on the riot arrestees, the most thorough of which were prepared by the California Department of Justice and the Governor of New Jersey's Select Commission on Civil Disorder.[19] Both reports relied heavily on arrest sheets (also known as blotters), written forms filled out by either the arresting officer or the booking officer, at the time of arrest or shortly after, on the basis of information supplied by the arrestees. The sheets include material not only about the arrest (time, place, charge, circumstances, arresting officer, and so forth), but also about the arrestee (age, sex, birthplace, occupation, and, among other things, prior criminal record). The California Department of Justice collected approximately four thousand sheets from the Los Angeles riots, and the Governor's Select Commission on Civil Disorder gathered roughly fifteen hundred sheets from the Newark riots. Both agencies then analyzed the arrest sheets and afterwards compiled profiles of the arrestees (and, by implication, of the rioters).[20]

These analyses also suffer from serious methodological problems. In the first place, they reveal a good deal about the characteristics of the rioters but very little about the extent of participation and the degree of community support. Although they do not depend on ex post facto data, they do depend on the reliability of the arrestees, who, according to one study,[21] are not consistently honest. Just as important, these studies assume the objectivity (or nonselectivity) of the arrest process, even though the police, through no fault of their own, apprehended only a small fraction of the rioters. Now there is little doubt that the arrest process is somewhat selective.[22] But there is much doubt whether the arrest process is highly selective: from the available evidence it is not even possible to tell whether the worst or the slowest rioters were more likely to be caught. What is more, the sheets are for arrests and not for convictions; they do not distinguish between guilty and innocent, nor do they allow for mistakes in the charge. And, as if this were not enough, arrest sheets, like police practices, vary considerably from one city to the next.

These methodological problems have certain substantive implications, too. Out of fear for their families, jobs, and futures, the arrestees may well have lied about their residence, employment, and prior criminal record. And in their determination to quell the rioting, the police may well have ignored the differences between the disreputable and respectable, though not to the extent of favoring the riffraff at the expense of the better-off. On the other hand, though the distinction between arrest and conviction cannot be lightly dismissed, the timing of the arrests, evidence from several cities indicates, coincides closely with the timing of the riots.[23] And the arrest sheets, for all their variations, contain several demographic items (such as age, sex, and race) and criminal charges (such as looting and arson) which are comparable from city to city. Rather than pursue the question further, it is safe to conclude that the arrest sheets are, if anything, biased in favor of the riffraff theory, too.

For an investigation of riot participation, then, two complementary, though not wholly satisfactory, sources of information are available, namely, survey research and arrest data. Unfortunately, these sources have not yet been analyzed for enough riots to permit generalizations. To take additional soundings of ghetto residents is not practicable either because the riots are already receding into the past. To make further studies of arrest sheets is another matter, however, because the sheets remain unchanged over the years. In any event, this was the conclusion reached late in 1967 by the National Advisory Commission on Civil Disorders (commonly known as the Kerner Commission). Accordingly the commission, with remarkable cooperation from police departments all over the country, gathered approximately twenty thousand arrest sheets from roughly a score of cities which had experienced rioting in the 1960s. The commission turned them over for analysis to me and Dr. Robert B. Hill of Columbia University's Bureau of Applied Social Research.[24] And our findings, supplemented by the surveys and studies described earlier, provide the basis for the most systematic evaluation yet of the riffraff theory of riot participation.

It is not hard to challenge the first point of the riffraff theory—that an infinitesimal fraction of the black population, no more than 1 or 2 per cent, actively participated in the riots. If only 1 or 2 per cent of the blacks rioted in Detroit or Newark, then, in view of the large number of persons arrested there, the police must have apprehended almost all the rioters,[25] a conclusion contradicted by the eyewitness accounts of these riots. Also, according to the University of Michigan's Survey Research Center, 11 per cent of the blacks fifteen years and older rioted in Detroit, and 45 per cent of the black males between the ages of fifteen and thirty-five rioted in Newark.[26] It is, however, much harder to reach a more precise estimate of how large a segment of the black population actively participated in the riots. For an estimate depends on the answers to two difficult questions: how many blacks might have joined in the riots? and how many blacks did join in the riots? Fortunately, the survey research and arrest data provide tentative answers to these questions and rough estimates of riot participation.

To determine how many blacks might have joined in the riots, it is incorrect to use the total number of blacks in the community. The reason why is illustrated by a brief discussion of the McCone Commission Report, which based its estimate of riot participation on all of Los Angeles County's 650,000 blacks.[27] This figure is wrong for two main reasons. First, the 1965 riots occurred principally in south-central Los Angeles, and not in Los Angeles County's small and dispersed black enclaves. Blacks from these communities should not have been counted any more than blacks from Chicago's South Side should be counted to determine how many might have joined in the West Side riots of 1966. Second, south-central Los Angeles contains a sizable number of residents who, for a variety of reasons, could not possibly have participated in the 1965 riots. Neither the infants and elderly, the lame, halt, and blind, nor the residents in prison, hospitals, and the armed forces should have been counted. Thus to determine how many blacks might have joined in the riots, it is essential to compute the number of potential rioters in the community.

The potential rioters are, to begin with, the residents of the riot area, not the metropolis, not the city, and not necessarily even the poverty area, but rather the neighborhood which experienced the rioting. To chart the riot area—or, in effect, to fix boundaries of the rioting, looting, arson, and assault—is an overwhelming task, one well beyond the scope of this brief essay. Fortunately, the Kerner Commission mapped the riot areas for Detroit, Newark, and several other cities in the course of its investigation.[28] And on the basis of the commission's maps the number of blacks living in the riot areas was computed. But, to continue, only some of the blacks living in the riot areas—namely, males and females between the ages of ten and fifty-nine inclusive—are the potential rioters. This definition is a broad one. It excludes children under ten and adults over fifty-nine not only for reasons of common sense, but also because they were only 1 per cent of the arrestees. And it includes the handicapped and the institutionalized, who are admittedly few in number, and women, even though they were less likely than men to join in the riots.[29]

The definition of potential rioters as all blacks living in the riot areas between the ages of ten and fifty-nine inclusive maximizes the base of the population and thereby minimizes the extent of participation. It is, if anything, biased in favor of the riffraff theory. And if this definition is applied to the dozen riots in which more than two hundred persons were arrested (and for which the arrest sheets were collected and the riot areas mapped) the numbers of blacks who might have joined in the riots are 166,400 in Los Angeles (August 1965), 149,000 in Detroit (July 1967), 90,700 in Philadelphia (August 1964), 46,500 in Newark (July 1967), 42,000 in Cincinnati (June 1967), 38,900 in Harlem (July 1964), 29,700 in Bedford-Stuyvesant (July 1964), 22,900 in Atlanta (June 1967), 13,700 in Chicago (July 1966), 15,300 in Rochester (July 1964), 12,600 in Cleveland (June 1966), and 5200 in New Haven (August 1967). It should be noted, however, that these figures, which are based on 1960 Census Tract data, probably underestimate the number of potential rioters.[30]

To determine how many blacks did join in the riots in these communities is much harder. The only data available are the U.C.L.A. survey of the Los Angeles riots and the University of Michigan surveys of the Newark and Detroit riots. About the other nine riots there is no information whatsoever. What is more, for the purpose of measuring riot participation among blacks between the ages of ten and fifty-nine even the available surveys are not particularly illuminating. The Newark survey included only black males between the ages of fifteen and thirty-five; the Detroit survey included only blacks above the age of fifteen; and the Los Angeles survey did not make explicit its age limits.[31] Notwithstanding these limitations, there is a way, albeit a highly speculative way, to derive estimates of riot participation from the survey research and arrest data. It requires two fairly simple, though not totally reliable, calculations. First, to find the ratio between the number of rioters in a given age group in Los Angeles, Newark, and Detroit and the number of arrestees in the same age groups in these cities. And second, to apply this ratio to these and the other nine cities—or, in effect, to multiply the number of arrestees by this ratio—and thereby estimate the number of rioters.

If this approach is applied, the results are as follows: of the 33,500 or so blacks in the Los Angeles ghetto between the ages of twenty-five and thirty-four, approximately 1200 were arrested in the 1965 riots, and, according to the Sears survey, roughly 22 per cent, or 7200, were active in the riots. Hence the ratio of rioters to arrestees in Los Angeles was about six to one. Of the 9800 or so black males in the Newark riot area between the ages of fifteen and thirty-five, approximately 900 were arrested in the 1967 riots, and, according to the Caplan survey, roughly 45 per cent, or 4400, participated in the riots. Hence the ratio of rioters to arrestees in Newark was about five to one. Of the 147,000 or so blacks in the Detroit riot area fifteen years and older, approximately 5400 were arrested in the 1967 riots, and, again according to the Caplan survey, roughly 11 per cent, or 16,200, joined in the riots. Hence the ratio of rioters to arrestees in Detroit was about three to one.

Whether the ratios which hold for Los Angeles, Newark, and Detroit would hold for the other cities is impossible to say. But if the ratio of six to one is applied to Los Angeles, the ratio of three to one to Detroit, and the ratio of five to one to Newark and the other cities, the numbers of blacks who participated in the riots are 23,200 in Los Angeles, 16,900 in Detroit, 1900 in Philadelphia, 6900 in Newark, 1800 in Cincinnati, 1100 in Harlem, 1800 in Bedford-Stuyvesant, 800 in Atlanta, 3900 in Rochester, 1900 in Chicago, 1600 in Cleveland, and 1800 in New Haven. And if these estimates are reasonably accurate, the proportions of blacks who participated in these riots are 14 per cent in Los Angeles, 11 per cent in Detroit, 2 per cent in Philadelphia, 15 per cent in Newark, 4 per cent in Cincinnati, 3 per cent in Harlem, 6 per cent in Bedford-Stuyvesant, 3 per cent in Atlanta, 25 per cent in Rochester, 14 per cent in Chicago, 13 per cent in Cleveland, and 35 per cent in New Haven.[32]

These estimates are highly speculative: riot areas have imprecise boundaries, ghetto residents are constantly moving, survey research is an inexact science, and police practices differ from one city to another. But these estimates are no more speculative than the personal impressions of courageous, but terribly harried, newspaper reporters or the official statements of concerned, but hardly dispassionate, public figures. These estimates also vary considerably from one city to the next, and, for reasons which are unclear,[33] they are lower in Detroit and Newark than in smaller communities which suffered much less serious rioting. But these estimates far exceed the riffraff theory's estimates; and, even more noteworthy, nowhere except in Philadelphia are they as low as 2 per cent of the black population. Hence the rioters were a minority, but a substantial minority—and, in view of the historic efficacy of the customary restraints on rioting in the United States, a significant minority too.[34] And to characterize them otherwise is not only to confuse the historical record but also to mislead the American public.

The second point of the riffraff theory—that the rioters, far from being representative of the ghetto community, were mainly the riffraff and outside agitators—has a certain plausibility. According to the arrest data, as the McCone Commission and other official agencies have noted, many rioters were young, unattached, unskilled, unemployed, uprooted, and, broadly defined, criminals.[35] But according to the census and other data, many blacks, rioters or non-rioters, are juveniles or young adults; many are single (or separated, divorced, and widowed), many unskilled and unemployed, and many recent immigrants; many have criminal records, too.[36] Hence to test the second point of the riffraff theory it is not enough just to ask whether many of the rioters fit into these categories; obviously they do. It is also necessary to ask whether a greater proportion of the actual rioters than the potential rioters fit into these categories. And to this question the arrest sheets from a dozen riots[37] over the past four years in which two hundred or more persons were arrested provide fairly reliable answers.

Although a majority of the arrestees (ranging from 68 per cent in the Cincinnati riots to 92 per cent in the New Haven riots) were adults, the rioters were a good deal younger than the potential rioters.[38] The difference was not manifested among the juveniles (defined, for the sake of consistency, as youths between the ages of ten and seventeen), who were a higher proportion of the arrestees than the residents in only four cities. Rather, the difference was manifested among the teen-agers and young adults from fifteen to twenty-four years of age. In four riots they were a majority (ranging from 52 per cent in the Bedford-Stuyvesant riots to 73 per cent in the Cincinnati riots); and only in the Rochester riots were they less than 40 per cent. The difference was also manifested among the young adults between the ages of twenty-five and thirty-four, who were considerably overrepresented in all but one riot where the fifteen to twenty-four age group was not a majority. Needless to say, the middle-aged and elderly from thirty-five to fifty-nine years of age (as well as the children from ten to fourteen years of age) were underrepresented in the riots. In sum, the teen-agers and young adults between the ages of fifteen and thirty-four, who are a minority of the potential rioters in every city except New Haven, were an overwhelming majority of the arrestees (ranging from 65 per cent in Harlem to 90 per cent in Atlanta) in all the riots.

At first glance the rioters also seem much more likely to be single, though much less likely to be separated, divorced, and widowed, than the potential rioters. In the seven riots for which information is available, single people were a majority (ranging from 57 per cent in the Atlanta riots to 76 per cent in the Cincinnati riots) in all except the Rochester and the Detroit riots.[39] By contrast, only about one in five of the potential rioters is single, though another one in five is separated, divorced, and widowed.[40] In view of the extremely heavy participation of the teen-agers and young adults, however, the difference is considerably less impressive. Indeed, if the arrestees in all the riots for which information is available are divided into two categories, one twenty-five years of age and under and the other twenty-six years of age and over, the difference virtually vanishes. Of the younger arrestees fully 78 per cent were single and only 20 per cent married; and of the older arrestees fully 54 per cent were married and only 31 per cent single. These proportions differ so little from the proportions for the ghetto residents that it is fair to say that, if age is held constant, the rioters were about as likely to be single as the potential rioters.

At first glance, too, the rioters seem much more likely to be unskilled and unemployed than the potential rioters. Although the unskilled are a minority (ranging from 28 per cent in Detroit to 48 per cent in Cincinnati) in every city save Atlanta, they were a majority (ranging from 50 per cent in the Detroit riots to 76 per cent in the Cleveland riots) in the ten riots for which information is available.[41] And although the unemployed are a small minority (ranging from 8 per cent in Chicago to 12 per cent in Newark) in the cities, they were a large minority (ranging from 18 per cent in the Atlanta riots to 43 per cent in the Chicago riots) in the eight riots for which information is available.[42] At a second glance, however, these differences are a good deal less impressive. The occupational distributions of the arrestees and the residents are quite similar; and the disparities partly reflect the extremely heavy participation of teen-agers and young adults who are somewhat more likely to be unskilled. Also, the Department of Labor's figures sharply underestimate unemployment in the ghettos;[43] and the remaining disparities largely reflect the exceptionally high unemployment among black teen-agers and young adults. So, if age is again held constant, the rioters were about as likely to be unskilled and unemployed as the potential rioters.

A great many rioters were also born in the South.[44] They were a majority (ranging from 51 per cent in the Chicago riots to 66 per cent in the Los Angeles riots) in five of the eight riots for which information is available and a large minority (ranging from 19 per cent in the Cincinnati riots to 47 per cent in the Harlem riots) in the other three. But a great many potential rioters were born in the South too. Indeed, the potential rioters were more likely to be born in the South in four of the eight cities; and in none of the other four were they less likely to be born there by much more than a few percentage points. Doubtless the extremely heavy participation of teen-agers and young adults, who were less likely to be born in the South, reduces the proportion of newcomers involved in the riots. But if the arrestees are again separated into two groups, with twenty-five years of age the dividing point, the difference, small to begin with, becomes negligible. Of the younger rioters 36 per cent were born in the South; and of the older rioters 62 per cent were born there; and these figures differ little from the figures for the ghetto residents of the same age. So, if age is held constant again, the rioters were about as likely to be born in the South as the potential rioters.

A majority of the arrestees (ranging from 57 per cent in the Detroit riots to 82 per cent in the Cleveland riots) also had prior criminal records in all but two of the eight riots for which information is available. But it is one thing to have a record and quite another to be a criminal; and there are a number of reasons why these figures do not prove that the arrestees were criminals. First, a criminal record in the United States simply means an arrest, as opposed to a conviction; probably no more than one half of the arrestees with a record had been convicted, and probably no more than one quarter for a major crime. Second, according to the President's Crime Commission, which has made the only estimate I know of, roughly 50 to 90 per cent of black males in the ghettos have criminal records.[45] And third, if the findings of the President's Commission on Crime in the District of Columbia are applicable elsewhere, the arrestees were much more likely to be employed and much less likely to have criminal records (and especially major criminal records) than convicted felons.[46] Hence to label the rioters as criminals is simply to brand most blacks (or at any rate most black males) as criminals.

If the firsthand descriptions of the riots are reliable, a few left-wing radicals and black nationalists encouraged the rioters and exploited the rioting. It would have been surprising had they not done so. But according to the arrest sheets, the overwhelming majority of the rioters were not outsiders. In none of the twelve riots did the proportion of the arrestees who resided in the stricken cities fall below 90 per cent. It ranged from 92 per cent in Newark to 100 per cent in Cincinnati. According to the Kerner Commission, too, most rioters were long-term residents of their cities.[47] The arrest sheets do not of course reveal whether or not a few agitators conspired to bring about the riots. But a good deal of other evidence is available on this point. The F.B.I. issued a brief report on the

1964 riots; F.B.I. director J. Edgar Hoover and Attorney General Ramsey Clark released public statements on the 1967 riots; and the Kerner Commission made a thorough analysis of the federal, state, and municipal reports on the 1967 riots.[48] And on the basis of this information, it is quite clear that the agitators did not secretly organize or effectively control the riots.

Hence the second point of the riffraff theory is inaccurate too. Depending on the riot, roughly two thirds to nine tenths of the arrestees were teen-agers or young adults, one half to two thirds single or otherwise unattached, one half to three quarters unskilled, one fifth to two fifths unemployed, and one third to two thirds uprooted; and one third to nine tenths had prior criminal records. But these figures do not sharply distinguish the rioters from the potential rioters; and to the extent that they do this reflects mainly the extremely heavy involvement of young adults who are more likely than their fathers to be single, unskilled, and unemployed (though not uprooted or previously arrested). That young men born and raised in the ghettos who reached maturity in the 1950s and 1960s participated so heavily in the riots is not surprising. What is surprising is that, in view of the historic efficacy of the restraints on rioting among blacks, fully one quarter to one half of the arrestees (again depending on the riot) were skilled or semiskilled, three fifths to four fifths were employed, and one third to two thirds were northern-born. Thus to claim that the rioters were mainly the riffraff and outside agitators rather than fairly typical young adult males is to seriously misinterpret the riots.

Before concluding the analysis of the second point of the riffraff theory, however, it is necessary to examine it from a somewhat different viewpoint. Even though the theory is disproved when the rioters are treated city by city, it may be confirmed if they are considered according to day of arrest, type of offense, year of the riot, or region of the country. In other words, even if the riffraff theory fails to account for the rioters as a whole, it might account for the rioters who were arrested on the first day or the second day, for looting or arson, in 1964 or 1967, or in the North or the South. It is impossible to tell whether there were differences from one region to another because not enough arrest sheets are on hand from the southern riots. But it is possible to say whether there were differences from one day to another, from one type of offense to the next, and from one year to another because day of arrest and criminal charge are included on the arrest sheets and the sheets are available from three or more riots in 1964, 1966, and 1967.[49] By so doing it is possible to evaluate further this point of the riffraff theory and in the process to learn more about participation in the 1960s riots.

If the arrestees[50] are broken down into blacks arrested on the first day, second day, and third day and after, their profiles are extremely perplexing. The blacks arrested on the first day were most likely to be under twenty-five years of age, single, unskilled, and unemployed and next most likely to have a criminal record; but they were also least likely to be born in the South. The blacks arrested on the second day were most likely to have a criminal record and next most likely to be under twenty-five years of age, unskilled, unemployed, and born in the South; but they were also least likely to be single. And the blacks arrested on the third day were most likely to be born in the South and next most likely to be single; but they were also least likely to be under twenty-five years of age, unskilled, and unemployed and to have a criminal record. Hence the blacks arrested on the first day bear the closest resemblance to the riffraff. But they were not only the least likely to be born in the South but also the most likely to be white-collar workers. In view of these inconsistencies it is safe to conclude that the riffraff theory is not confirmed if the arrestees are classified according to day of arrest.

A few patterns do emerge, however. The relatively young, single, unskilled, and unemployed blacks were more active on the first day of the riots than on the second day and more active on the second day than on the third day. The opposite is true for the relatively old, married, skilled, and employed blacks. Perhaps even more revealing, this pattern is reversed if the rioters are classified according

44

to birthplace. The blacks born in the North were more active on the first day of the riots than on the second day and more active on the second day than on the third day. Again, the opposite is true for the blacks born in the South. If the arrest sheets are reliable, then, the upcoming (and presumably more militant)[51] generation of urban blacks started the rioting. And only later on did the current (and presumably less militant) generation of urban blacks overcome its inhibitions and join its children in the streets of the ghettos.

If the arrestees are broken down into rioters,[52] looters, arsonists, and assaulters,[53] their profiles are once again rather inconsistent. The rioters were most likely to be unskilled and born in the South; but they were also least likely to be under twenty-five years of age and unemployed. The looters were most likely to be unemployed and second most likely to be single, unskilled, and born in the South and to have a criminal record; but they were also least likely to be under twenty-five years of age. By contrast, the arsonists were most likely to be under twenty-five years of age and single and to have a criminal record; but they were also least likely to be unskilled, unemployed, and born in the South. The assaulters were second most likely to be under twenty-five years of age and unemployed; but they were also second least likely to be single, unskilled, and born in the South and to have a criminal record. Thus the rioters, looters, arsonists, and assaulters all differ enough from the riffraff that it is fair to say that the riffraff theory is not confirmed if the arrestees are classified according to criminal charges.

A few patterns also emerge here, however. Leaving aside the rioters arrested for curfew violation and the other relatively minor offenses lumped under rioting, the looters were probably the least dangerous and disaffected of the participants. Hence it is noteworthy that, as the blacks least likely to be under twenty-five years of age and second most likely to be born in the South, they bear the closest resemblance to the current (or passing) generation of urban blacks. That they were most likely to be unemployed and the second most likely to be unskilled suggests that they looted out of an immediate sense of economic deprivation rather than a profound sense of racial exploitation.[54] Also, leaving aside the snipers, whose involvement in the riots was greatly exaggerated and whose representation among the arrestees was virtually nil, the arsonists were the most dangerous and disaffected. It should therefore be noted that, as the blacks most likely to be under twenty-five years of age and least likely to be born in the South, they bear the closest resemblance to the upcoming generation of urban blacks. That they were least likely to be unskilled and, by a wide margin, unemployed suggests that intense racial militancy is not inconsistent with relatively sound economic position.[55]

If the arrestees are broken down into the blacks who rioted in 1964, 1966, and 1967,[56] their profiles are again quite perplexing. The 1964 rioters were most likely to be unskilled and next most likely to be under twenty-five years of age, single, and unemployed. By contrast, the 1966 rioters were most likely to be born in the South and to have a criminal record, but only next most likely to be under twenty-five years of age, single, unskilled, and unemployed. And the 1967 rioters were most likely to be under twenty-five years of age, single, and unemployed, but also least likely to be unskilled and born in the South and to have a criminal record. Hence none of these groups—nor, for that matter, the Los Angeles rioters—consistently (or even remotely) resembles the riffraff. And it is reasonable to conclude that the riffraff theory is not confirmed if the arrestees are classified according to year of the riot either.

A few patterns also emerge here, however. The young and single blacks were more active in the 1967 riots than in the 1966 riots and more active in the 1966 riots than in the 1964 riots. So were the unskilled blacks. The opposite is true for the mature and married blacks. It is also true for the unemployed blacks. Perhaps even more noteworthy, the blacks born in the North were more active in the 1967 riots than in the 1966 riots and more active in the 1966 riots than in the 1964 riots. And the opposite is true for the blacks born in the South. In 1964, 51 per cent of the rioters were born in the South and 44 per cent in the North; in 1966, the year of the Atlanta riots,[57] 52 per cent were born in the South and 47 per cent in the

North; and in 1967, 33 per cent were born in the South and 64 per cent in the North. Leaving aside the inconsistency in occupational and employment status, which I cannot explain, the arrest sheets suggest that the upcoming generation of urban blacks has played an increasingly active role in the riots.

To sum up, the arrest sheets do not confirm the second point of the riffraff theory if the arrestees are classified according to day of arrest, type of offense, or year of the riot. But they do suggest a few patterns in the riot process. Apparently the upcoming generation of urban blacks, the young and single blacks born in the northern ghettos, joined in the riots first; and it was particularly active in the rioting and burning. The current generation of urban blacks, the mature and married blacks born in the rural South, joined in thereafter; and it was particularly active in the rioting and looting. What is more, the upcoming (and presumably more militant) generation has increased its participation over time much more rapidly than the older generation. Hence the fairly typical young adults born and raised in the northern ghettos who reached maturity in the 1950s and 1960s were not just the main source of rioters. They were also the rioters who joined in at the beginning, who engaged in the most serious forms of violence, and who, in all likelihood, will predominate in future riots.[58]

The third point of the riffraff theory—that the overwhelming majority of the black population, the 98 or 99 per cent who did not join in the rioting, unequivocally opposed the riots—also has a certain plausibility. A sizable majority of the potential rioters refrained from rioting, and their restraint could be construed as a repudiation of the riots. In one city after another, too, many moderate black leaders—among them, James Farmer of New York, John A. Buggs of Los Angeles, James Threatt of Newark, and Nicholas Hood of Detroit—labored valiantly to restrain the rioters.[59] And many ordinary blacks registered sharp protest against the violence while the rioting was under way and expressed extreme dismay at the consequences when it was over. From Washington, too, a group of national black leaders, including Martin Luther King, Jr., A. Philip Randolph, Roy Wilkins, and Whitney Young criticized the riots as "ineffective, disruptive and highly damaging" and called on the blacks to "forego the temptation to disregard the law."[60] This evidence, it could be argued, proves that the overwhelming majority of the black population unequivocally opposed the riots.

And yet it could also be argued that this evidence proves nothing of the kind. About one out of five potential rioters did join in the riots, and the other four might have refrained from rioting more because they feared the local policemen and National Guardsmen than because they disapproved of the riots. Moreover, the moderate black leaders labored in vain to restrain the rioters: no matter how strongly committed to their race or how deeply concerned about their community, they had little impact on the course of the riots.[61] Also, many ordinary blacks objected to the violence not so much because they sympathized with the authorities as because they suspected that blacks, not whites, would suffer the worst losses. If Martin Luther King, Jr., and other moderates appealed for nonviolence, Stokely Carmichael and other militants did not; and by the end of the summer of 1967 it was not clear which, if either, of them spoke for the black people.[62] Hence the evidence proves nothing conclusively—except perhaps that to gauge community sentiment about the riots with any accuracy it is essential to raise more revealing questions, probe more relevant sources, and offer more tentative answers.

To begin with, it is not particularly enlightening simply to ask whether the black population supported or opposed the riots. To do so is to assume that the blacks felt clearly one way or another about the rioting, when, in all probability, they had mixed feelings, and that the blacks agreed basically about the rioting, when, in all likelihood, they had sharp disagreements. It is more illuminating to ask whether the blacks believed that the riots were beneficial or essential or, even if not, inevitable, and whether the blacks objected to the rioting mainly on principled or pragmatic grounds. It is also more illuminating to ask what proportion of blacks (and especially of blacks who did not participate as rioters or counter-rioters) and which groups of blacks considered the rioting beneficial, essential, and inevitable. To phrase the questions in these ways is to allow for the ambiguities in the black positions and the differences among the ghetto residents which are at the core of the black community's attitudes toward the riots.

Unfortunately the information available is extremely scanty. The position of the moderate black leaders is well documented; so is the ideology of the militant black leaders. The activities of the rioters are also well known; and so are the efforts of the counter-rioters. But the leaders and the participants are a minority, even if a substantial one, of the ghetto population. And about the position and activities of the rank-and-file and uninvolved blacks, not much is known. Nor are the studies of arrest sheets particularly helpful. There are, however, a few local and national opinion surveys taken in the ghettos during the 1960s[63] as well as some firsthand descriptions of the riots and on-the-spot interviews with the ghetto residents made during or shortly after the rioting.[64] And these opinion surveys and impressionistic accounts convey with reasonable accuracy the black community's sentiments about the riots.

According to the opinion surveys, the black community's attitude is ambivalent. Of the blacks in Los Angeles interviewed by U.C.L.A.'s Institute of Government and Public Affairs in 1965, only one third favored the rioting, yet two thirds believed that it would increase the whites' awareness and sympathy and improve the blacks' position; only one eighth thought that violent protest was their most effective weapon, yet two thirds believed that the riots had a purpose and five sixths that the victims deserved their treatment; three fourths preferred negotiation and nonviolent protest, yet only one fourth believed that there would be no more riots in Los Angeles.[65] Of the blacks interviewed across the nation by Louis Harris and Associates in 1966, 68 per cent felt that they stood to lose by the rioting; yet 64 per cent felt that it has helped their cause, 20 per cent that it has hurt, and 17 per cent that it has made no difference;

59 per cent were confident that they will win their rights without violence, but 21 per cent were convinced that violence will be necessary and 20 per cent were not certain; 61 per cent predicted that there will be further rioting, 31 per cent were not sure, and only 8 per cent predicted that there will be no rioting in the future.[66]

According to the Institute of Government and Public Affairs, moreover, the blacks in Los Angeles objected to the rioting mainly on pragmatic rather than principled grounds: they disapproved of the consequences of the riots rather than the riots themselves. Whereas 29 per cent disliked the burning and 19 per cent the looting, 21 per cent protested the shooting and the killing and 13 per cent the police action, and only 1 per cent objected to the rioting and 1 per cent to the assault.[67] According to the Institute of Government and Public Affairs, too, the relatively well-to-do and well-educated supported the Los Angeles riots as much as the less well-off and less well-educated, though in Detroit, according to the University of Michigan's Survey Research Center, the counter-rioters tended to be more affluent and better educated than the rioters. And according to the Harris organization, lower- and lower-middle-income blacks were a bit more likely to regard the riots favorably than middle- and upper-middle-income blacks; and blacks thirty-four years and younger were much more likely to do so than blacks fifty years and older and even more than blacks between the ages of thirty-five and forty-nine.[68]

These findings are consistent with the impressionistic accounts of the riots. Firsthand descriptions of the riots and on-the-spot interviews with ghetto residents reveal a great deal of tacit support for the rioters among the non-rioters. Apparently many of them also saw the rioting as a legitimate protest against ghetto grievances, a protest which, if need be, would be delivered again. Their feelings were well articulated by a middle-age black woman who ran an art gallery in south-central Los Angeles: "I will not take a Molotov cocktail," she said, "but I am as mad as they (the rioters) are."[69] These findings are also consistent with a common-sense approach to the riots. After all, is it conceivable that several hundred riots could have erupted in nearly every black ghetto in the United States over the past five years against the opposition of 98 or 99 per cent of the black community? And is it conceivable that militant young blacks would have ignored the customary restraints on rioting in the United States, including the commitment to orderly social change, unless they enjoyed the tacit support of at least a sizable minority of the black community?

If the survey research, arrest data, and impressionistic accounts are indicative, the rioters were a small but significant minority of the black population, fairly representative of the ghetto residents, and especially of the young adult males, and tacitly supported by at least a large minority of the black community. Hence the riots were a manifestation of race and racism in the United States, a reflection of the social problems of black ghettos, a protest against the essential conditions of life there, and an indicator of the necessity for fundamental changes in American society. If the riffraff theory has been inaccurate in the past, it will probably be invalid in the future too. The riots appear to be gaining support from many segments of the black community. Of the blacks asked by Louis Harris in 1966 if they would join in riots, 15 per cent replied that they would, 24 per cent that they were unsure, and 61 per cent that they would not. Moreover, the lower-middle-, middle-, and upper-middle-income blacks were more likely to respond affirmatively than the lower-income blacks. And of the blacks thirty-four years and younger, the upcoming generation, fully 19 per cent said that they would join a riot, 24 per cent that they were uncertain, and only 57 per cent that they would not. At the start of the 1970s these responses are anything but reassuring.[70]

3: From Resentment to Confrontation

With a few notable exceptions—among them the Chicago riots of 1965, which erupted after a black woman was accidentally killed by a fire engine, the Dayton riots of 1966, which broke out after a black man was deliberately gunned down from a passing car, and the Washington riots of 1968, which followed the assassination of Martin Luther King, Jr.—the 1960s riots were precipitated by police actions. Some were extremely grave. In New York (1964) an off-duty policeman killed a black youth; in Atlanta (1966) a patrolman seriously wounded a black suspected of auto theft; and in Tampa (1967) a policeman shot a black suspected of burglary. Some were misguided and unjustified. Only in New York was the victim allegedly armed, and with a knife not a gun; in the other cities the blacks were killed in flight; and nowhere were the crimes committed by the suspects or the dangers faced by the policemen serious enough to warrant the ultimate sanction.[1] In any event, if most of the 1960s riots had been precipitated by extraordinary police actions it would not be hard to account for the blacks' reactions. Nor would it be difficult to devise recommendations to prevent, or at any rate to inhibit, such incidents in the future.

This was not so, however. Most of the riots were triggered by routine police actions, if anything, a more perplexing and less reassuring pattern. The Rochester (1964), Philadelphia (1964), and Los Angeles (1965) riots are cases in point. So are the Jersey City riots of 1964, which erupted after the police attempted to break up a fight between two black women; the Omaha riots of 1966, which broke out after the police stopped a fireworks display on the July Fourth weekend; the Chicago riots of 1966, which started after the police turned off fire hydrants on a hot summer evening; and the Detroit riots of 1967, which erupted after the police raided an after-hours drinking spot.[2] Moreover, most of these actions were taken in response to complaints by blacks. They may or may not have been wise, but they were certainly not extraordinary; the police break up fights, stop fireworks displays, turn off fire hydrants, and raid saloons all the time. Nor did the press reports reveal that the police used excessive force, showed insufficient respect, or otherwise behaved improperly in most of these incidents.

Routine or not, these police actions evoked an extraordinary response. Blacks converged on the site, shouted abuse, hurled bricks, and otherwise assaulted patrolmen, stoned and overturned police cars, and, when the opportunity arose, attempted to prevent the arrests and, failing that, to free the prisoners.[3] In the meantime wild rumors circulated through the ghetto—in south-central Los Angeles the police arrested a woman barber dressed in a smock, and word went out that they had attacked a pregnant woman; the rumors infuriated many blacks and attracted some to the scene.[4] In a few cases the police withdrew for a while, hoping to restrain the rioters by removing their targets; but in most cases they held their ground, arrested the most aggressive rioters, and, when the crowds grew larger and more menacing, summoned reinforcements. Sometimes, as in Indianapolis, Los Angeles, Kansas City, and Philadelphia in 1966, the reinforcements managed to restore order; more often, however, they succeeded only in inciting the people involved and in arousing many others.[5] In the end, a point was reached at which the police perceived the confrontation as a test of their authority and the blacks perceived it as a challenge to their pride and loyalty.

Moreover, once full-scale rioting was under way the blacks directed a great deal of violence at the police. During the day they glared at them with contempt; and at night they threw bricks and stones and, on occasion, fired rifles at them. The response to police action should not be exaggerated, however. Most blacks did not have the inclination, not to mention the arms, to murder or seriously harm the police; otherwise police casualties would have been much higher, though this is scant consolation to the few dead and injured policemen. But neither should the response to police action be dismissed on the grounds that during the rioting the policemen often exceeded their authority and the blacks sometimes fought to defend their families and friends.[6] For if this point is emphasized, it obscures one of the salient lessons of the 1960s riots: that from the beginning to the end of the rioting the police were among the principal targets. Indeed, it is impossible to conceive of the riots erupting with the same frequency or assuming the same form were it not for the ghetto's intense resentment of the police.

Many prominent blacks have attempted to explain this resentment to the U. S. Commission on Civil Rights, the Governor's Commission on the Los Angeles Riots, and other official investigative bodies. They have made three main points. First, that most blacks have long been, and indeed still are, subjected to brutality, harassment, and other forms of police misconduct in both the North and the South. Second, that most blacks are convinced that the police enforce the law less rigorously in black ghettos than in white communities. And third, that most blacks are persuaded that they have no effective way to protest, much less to remedy, brutality, harassment, and inadequate law enforcement. It is, as Los Angeles Assemblyman Mervyn M. Dymally told the McCone Commission, because black people have "generally expected the worst from the police and generally received it" that they intensely resent the police.[7] To allay this resentment, Dymally and other black spokesmen have forcefully urged that brutality and harassment be eliminated, law enforcement tightened, and police complaint procedures revised.

Police administrators have flatly denied these charges and in some cases even countercharged that these criticisms are manifestations of dwindling respect for law and order and attempts to undermine the effectiveness of law enforcement. In police departments, as in other large organizations, there are occasional lapses by misguided individuals who are promptly reprimanded and, if need be, punished —that and nothing more. The blacks' resentment, the police have explained, is due to their mistreatment in the South, their maladjustment in the North, and their misunderstanding of the police, and not to the misconduct of patrolmen. The rioters vented their violence at patrolmen not as patrolmen but as representatives of white society; the police are the recipients rather than the source of the blacks' resentment.[8] Past practices aside, police administrators have assured the Civil Rights Commission and the McCone Commission the blacks have few, if any, legitimate grievances against the police.

There is something to be said for this position. Police misconduct is less common and law enforcement stricter today than a generation ago.[9] Police administrators are less subject to political interference, ordinary patrolmen are better educated and better trained, and police departments as a whole are more aware of their limitations and responsibilities; the police are, in a word, more professional. The great majority of American policemen cannot be blamed for a small, if notorious, number of racist southern sheriffs;[10] nor can they be held accountable for the insufficient opportunity, inferior education, and inadequate housing which, it is widely assumed, underlie the high rate of crime in the black ghettos. For most blacks the patrolmen are the principal (and, after the merchants lock up for the evening, the only) representatives of white society in the ghettos. So by virtue of their presence alone, the police bear a heavy brunt of the blacks' hostility to white America.

But there is even more to be said against this position. First of all, most blacks, and not only lower-class blacks, do not believe the claims of police authorities; and their beliefs, whether correct or not, are crucial because, like most people, they act on what they believe to be true. Even more important, there is a great deal of evidence indicating that in spite of improved policing many blacks are subjected to brutality and harassment, few ghettos are adequately protected, and few complaints are impartially processed. This resentment of the police is not a rejection of policing. Not even blacks highly critical of the police, a recent survey taken in San Diego reveals, thought that policing should be abandoned; for all their criticism of police practices, none questioned the legitimacy of the police function.[11] Nor is this resentment of the police a repudiation of public authority. Aside from protesting that the National Guard is ordered in to protect white property in the North but not black lives in the South, most rioters treated the guardsmen with respect (or at any rate without sharp hostility).[12] If the outbreak and subsequent development of the riots are to be understood, then, it is essential to analyze the reasons why so many blacks keenly resent the police.

Perhaps the most familiar of these reasons is police brutality, or, simply defined, the excessive use of force against civilians. To find allegations of brutality is fairly easy. The U. S. Civil Rights Commission has received hundreds of complaints charging that policemen have barged into homes and terrorized inhabitants, beaten suspects beyond the point of resistance, shot fleeing juveniles suspected of minor offenses, broken up nonviolent demonstrations in a violent way, and even applied third-degree techniques in the station house.[13] But to prove these allegations is much harder. Nevertheless, the Civil Rights Commission found enough cases where the issue was beyond reasonable doubt to conclude that police brutality is a serious problem today.[14] Brutality is not a new, or even a growing, problem; it is not a regional problem, though it is more common in the South and more explosive in the North; and it is not strictly a class problem either, though the lower class is more likely to experience it and the middle class more likely to complain about it. Brutality is, however, a racial problem because blacks are much more likely to be victims than whites.

And blacks are well aware of this. In Detroit, Newark, Cleveland, and other cities where the Civil Rights Commission held hearings on criminal justice many blacks, especially middle-class blacks, complained vigorously about police brutality.[15] Indeed, they complained as vigorously about police brutality as about excessive unemployment, inferior education, and inadequate housing. What is more, recent surveys have revealed that their attitude is widely shared in the ghetto. Of the blacks in south-central Los Angeles who replied to the question "How much brutality is there in the community?" John F. Kraft, Inc., reported that 36 per cent said a lot, 40 per cent a little, and only 20 per cent none at all. The response was much the same in Harlem. Of the black men in Washington, D.C., who maintained that black people were treated differently by the police, the Bureau of Social Science Research found that 49 per cent thought this difference was manifested in brutality. This finding was confirmed by surveys in Philadelphia, San Diego, and other cities.[16] Taken together, the evidence indicates that a substantial minority of blacks, and not only southern blacks, believes that police brutality is a common practice today.

Whether they are right is another matter. Most police officials, pointing out that very few persons submit complaints about brutality and that very few complaints are substantiated, contend that the blacks are wrong. But this reasoning is not convincing. Most victims of brutality are not only black but also poor and powerless; they do not know how to lodge a complaint, nor do they believe it would do much good anyway.[17] Also, most policemen are so sensitive to the sanctions against brutality that they seldom mistreat civilians before witnesses or leave marks of their handiwork behind. There is other evidence supporting the blacks' position too. Of the south-central Los Angeles residents interviewed by the U.C.L.A. Institute of Government and Public Affairs, 47 per cent had seen police brutality, 43 per cent knew someone so mistreated, and 9 per cent had themselves been victims. According to data gathered by the American Civil Liberties Union, the situation is just as bad, if not worse, in Boston, Chicago, and New Orleans.[18] The evidence is crude, but, considered with the report of the President's Crime Commission, which found that excessive force was often used in Washington, D.C., it indicates that a small but significant minority of blacks is subjected to police brutality.

Contrary to the claims of the police, the source of brutality is not so much the volatility of a few wayward patrolmen as the ideology and experience of the police as an occupational group. For the police feel profoundly isolated from a public, which, in their view, is at best apathetic and at worst hostile, too solicitous of the criminal and too critical of the patrolmen. They also believe that they have been thwarted by the community in the battle against crime, that they have been given a job to do but deprived of the power to do it.[19] Excessive force is a way to even the score. Moreover, the police, who in America are regarded as employees of the taxpayers rather than representatives of the law, do not receive the deference accorded them in most Western European countries. Held in such low esteem that they cannot command respect merely by virtue of their position, they must rely on a personal, as opposed to a professional, claim to authority.[20] They must be tough. This sense of isolation and absence of respect render it very difficult for most American policemen to maintain law and order and at the same time apply minimal physical force.

This situation is at its worst in the black ghettos. Nowhere else do the police have better reason to feel isolated; so deep is their hostility that many blacks refuse to cooperate with the police. Nowhere else do the police have greater cause to sense a lack of respect too; so intense is their resentment that many blacks regard the police with outright contempt.[21] Besides, the ghetto is a very dangerous place; the rate of crime, especially violent crime, is higher there than anywhere else in the city. To deal with this problem the police rely on stereotyping, a standard practice by which they judge the individuals in a community by the reputation of the community as a whole. Stereotyping works fairly well in white neighborhoods. But applied to black ghettos it leads most policemen, particularly prejudiced policemen, to conclude that all blacks are lawless, prone to resist the police and likely to require rough handling.[22] From the perspective of these policemen, it is virtually impossible to patrol the ghettos without sometimes using excessive force.

59

In practice, then, the police regard excessive force as a special, but not uncommon, weapon in the battle against crime. They employ it to punish suspects who are seemingly guilty yet unlikely to be convicted and to secure respect in communities where patrolmen are resented, if not detested. They justify it on the grounds that any civilian, especially any black, who arouses their suspicion or withholds due respect loses his claim to the privileges of law-abiding citizens.[23] There are of course sanctions against brutality—a policeman can be suspended or dismissed from the force; he can even be sued for damages by the victim but they are not very effective. The victim who presses charges is rare indeed; rarer still is the police administrator who accepts a civilian's accusation in the face of a patrolman's denial. Moreover, the only witnesses are usually other policemen whose loyalty to their fellow officers is so strong that they are seldom willing to substantiate allegations of brutality.[24] Hence the police use excessive force for personal, as opposed to professional, ends (especially, but not exclusively, in the black ghettos) because the risks are not commensurate with the benefits.

The extent of police brutality can be exaggerated, however, if considered outside its historical context. A long-standing practice, it can be traced back into the nineteenth century when the first official police forces were established in the United States. A persistent practice, it was sharply condemned by the National Commission on Law Observance and Enforcement in 1931 and by the President's Committee on Civil Rights in 1947.[25] And viewed in perspective, police brutality is on the wane. Except in some southern states the police do not assault blacks on the streets or beat them in the station houses as frequently as they did a generation ago. Nor do they so casually dismiss charges of excessive force and other illegal activities on the grounds of increased efficiency. The decline in brutality has several causes. Police administrators have labored long and hard to persuade their personnel that excessive force is incompatible with professionalism. The courts have refused to accept evidence secured by third degree techniques, improper searches and seizures, and other unlawful tactics. And, perhaps more important, the black leadership and rank-and-file have served notice that they will no longer tolerate excessive force.[26]

To say that brutality is on the wane is not to deny that it remains a grave irritant of police-community relations in the ghettos. According to the Bureau of Social Science Research's survey of Washington, D.C., blacks who have witnessed (without, it should be noted, experiencing) brutality and other official misconduct are much less respectful of the police than blacks who have not.[27] Brutality is plainly inconsistent with the function of a police force in a democracy, too. Can anything be more infuriating to an American than to be beaten and otherwise mistreated by the very authorities who have been entrusted with a monopoly of physical force for the express purpose of protecting him? Finally, to say that brutality is on the wane is not to deny that the pace could be hastened or that public policy could be improved. Among police administrators, civil libertarians, and black spokesmen, however, there is a great deal of disagreement about the gravity of the problem, the responsibility for the situation, and the prospect for reform. And rather than enter into this controversy here, it is sufficient to conclude that brutality is one reason for the ghetto's intense resentment of the police.

Another reason, no less important though much less well known, is police harassment, or, roughly defined, the denial of ordinary respect to blacks because of their color and the presumption of their criminality without sufficient cause. Harassment assumes many forms. It is harassment when the police refer to a black as "nigger" or to an adult as "boy," when they treat a hard-working man as a loafer and a respectable woman as a tramp, when they detain, question, or arrest a black youth for no apparent reason, and when they force him to spread-eagle against a wall or a car for frisking.[28] Harassment is verbal as well as physical; and sometimes the only distinction between harassment and proper patrolling is nothing more tangible than the tone of a policeman's voice. Harassment is also extremely widespread; it is practiced in the North as well as the South and

61

experienced by middle-class blacks as well as lower- and working-class blacks. Indeed, the available evidence leaves little doubt that no one, white or black, resents harassment more than respectable blacks.[29] Harassment is also a racial problem because blacks are much more likely to be mistreated than whites.

And if the U. S. Civil Rights Commission's hearings are indicative, harassment is a very serious problem too. For every complaint about brutality received by the commission (and by state civil rights commissions and the McCone Commission as well) there are several complaints about harassment. Taken together, these complaints describe a continuous round of petty (and not so petty) insults and other indignities even more oppressive than the less frequent incidents of brutality.[30] These indignities are exceedingly frustrating not only because many are blatantly racial but also because, to anyone other than a black, some often appear trivial. This testimony is substantiated by recent public opinion surveys. Of the Washington, D.C., residents interviewed by the Bureau of Social Science Research, over one half of the blacks, as opposed to about one quarter of the whites, thought that the police needlessly push people around. Of the Los Angeles blacks questioned by the U.C.L.A. Institute of Government and Public Affairs, fully eight of ten claimed that the police use insulting language in the south-central ghetto.[31] These findings, which are consistent with other surveys of attitudes toward the police, indicate that a substantial majority of blacks believe that harassment is a common practice.

Whether they are right is hard to say because harassment is very difficult to measure. There are millions of contacts between blacks and policemen, and what is harassment to one is usually proper patrolling to the other; even to an observer the dividing line is often extremely vague. Moreover, the studies and statistics which would provide the basis for measurements are not available. There are few interviews of blacks and patrolmen and even fewer observations of field encounters; nor are there many police statistics about detention, interrogation, arrest, and disposition by race. There is, nonetheless, some evidence from Los Angeles, which boasts a highly professional police force, supporting the blacks' position. Of the blacks interviewed by U.C.L.A.'s Institute of Government and Public Affairs, fully one half had witnessed harassment and over one quarter had experienced it. Also, about twice as many persons are arrested per crime in the south-central ghetto as in the surrounding white communities; and fully one third of them are not subsequently charged.[32] If these figures suggest that harassment is fairly common in south-central Los Angeles, the report of the Task Force on Police to the President's Crime Commission implies that this is also true in other ghettos.

Again, contrary to the claims of the police, the source of harassment is not so much the prejudice of a few misguided patrolmen as the occupational anxiety of the police and the personal sensitivity of the blacks. The anxiety of the police stems from their inability to reconcile the public's ranking of their occupation, which, while slowly rising, is still rather low, with their own more elevated estimate.[33] Somewhat authoritarian in temperament, and increasingly so with length of service, most patrolmen are extremely sensitive to any sign of disrespect, any slight whatever, to their profession.[34] A large majority of them are convinced that it is harder to maintain public order today than ever before, that the criminals are more active, the public less cooperative, and the courts too lenient. For these reasons the police vigorously assert their authority and intensify their surveillance in high-crime neighborhoods; only by these means, they assume, can patrolmen insure respect and reduce crime. And though the police argue that the public should approve, and trust that all law-abiding citizens will do so, they do not consider public approval essential.[35]

Whether intensive patrolling develops into outright harassment depends on two things: how the patrolman approaches the civilian and how the civilian responds to the patrolman. Now the police do not treat everyone alike. Other things being equal, they are more likely to harass blacks than whites, juveniles than adults, men than women, the poor than the rich, and the deviant than the respectable. But, according to the squad-car sociologists, in high-crime communities the patrolman's approach is shaped largely by the civilian's response.[36] The patrolman is more inclined to behave properly if the civilian is sober and deferential, or at least civil, than if he is drunk, antagonistic, or simply disrespectful. And blacks are less respectful of the police than whites. The blacks left the South with a long and sorrowful history of police treatment; to them the patrolman was the principal agent in perpetuating racial subordination and segregation. Once in the North, moreover, the blacks are just as anxious about their status as the police; a racial (indeed, in America the racial) minority, they too are touched by acute and sometimes undue sensitivity.[37] They are quick to take offense and slow to hide resentment.

What aggravates this situation is that most policemen are prejudiced against blacks, that, as Richard Simon of the Los Angeles Police Department admitted to the McCone Commission, they do not perceive them as individuals.[38] That is, most policemen, who deal with blacks professionally as lawbreakers and personally not at all, cannot differentiate between ordinary blacks and black criminals; to them few blacks are worthy of respect and even fewer are free of suspicion. Accordingly, police discretion, which is applied everywhere in urban America and with satisfactory results in white neighborhoods, breaks down in black ghettos because the police, not knowing which blacks to ignore, check them all. This procedure is crude as well as unjust; and when law-abiding blacks request an explanation, most patrolmen believe that their authority is being challenged. A confrontation develops because few groups are less willing to hear a reasonable gripe than the police, few are less ready to accept an honest error than the blacks, and, though each would prefer to avoid a showdown, neither is secure enough to concede the issue.[39]

Although harassment is less common now than in the past, it is, in view of the blacks' current militancy, a more serious problem than ever before. Also, by virtue of its low visibility, harassment is very hard to restrain. The police are publicly opposed to racial discrimination; but the courts are ill prepared to review everyday patrolling, and the blacks are hard pressed to transform minor insults into major issues. Moreover, the community relations commissions established in several large cities have not relieved the anxiety of the patrolmen or soothed the sensitivity of the blacks.[40] Nor have they persuaded the police to halt field interrogations, stop-and-search maneuvers, and the other patrolling techniques which, in the name of vigorous law enforcement, subject the blacks to unjustified suspicion and unwarranted surveillance. Hence the situation in the ghetto is paradoxical. The police have curtailed racial discrimination and at the same time institutionalized preventive patrolling; in other words, they have replaced harassment by individual patrolmen with harassment by entire departments.[41]

This not only undermines public order in the ghettos; it also generates intense resentment among the blacks. The United States is not an occupied territory; it is a policed society, a society in which police authority is severely limited and police action is essentially responsive. Accordingly the fundamental basis of public order is not law enforcement, which is the penultimate sanction, but what Allan Silver aptly describes as the "moral consensus" of the community.[42] Put negatively, this means that the authorities cannot maintain law and order in the face of the widespread indifference, not to mention the out-and-out opposition, of the populace. By denying the blacks respect and presuming their criminality, the police are undermining the already unstable moral consensus in the ghettos; by practicing preventive patrolling in the ghettos they are treating these communities as occupied territories. And in these ways the police are engendering the intense hostility the blacks pointedly directed at their ranks during the 1960s riots.

In view of the fact that the police justify the use of extraordinary tactics in the black ghettos on the grounds that they cannot otherwise preserve order, it is ironic that still another reason the blacks resent the police is that they believe that the ghettos are inadequately protected. By this charge, which has been made to the U. S. Civil Rights Commission, the state civil rights commissions, and the

McCone Commission, the blacks mean two things. First, that the police maintain a much less rigorous standard of law enforcement in black ghettos than in white communities, that they ignore a wide range of illegal activities there, including drug addiction and prostitution, that they do not tolerate elsewhere. Second, that the police treat complaints and appeals with much less urgency in black ghettos than in white neighborhoods, that they answer calls much more slowly there, if indeed they answer them at all, than anywhere else.[43] According to black spokesmen, it is due to this dual standard of law enforcement that life and property are so precarious in the black ghettos.

If recent public opinion surveys are indicative, this belief is widely shared by the black rank-and-file. The University of California School of Criminology found that blacks in Philadelphia and San Diego are convinced that the police apply a different standard of law enforcement in the ghettos. John F. Kraft, Inc., reported that blacks in Harlem and south-central Los Angeles mention inadequate protection more often than brutality or harassment as a reason for resenting the police. And the National Opinion Research Center concluded that only one black in five, as opposed to about one white in two, regards police protection in his community as very good.[44] The black rank-and-file also acts as if it lacks confidence in the police and fears for its safety. According to a nationwide survey prepared for the President's Crime Commission, blacks are somewhat less likely than whites to report crimes to the police. Among Washington, D.C., residents, about one third of the blacks, as opposed to only one eighth of the whites, stay home at night because of fear. And blacks in Fillmore and Roxbury are more likely to carry weapons than are whites in comparable high-crime districts of Chicago and Boston.[45]

The available evidence indicates that this concern is well founded. Among Chicago's twenty-one police districts, the West Side ghetto, the site of a few recent riots, ranked first in homicide and rape, second in aggravated assault and burglary, third in robbery, and second, behind the Loop, in all serious crimes in 1965. It was closely followed by the South Side ghetto. In Los Angeles, 44 per cent of the murders, rapes, and aggravated assaults, 40 per cent of the robberies, 33 per cent of the thefts, 24 per cent of the burglaries, and 27 per cent of all serious crimes were committed in the south-central ghetto in 1965. Yet only 17 per cent of the population lived there.[46] According to a study prepared for the President's Crime Commission, too, black men are six times as likely as white men—and black women eight times as likely as white women and even four times as likely as white men—to be victims of a serious crime.[47] And as this differential exists at every income level, it is safe to conclude that the incidence of crime and the danger to life and property are inordinately high in the black ghettos.

But it does not necessarily follow that the police enforce the law less rigorously there. This was the case in black ghettos a generation ago (as well as in Irish, Italian, and other ethnic ghettos earlier). At that time the police ignored many kinds of crimes there that they did not tolerate in white, particularly middle-class white, neighborhoods. To most policemen a crime against a black was not a police matter; to most whites it was not, except in special circumstances, a public affair. So long as whites were insulated from blacks and crime was confined to the ghettos, nearly everyone assumed that the police were doing their job. The police also protected many criminals, especially, but not exclusively, white criminals, who operated illegitimate enterprises in black ghettos. Indeed, policemen and criminals were often connected with politicians and businessmen in an intricate network of underworld activities. The patrolman who overlooked these activities was well rewarded; the patrolman who interfered with them was soon transferred to another precinct.[48] The concept of limited responsibility and the practice of systematic corruption were at the core of the dual standard of law enforcement which prevailed in most cities down through World War II.

Since then, however, the professionalization of the police has made the dual standard anachronistic. Not that the police enforce the law in exactly the same way in black communities as in white neighborhoods; the incidence of crime, particularly violent crime, is so high in the ghettos that the police often respond to major crimes too late and disregard minor crimes altogether.[49] Not that there are no corrupt or incompetent policemen either; the major scandals which shocked Denver, Chicago, Indianapolis, Buffalo, and a few other cities not long ago clearly indicate that this is not so.[50] And not that the police are free of racial preconceptions; a survey prepared for the President's Crime Commission in 1967 leaves little doubt that the overwhelming majority of patrolmen are prejudiced against blacks.[51] Nonetheless, the police have by now recognized that a crime is a crime whether the victim is black or white, eliminated the more systematic and institutionalized forms of corruption, and thereby revitalized their commitment to law enforcement. And though some police departments, principally in the South, have not as yet conformed, a single standard of law enforcement is fairly well established in most of the country today.

So deep is their pride in these changes that the police have reacted extremely sharply to charges that black communities are less vigorously patrolled than white neighborhoods. Their spokesmen have stressed two points. One, that the police are seriously handicapped in fighting crime in the ghettos because blacks are seldom willing to cooperate unless their own lives or property are at stake. The other, that the police have no responsibility for the conditions underlying crime, that, to apply one criminologist's distinction, the police can prevent the opportunities but not the motives for illegal activities.[52] Concerning the first point, many blacks are reluctant (and, in view of their long history of mistreatment, understandably so) to get involved with government authorities (and, above all, with the police). And the extraordinary tactics employed in the ghettos under the rubric of preventive patrolling have greatly intensified their suspicion. Hence the police bear no small part of the responsibility for society's failure to tap what recent public opinion surveys describe as an enormous concern for public safety among blacks.[53]

68

With respect to the second point, the excessive rate of crime, especially violent crime, in black ghettos is essentially a function of poverty and discrimination and only incidentally of the quality of law enforcement. Like other impoverished immigrants, the blacks resorted to underworld enterprises when they found the legitimate channels to success narrow and clogged. The instability of their families, the weakness of their voluntary associations, and the attractions of street life eased this transition. Also, even more than the European immigrants, the blacks suffered from chronic discrimination which gave rise to severe and widespread frustration. For several generations they directed their aggression not at whites, who were either unavailable or too dangerous, but rather at other blacks (often relatives and friends).[54] And these tendencies toward crime and violence were accelerated by many policemen and correctional officers who, operating on the principle that blacks are inherently criminal, prematurely classified them as delinquent, jailed them and branded them, and thereby left them no alternative but crime.[55]

Hence the police are right in claiming that their responsibility does not extend beyond limiting the opportunities for criminal activity. But they are wrong in arguing that to meet this responsibility they must resort to preventive patrolling and other extraordinary tactics. Surely the police cannot accept the restraints of the policed society in one case and reject them in the other. The blacks, for their part, are mistaken in attributing high levels of crime and violence to a dual standard of law enforcement. But they have long held this belief and still encounter a few policemen whose behavior confirms it. In any case, the blacks cannot be expected to change their opinions in a moment when it took the police over a generation to revise their practices. Without pursuing the matter further, one point is clear. However hard it is for the blacks to submit to brutality and harassment under ordinary circumstances, it is even harder when the police do not provide the protection which might excuse occasional mistreatment. Which is another way of saying that inadequate protection is one more source of the keen resentment manifested in the outbreak and subsequent development of the riots.

This resentment is greatly intensified because most blacks believe they are powerless to protest and remedy these grievances. There are of course complaint procedures. According to a survey undertaken by Michigan State's Center on Police and Community Relations, nine police departments of every ten require an investigation of civilian complaints.[56] These procedures vary considerably from one department to the next. Roughly one half maintain special units to handle civilian complaints, whereas the other half delegate responsibility to ordinary supervisors. The findings are transmitted to internal advisory boards; some hold formal hearings, which are generally closed to the public, but most do not. Sometimes these boards enforce their decisions; more often final authority is vested in the police chiefs or the division heads.[57] But the principle underlying these complaints procedures is much the same everywhere (except in the few cities which have established civilian, or civilian-controlled, review boards). And that is, that the responsibility to receive, process, and dispose of complaints against the police should be entrusted to the police, and to them alone.

That few blacks have much confidence in police complaint procedures was made quite clear at the U. S. Civil Rights Commission hearings in Newark, Detroit, and Cleveland. Testimony taken by the commission's state advisory committee in Minnesota corroborated this. So did surveys in Philadelphia and San Diego by the University of California School of Criminology, statements to the McCone Commission, and studies by the American Civil Liberties Union (or its regional affiliates) in Atlanta, Boston, and New York.[58] Most blacks have grounds for their distrust. It is true that very few submit complaints to the police, that even fewer carry their cases to a conclusion, and that there is a wide variation in the disposition of civilian complaints in different police departments. But it is also true, as candid police administrators sometimes concede, that it is so rare as to be an occasion when a policeman is found guilty and punished on the basis of a complaint by a black (or by any civilian).[59]

There are several reasons why. First of all, none of the nation's municipal agencies, not housing, education, traffic, and certainly not welfare, solicit or encourage complaints from civilians. Well insulated from political pressure, these bureaucracies are not very responsive to public opinion; indeed, most bureaucrats consider demands from outside unwarranted interference. Hence it is not easy for civilians (even white civilians), no matter how affluent, well informed, and persistent, to protest and remedy flagrant misconduct, let alone simple incompetence.[60] For blacks it is much harder. Like other predominantly lower- and working-class groups, they are exceedingly pessimistic about the likelihood of redressing grievances through administrative channels. Short of funds, information, and time, they are understandably reluctant to entangle themselves in expensive, complicated, and often interminable complaint proceedings.[61] Hard as it is to submit complaints and carry them to successful conclusions in most municipal agencies, however, it is even harder to do so in most police departments.

For this the police bear the brunt of the responsibility. Until recently they arrested civilians for filing false complaints in Los Angeles, charged them with criminal libel in New York, and, among other reprehensible practices, demanded they take lie detector tests in Cleveland.[62] Even now the police employ a variety of tactics designed to discourage, if not to prevent, civilians, and especially blacks, from making complaints. If a civilian submits a complaint, the policeman who investigates the charges often intimidates him and his witness. If the complainant still insists on a hearing, most police departments neither provide him with counsel nor permit him access to their files. What is more, patrolmen seldom testify against one another, and police authorities often treat the complainant as if he, not the policeman, were the defendant. A decision is not reached for several months, and the policeman is acquitted in most cases; and when he is convicted the police do not publicize the verdict. More often than not, they do not even notify the complainant.[63]

It is hardly likely that the police will change these procedures in the near future. Civilian complaints bring the deepest anxieties of the police to the surface in a way that more rigorous self-policing measures directed at tardiness, sloppiness, and narrowly professional or strictly internal matters do not.[64] To most officers civilian complaints pose a serious threat to professionalism, to their determination to set their own standards, judge their own members, and maintain their own discipline. They perceive a complaint against a single patrolman as a challenge to the entire profession. Civilian complaints also intensify the policeman's distinction between the police and the public, especially when the complainant belongs to a group which, in the policeman's view, is the greatest source of criminal activity and the gravest danger to public order. Moreover, civilian complaints may do irreparable damage to an officer's career and, by implication, to every officer's career; at one time or another they too may be called on to defend themselves.[65] For these reasons most policemen stand together in opposition to civilian complaints.

So intransigent are the police that many black spokesmen and civil libertarians have proposed that civilian review boards be established to handle complaints. They have offered the following reasons. One, a small but significant minority of patrolmen engage in brutality, harassment, corruption, and other illegal, or at least nonprofessional, practices. Two, most Americans, especially black Americans, have little confidence in police complaint procedures and less knowledge about judicial and federal remedies. Three, the special character of police work, the right to employ physical force, renders it imperative that civilians feel free to call police actions into question. Four, the creation of civilian review boards would discourage police malpractice, restore civilian confidence, and thereby improve police-community relations. Five, civilian review boards would be better qualified than internal investigative units to assure complainants and patrolmen alike an impartial investigation.[66] Civilian review boards would only offer recommendations anyway, the black spokesmen and civil libertarians have assured the police; the departments would retain final authority.

The police have vigorously challenged these arguments. The amount of misconduct is tremendously exaggerated, they have insisted; the cries of brutality and harassment are often nothing but attempts to undermine the effectiveness of law enforcement. The existing complaint procedures in police departments, courts, and the Justice Department provide citizens with ample opportunity to secure redress. The police should not be singled out for special treatment, nor should they be made the scapegoat for broader social problems. What is more, the police have claimed, civilian review boards will demoralize the police, weaken their authority, impair their efficiency, and thereby increase crime in America. Police work is so complicated that it is intolerable for anyone without special expertise and practical experience to sit in judgment on a patrolman.[67] Rather than inject politics into law enforcement, the police have answered, black spokesmen and civil libertarians should promote efforts to professionalize the police and spread understanding of their role.

The controversy over independent review boards cannot be resolved at this point. But it can be clarified by noting that black spokesmen and civil libertarians have exaggerated the benefits almost, though clearly not quite, as much as the police have exaggerated the liabilities. Illuminating here is the experience of Philadelphia, which established a civilian review board in 1958. Contrary to the claim of the New York City Patrolmen's Benevolent Association, the Philadelphia Police Department, as Howard R. Leary (former Philadelphia Police Commissioner and now New York City Police Commissioner) has stated, is as effective as ever.[68] But if the 1964 rioting is indicative and if a 1966 survey by the University of California School of Criminology is reliable, the Philadelphia review board has not soothed the ghetto's resentment of the police or restored its confidence in complaint procedures.[69] Hence civilian review boards can probably promote but hardly guarantee improved police-community relations. In any event, the police have blocked them in all but a handful of cities, and not even there do blacks have the confidence in complaint procedures which might relieve the intense resentment generated by brutality, harassment, and inadequate law enforcement.

Granted that these police practices (or, to be more accurate, the blacks' perceptions of them) underlie the triggering incidents of the 1960s riots, two additional questions should be raised. First, if it is true—and I believe it is—that many other ethnic minorities have been severely mistreated by the police at one time or another, why have only the blacks responded so violently to routine police actions? Second, if it is also true—and again I believe it is—that blacks were treated worse by the police in the 1930s, 1940s, and 1950s, why have they resorted to riotous protest for the first time in the 1960s? In other words, why have blacks reacted in a way unprecedented not only for themselves but for other minority groups as well? Unfortunately, satisfactory answers cannot be offered at this point. The history of ethnic minorities in America is extremely sketchy; and, despite a recent rash of fairly impressive books and reports, the sociology of the police in America is only just under way. Nonetheless, certain broad differences can be discerned, and a few tentative conclusions can be suggested.

There is little doubt that many other ethnic minorities have been severely mistreated by the police at one time or another.[70] Irish, Italian, and Jewish suspects were subjected to third-degree practices in the precinct house in the late nineteenth and early twentieth centuries; so were Mexicans and Puerto Ricans in the middle twentieth century. Until quite recently these newcomers were also subjected to vicious ethnic slurs; the Irish were referred to as "Micks," Italians as "Wops," Jews as "Kikes," and, a generation or two later, Mexicans as "Panchos" and Puerto Ricans as "Spics." The ethnic ghettos were (and, in some cases, still are) extremely dangerous, too; down through the early twentieth century they were not patrolled systematically, if indeed they were patrolled at all. And if police complaint procedures are ineffective today, they were virtually nonexistent in the past (though occasionally injured civilians pre-

vailed on political bosses to even the score with individual patrolmen). Yet with notable exceptions, among them the Puerto Ricans
who recently assaulted the police in New York and Chicago,[71] only
the blacks have responded so violently to routine police actions.

To explain these differences requires a historical and sociological
examination of the relationship between the police and minority
groups which is well beyond the scope of this survey. But a few
points can be made other than the obvious one that the blacks are
more militant than the other minorities and that their militancy
shapes their attitude toward the police. Even if brutality and harassment are not more common in the black ghettos today than in the
ethnic ghettos yesterday, the blacks are more inclined to view police
mistreatment as a racial issue. For, except in Philadelphia and a few
other cities, the police are about as white as the ghettos are black.[72]
What is more, by virtue of the professionalization of the police and
the pressure of the community, the black ghettos are patrolled more
extensively nowadays than the ethnic ghettos were in the past. And
though this change improves the quality of law enforcement, it also
increases the opportunity for conflict between patrolmen and civilians.[73] These differences do not fully explain why the blacks have
responded so violently to routine police actions, but they do indicate
a few reasons why resentment of the police is stronger in the black
ghettos now than in the ethnic ghettos a generation or two ago.

Nor is there much doubt that the blacks were treated worse by
the police in the 1930s, 1940s, and 1950s. If the report of the National
Commission on Law Observance and Enforcement is reliable, outright brutality was much worse a generation ago. And if the novels
of Richard Wright, Ralph Ellison, and other black authors are accurate, verbal abuse was more common then than now. Also, many
police departments maintained a separate standard of law enforcement in the black ghettos down through World War II.[74] And police
complaint procedures, however ineffective they are today, were, as
I have pointed out, virtually nonexistent in the past. Indicative of
these changes, most police departments now recognize the blacks'
right to participate in nonviolent demonstrations. How much more

professionally they handled the march against residential segregation in Cicero, Illinois, in 1966 than the protest against the Scottsboro incident in New York City in 1934.[75] And yet the blacks—who previously employed a variety of strategies, some violent and others nonviolent, to express their resentment of the police[76]—have engaged in riotous protest for the first time in the 1960s.

To explain so momentous a change requires an extended analysis of the relationship between the police and the blacks in the twentieth century which is also well beyond the scope of this survey. But a few observations can be made besides the obvious one that, for reasons which I will discuss later, violent protest has recently gained increasing legitimacy in the ghettos. At present many blacks, especially second-generation blacks born and raised in northern ghettos since World War II, measure police practices by the standards of the urban North and not the rural South. And by these standards the police record has been deplorable.[77] These blacks are not frightened of the police, either; they derive a great deal of protection not only from the sheer size of the ghetto but also from the professionalization of the police. For the first time they can count on a certain restraint by most patrolmen. These blacks are more proud of themselves, too, more inclined to view police mistreatment as a racial issue and to respond actively, as a group, rather than passively, as individuals. These differences do not fully explain why the blacks have resorted to riotous protest for the first time in the 1960s; but they do suggest a few reasons why resentment of the police is much keener in the black ghettos nowadays than a generation or two ago.

In any case, if the triggering incidents and the riots themselves are indicative, the blacks are prepared, even determined, to respond to unjust police action with violence no matter what the cost.[78] They have served notice that they will resist oppression, openly and, in their view, honorably, rather than submit to brutality and harassment by policemen who do not adequately protect them. So long as they are arrested without due cause, they will challenge ordinary arrests; so long as they are subjected to verbal abuse and excessive force, they will shout back racial obscenities and launch out-and-out assaults; and so long as they are denied redress, they will protest and, if need be, protest violently. If this leads to rioting, so be it. Hence the long-standing tradition of passive resistance, eroded by generations of intolerable treatment and bureaucratic indifference, has vanished beneath a barrage of bricks, stones, Molotov cocktails, and bullets. And whatever doubts about this remained after the Harlem and Bedford-Stuyvesant riots and even after the Los Angeles riots were dispelled by the Newark and Detroit riots.

Under these circumstances it is not surprising that the blacks have resorted to collective violence to protest police practices in the ghettos. What is surprising is that, in view of the extreme vulnerability of the police in urban America and the wide range of violence available to disaffected minorities, the blacks have acted with such restraint and selectivity. For all the violence of the 1960s riots, even including the sniping in Newark and Detroit in 1967, it is beyond dispute that few, if any, blacks attempted to murder policemen. They obstructed them, insulted them, and even attacked them, but they did not kill them, and not for lack of opportunity but, as the first-hand accounts of the riots reveal, for want of intent.[79] The blacks also directed their aggression principally at local policemen, the source of their immediate grievances, and only incidentally at National Guardsmen and federal troops, the symbols of society's ultimate sanction.

Whether in the future the blacks will arm themselves and, openly or otherwise, kill local policemen, wage war on National Guardsmen and federal soldiers, and in these ways deny the legitimacy of outside authority in the ghettos is impossible to say. But the responsibility for avoiding the course rests not only with blacks, who must realize that occasional mistreatment will accompany intensive patrolling, and with whites, who must alleviate the conditions generating crime and violence in the ghettos, but also with the police. It is incumbent upon them to promote professionalism so that brutality is eliminated as rapidly as possible, a single standard of law enforcement is maintained everywhere, and complaint procedures are revised to provide opportunity for redress. But it is also incumbent upon them to recognize the limitations of professionalism, especially when it is used to rationalize the employment of preventive patrolling and the other extraordinary tactics which transform the black ghettos into occupied territories. Otherwise police actions may again trigger full-scale riots there.

4: The Ghetto's Grievances

Once the police and the blacks confronted one another the rioters filled the streets, defied the patrolmen, denounced the authorities, threatened the reporters, and participated in the other forms of low-level violence which prepared the way for more serious attacks on property and persons. They also broke into stores in the ghettos (and only into stores and only in the ghettos) and, in an open, unashamed, and orderly manner, stole the merchandise; they often deliberately burned the looted stores (and sometimes accidentally destroyed the adjacent buildings). At the same time the rioters not only assaulted white passers-by and overturned their automobiles, but also tossed bricks and stones, hurled Molotov cocktails, and, in Los Angeles, Newark, Detroit, and a few other cities, fired rifles at local policemen and other law enforcement officials.[1] By the time the rioters were finished the ghettos were in shambles and white society was in shock.

The violence differed somewhat from one ghetto to another. The differences between the Los Angeles (1965), Newark (1967), and Detroit (1967) riots, on the one hand, and the Rochester (1964), Chicago (1965), and Cleveland (1966) riots, on the other, are obvious. They can be measured by scores killed, thousands injured and arrested, and millions of dollars of property destroyed. Less obvious, but more noteworthy, are the differences among the riots of similar magnitude. There was more looting in Cleveland than in Rochester and Chicago, more burning in Los Angeles than in Newark, and more sniping in Detroit than in all the other cities combined.[2] Given the diversity of the ghettos, this is not surprising. What is surprising

79

is that no matter where the riots erupted the rioters engaged in similar violence, namely, rioting, looting, arson, and assault. And these acts of violence—particularly the looting and arson, the sources of the riots' most memorable slogans and symbols—transformed the triggering incidents into full-scale disorders.

This transformation was not inevitable. For well over a century Americans (especially adolescent members of ethnic minorities) have intermittently challenged police authority without provoking widespread disorder. The Puerto Rican and black gangs organized in New York, Chicago, and other cities after World War II are a recent case in point.[3] Not every confrontation between the police and the blacks has led to full-scale rioting. For each severe disturbance in Rochester's Third and Seventh wards, one close observer of that ghetto has estimated, there have been at least a dozen precipitating events.[4] And not all the rioters were inspired by the triggering incidents. If the available evidence is reliable, very few actually witnessed the initial confrontation—though many more probably heard the rumors that spread through the ghettos afterwards.[5] Thus, unlike the outbreak of the riots, the subsequent course cannot be explained simply as a manifestation of the blacks' intense resentment of the police.

Nor can the looting, arson, and assault be explained as simply a consequence of the breakdown of public order. It is true that rioting generated an atmosphere conducive to looting, arson, and assault; and it is also true that looting, arson, and assault enhanced the opportunities for rioting. But according to the extensive historical and sociological literature on European and American disorder, neither looting nor arson, and not even assault, is an automatic consequence of the breakdown of public order. There are too many instances of rioting without looting, arson, and assault, of looting without arson, and even, witness events in Chicago during the winter of 1967–68, of looting without rioting. If the available literature suggests anything at all, it is that there are no predetermined patterns of violence in riots.[6] And if this rule holds true in America nowadays—and I believe it does—the violence of the 1960s riots can only be understood as a manifestation of the grievances of the black ghettos.

The riots can be partially explained without reference to the ghetto's grievances. The vast majority of the disorders broke out on those extremely hot and humid summer days which leave most Americans extremely irritable, if not highly inflammable, very long on resentment and equally short on patience.[7] Also, like many Mexicans, Puerto Ricans, and other lower- and working-class people, whose lives revolve around peer groups and whose homes lack space for neighboring, many blacks spend a great deal of their leisure time on the streets.[8] Hence they were already on hand at the time of the triggering incidents. And once the riots were under way the black mobs assumed many of the extraordinary characteristics attributed to mobs in general by the French social-psychologist Gustave Le Bon more than half a century ago.[9] That is, they exhibited a touch of the demonic, a sense of overwhelming power and a feeling of excitement bordering on abandon, which encouraged the rioters to act according to the passions of the crowd rather than the rules of the society.

But the significance of summer weather, social class, and crowd psychology can easily be exaggerated. To begin with, the relationship between these variables and the riots is ambiguous. The number of disorders which have erupted in the spring and fall (as well as on temperate summer days) has increased year by year. Although Mexicans, Puerto Ricans, and other lower- and working-class groups also socialize on the streets, only blacks have resorted to violent protest. The mobs have also displayed a restraint and selectivity which stands in sharp contrast to the findings of Le Bon and more contemporary social scientists.[10] What is more, summer weather, social class, and crowd psychology are fairly constant variables. The weather may vary from one summer to another, but each will have its hot and humid days; in which case the blacks will seek relief and company on the streets; and if from time to time they engage in rioting they will behave as rioters. And this, it seems to me, is just another way of saying that if there are riots there will be violence.

These variables cannot account for the critical features of the riots either. They cannot explain why, according to the findings of field surveys and analyses of arrest sheets, the rioters were a substantial minority of the blacks, fairly representative of the young adult males, which received considerable support in the ghettos.[11] Nor can they explain why, if the newspaper accounts, police reports, and other firsthand descriptions are trustworthy, the rioting and assault were so restrained, the looting and arson so selective, and the disorders as a whole so articulate.[12] In other words, these variables do not enhance our understanding of the riots because they do not regard them as violent protests against genuine grievances in the black ghettos. And if any doubts remain about this interpretation after six summers of rioting, they should be dispelled by the many blacks who have pointed out that the violence was directed at the sources of their most profound grievances.

These conclusions should not be carried too far. The rioters were not always restrained and selective; nor was the violence unaffected by matters other than ghetto grievances. Among the most noteworthy were the availability of targets, the intensity of resentment, and the consequences of destruction. The rioters rarely attacked jails and courthouses because these facilities are located outside the ghettos and not because they are satisfied with the system of criminal justice. The rioters generally burned down stores rather than schools because consumer exploitation is even more humiliating and infuriating than inferior education. And the rioters normally spared their homes and apartments not because they are content with their accommodations but because inadequate accommodations are better than none at all.[13] Notwithstanding these qualifications, the rioters chose their targets with a consistency which suggests that a look at the violence will reveal the nature of the grievances and thereby clarify the meaning of the riots.

Of all the types of violence, the most common was rioting itself. By rioting I mean milling in the streets, defying the patrolmen, denouncing the authorities, threatening the reporters, violating the curfews, and engaging in the other low-level violence which created the setting for more serious attacks on property and persons. Less destructive than looting, arson, and assault, rioting was no less important. To begin with, rioting not only provided the first outlet for the rioters but also stimulated them to seek other outlets later on. What is more, rioting went on all through the riots, though it was more prominent just after the triggering incidents and less conspicuous once the looting, arson, and assault were under way. And besides, rioting, as an analysis of the arrest sheets indicates, attracted especially the young adult males born and raised in the ghettos who reached maturity in the 1950s and 1960s.[14]

The rioting was characterized not only by resentment, excitement, and bravado, but also by a few other less predictable yet more revealing emotions and attitudes. First, an outpouring of fellow feeling, of mutual respect and common concern, which was well described by a black psychiatrist from Los Angeles as camaraderie.[15] Second, a display of what Governor Richard J. Hughes of New Jersey denounced as carnival spirit but what was actually exhilaration so intense as to border on jubilation.[16] Third, a sense of pride, purpose, and—in spite of, or perhaps because of, the ransacked stores, smoldering buildings, and police and military patrols—accomplishment.[17] Camaraderie, jubilation, and accomplishment were, I realize, only a few of the many emotions and attitudes exhibited by the rioters.[18] But few others which are witnessed so rarely in the ghettos were observed so frequently in the riots that a brief discussion of them may well enhance our understanding of the rioting.

The outpouring of camaraderie was triggered not only because the rioters issued the protest and faced the danger together but also because the rioting revealed the common fate of blacks in America. For most blacks, and particularly northern blacks, racial discrimination is a highly personal experience. They are denied jobs, refused apartments, stopped-and-searched, and declared ineducable because —or so they are told—they are inexperienced, unreliable, suspicious, and culturally deprived and not because they are black. Few blacks are persuaded by these reasons, but only the most confident or in-transigent are absolutely convinced that all employers, landlords, policemen, and teachers are prejudiced. The rest are left to wonder from time to time whether they themselves are not somehow inade-quate, whether other blacks are not somewhat at fault, and whether racial subordination and segregation are not, as many whites be-lieve, partially justified.[19]

But once thousands of blacks rushed into the streets and joined in the riots, they realized that all blacks have suffered similar in-justices, that racial discrimination, though personal in its impact, is social or institutional in its origin. They also realized what Malcolm X told his audiences time and again: "You don't catch hell because you're a Methodist or a Baptist, you don't catch hell because you're a Democrat or a Republican, you don't catch hell because you're a Mason or an Elk, and you sure don't catch hell because you're an American, because if you were an American you wouldn't catch hell. You catch hell because you're a black man. You catch hell, all of us catch hell, for the same reason."[20] These realizations removed all doubt that color, and nothing else, prevents them from enjoying the full rights and privileges of American citizens. Their common predicament revealed in the rioting, blacks looked again at one an-other and saw only brothers.

The display of jubilation was generated by more than simply the frenzy of the rioting, the defiance of the law, and, by the rioters' criteria, the success of the riots. It was also generated by the extreme clarity of the conflict. The blacks' struggle for social justice is widely endorsed in America today; nowhere except in the rural South are ordinary civil rights withheld, and even there white supremacy is on the defensive. Yet most blacks learn that employers have few, if any, decent jobs, landlords few, if any, decent apartments, and govern-ment agencies nothing but forms. If the nation's ideology and tradi-tion honor progress and equality, the blacks wonder, why does every-thing change so slowly and why are they still at the bottom? Who is responsible, individuals or institutions, whites or blacks, everyone or no one? Lacking answers to these questions, most blacks find it extremely hard to identify their oppressors and, by striking out directly at them, relieve their frustration.[21]

But once the rioting erupted, and especially once the local police and national guard occupied the ghettos, the situation changed radically. The conflict was clear, and the issue was joined. Blacks were allies, and whites, especially white patrolmen, merchants, and passers-by, were enemies; there were no shades and no neutrals. The official response reinforced this conviction. And by the end of the riots many blacks were convinced that they were defending themselves and their families against white aggression. It was as Elijah Muhammad told his congregation over and over again: the white man is a devil; he always has been, and he always will be.[22] Unfortunately, under the terrible pressure of these events some whites confirmed his predictions. In any event, once the enemy was visible and the targets were at hand, the blacks focused their resentment, released their hostility, and, for a long moment, knew great jubilation.

The sense of accomplishment was not derived from a profound passion for destruction or doctrinaire commitment to revolution but rather from a singularly successful attempt at communication. For well over half a century blacks have repeatedly resorted to marches, appeals, pickets, petitions, demonstrations, and other nonviolent protests to call attention to their grievances. And, what with the Montgomery bus boycott, the Greensboro sit-ins, and the Washington Resurrection City, they have probably launched more protests in the 1950s and 1960s than ever before. Yet if the public statements of the Reverend Fred C. Shuttlesworth and other moderate black leaders are reliable, these protests have had relatively little impact, especially in the northern ghettos.[23] For this reason many blacks have lost confidence that nonviolent protest can direct the attention of white society to ghetto grievances in the 1960s as effectively as it had directed it to southern injustices in the 1950s.

But once the riots were under way white society did pay attention (even if many white leaders did nothing but denounce the rioters and suppress the rioting). Reporters and cameramen rushed into the ghettos; elected and appointed officials followed behind; and sociologists and other scholars arrived shortly after. The President established a riot commission; so, to list only a few, did the Governors of California and New Jersey and the Mayors of Detroit and Chicago. Henceforth the riots and, by implication, the ghettos were urgent issues; ghetto characters were national celebrities, and ghetto conditions national scandals. With reason, though without mercy, young militants boasted that they had accomplished in a few days what older moderates had failed to do in a few decades.[24] And for many blacks—who had long assumed, rightly or wrongly, that once white America was fully aware of the grievances of ghetto life it would promptly rectify them—this was no mean accomplishment.

Aside from rioting, looting was the most common and least serious type of violence. It was directed at property and not people (which makes it ironic that many of the blacks killed during the riots were looters); and it was inexpensive compared with arson. By the same token, however, looting happened in just about all the riots; and it attracted a large and broad segment of the ghetto population (including, according to the arrest sheets and firsthand descriptions, middle-age men and women as well as young male adults).[25] The character of the looting was particularly revealing. The looters did not steal furtively, as if ashamed, but openly, as if convinced that the merchandise was theirs all along; they felt no remorse, only regret, if caught by the police. Nor did they take food as often as clothing, furniture, appliances, and other durable goods; they were driven not by starvation but by acute and chronic economic deprivation.[26] Scores of blacks made this point during and after the rioting. But few did so more clearly than one woman from Philadelphia who, loaded down with clothing stolen during the 1964 riot, replied to an appeal for restraint by the local N.A.A.C.P. president, "Listen man, this is the only time in my life I've got a chance to get these things."[27]

For a great many blacks—the roughly 40 per cent or ten million classified impoverished by the Social Security Administration—this deprivation is absolute. It is worse on southern farms than in northern cities. But even there, a Department of Labor survey of a dozen ghettos all over the country recently found, fully 10 per cent of the blacks are unemployed, about three times the national average. And this figure, the department acknowledged, is a gross underestimate. Moreover, around 7 per cent of the employed work part-time because they cannot find full-time jobs, and about 21 per cent of the full-time workers earn less than sixty dollars a week. Combined into a single index, these findings show that fully one third of the blacks are unemployed, underemployed, underpaid, or otherwise "sub-employed."[28] Some (though, as several studies have recently revealed, far fewer than are eligible) supplement earnings with unemployment insurance, welfare payments, and other public assistance. But these allotments are so small that nowhere, not even in New York and California, the two most generous states, do they raise the recipients' incomes above the poverty level.[29] For these people looting offers a unique opportunity to acquire goods otherwise unattainable.

For most blacks—the other fourteen million, or 60 per cent, less a few college graduates and government employees—this deprivation is relative. Blacks have made considerable economic progress since World War II: their income has more than doubled, and their occupational range has been markedly upgraded. Yet these advances largely reflect the economy's overall expansion and structural transformation and the black migration from the rural South to the urban North. Vis-à-vis the whites, the blacks have gained little.[30] They earn only 60 per cent as much nationally, an increase of roughly 10 per cent since 1947 (and an uneven one at that); and they do only slightly better in the large eastern and western cities. Compared with whites, they are much more likely to be found in unskilled, semiskilled, and menial service jobs than in skilled, managerial, entrepreneurial, and professional positions. Even with the same education and training, one study of automotive mechanics in Baltimore shows, blacks are not paid as much as whites for the same work. As Herman P. Miller of the Census Bureau has written, "White men earn more simply because they are white."[31] For Americans, white and black, who regard goods as a sign of status and manhood, relative deprivation is as sore a grievance as absolute deprivation and as good a reason for looting.

Despite a rash of books and studies, there is no simple explanation for this situation. It is clear that economic deprivation is not a reflection of personal immorality and even, as Elliot Liebow has shown, that what seems to be laziness or unreliability may often be physical or mental illness.[32] Yet it is also clear that economic deprivation is more than just a function of inferior education and inadequate training, the comforting assumption which underlies the government's manpower program. If the recent exposés of the New York, Boston, Los Angeles, and Washington public schools are accurate, many blacks are poorly educated.[33] And if the situation whereby thousands of unskilled blacks are unemployed while thousands of semi- and highly-skilled jobs are unfilled is indicative, many blacks are improperly trained as well. According to the Department of Labor, however, black high school graduates are more likely to be unemployed than white drop-outs, and blacks, regardless of qualifications, are less likely to hold white-collar positions than whites.[34] Without denying the relevance of inferior education and inadequate training, then, it is fair to conclude that there are other reasons for economic deprivation in the ghettos.

One reason is racial discrimination, a practice which denies blacks employment opportunities because they are black. Racial discrimination is much less common now than ever before. By virtue of civil rights agitation, fair employment legislation, and enlightened corporate management, the United States has made impressive progress toward eradicating discrimination in the last few decades. No longer do the great majority of employers, private and public, pursue policies by which blacks are hired last and fired first as well as relegated to the least responsible and remunerative positions.[35] Despite these advances, however, racial discrimination is still all too common today. According to the U. S. Civil Rights Commission, it is extremely widespread, indeed just about ubiquitous, in the apprenticeship programs of most craft unions (and especially the building trades).

It is also common, though not as widespread, in the personnel practices of corporate enterprise, and it is even known, though quite rare, in the civil service procedures of government agencies.[36] Real and imagined, racial discrimination severely restricts the blacks' employment opportunities.

Another reason for economic deprivation is statutory unemployment, a policy which deprives blacks of jobs because they have criminal records. How this works can be briefly described. A large and growing number of firms, including truckers and department stores as well as banks and insurance companies, require that employees be bonded. Yet the surety companies, for all their claims that each application is considered on its own merits, reject most applicants with criminal records.[37] Also, most municipal, state, and federal agencies insist that applicants for civil service positions say whether they have ever been arrested or convicted. And the civil service administrators, for all their claims that no one is rejected outright for a minor offense, discriminate against most applicants with criminal records.[38] These practices strike particularly hard at black males because the overwhelming majority of them—between 50 and 90 per cent, according to the President's Crime Commission—have been arrested at one time or another. Hence statutory unemployment, which is probably more pervasive now than ever before, sharply reduces the number of jobs available to blacks.

Yet another reason for economic deprivation is residential segregation, the process which confines urban blacks to the central cities. This process, which, as Karl and Alma Taeuber have shown, has accelerated considerably in the recent past and is now common to American cities in every region and of every size, has a profound impact on the blacks' economic status.[39] The increase in new jobs today, and especially in the semiskilled manufacturing and service jobs for which many blacks are well qualified, is not taking place in the central cities. According to a recent study of employment in New York, Philadelphia, Baltimore, St. Louis, and San Francisco made by the National Committee Against Discrimination in Housing, they are barely holding their own. Rather the increase is taking place largely in the outlying suburbs which systematically exclude blacks.[40] Hence few blacks are aware of employment opportunities there; and, given the distance between the ghettos and suburbs and the time and cost of commuting, even fewer can take advantage of them. Combined with business decentralization, a long-term and probably irreversible trend, residential segregation seriously inhibits the blacks' economic progress too.

Even if these artificial barriers were removed, many blacks would be stymied by a severe shortage of unskilled and semiskilled jobs which pay enough to support a family above the poverty level. For this the federal government bears a heavy responsibility. The postwar administrations have placed so high a priority on controlling inflation, as opposed to maintaining full employment, that private enterprise cannot operate at capacity. Democratic and Republican alike, they have also proven so reluctant to raise taxes (except, of course, for military purposes) that the public sector cannot pick up the slack. Notwithstanding sustained economic expansion, the rate of unemployment has therefore averaged 4 to 5 per cent for whites and fully twice as high for blacks since 1947.[41] An exceedingly conservative estimate, this figure would probably be considered a national emergency in most of the industrialized countries of Western Europe. Which means that overall unemployment, often aggravated by inferior education and inadequate training, is one more reason for economic deprivation in the ghettos and, by implication, for widespread looting in the riots.

Less widespread than looting, arson was more destructive. It did not occur in as many riots (and not, to cite one, in the Newark riots); nor did it engage as large or broad a group of ghetto residents (and, to be specific, few other than teen-age and young adult males). By the same measure, however, arson left much more damage and even took a few lives.[42] The selectivity of the arson was especially noteworthy. According to most observers, the arsonists burned only stores, particularly stores which charged excessive prices and sold inferior merchandise. They did not intentionally fire houses, churches, or, somewhat more surprising, schools, hospitals, and other government facilities. The arsonists also bypassed shops which displayed signs reading "Blood Brother" or just plain "Blood" or otherwise identified the owners as blacks.[43] This selectivity can be exaggerated; a few private homes and black-owned shops were deliberately destroyed. But, in view of the ferocity of the riots, what is remarkable are not the exceptions but the overall pattern and the pervasive and intense sense of consumer exploitation underlying it.

To most blacks consumer exploitation means two distinct, though closely related, things. First, that most ghetto merchants are whites who live outside the black community and are indifferent to its welfare. As a middle-age militant, echoing Malcolm X and other black nationalists, told an interviewer after the Buffalo riots of 1967, the white shopkeepers "are siphoning off all the money and taking it out of the neighborhood and sucking the neighborhood dry." "That," he said, "is the main grievance there."[44] Second, and even more important, that most ghetto merchants are unscrupulous, that they charge excessive prices, sell inferior merchandise, and otherwise exploit customers. As a respectable woman informed her pastor after the Los Angeles riots of 1965, "it dawned on me at the height of the hysteria, as I was passing a certain store, that I have been paying on my present television set for more than five years. And [therefore] that store owed me five televisions. So I got three and I still believe they owe me two."[45] For most blacks consumer exploitation is a personal as well as a social grievance: it weakens their families' purchasing power and at the same time undermines their communities' economic position.

Many, if not most, ghetto merchants are, as the blacks protest, white—though precisely how many varies from one city to the next and from one enterprise to another. Even in Harlem, perhaps the oldest and most stable ghetto in the United States, whites own about 50 per cent of the businesses and an even higher per cent of the large-scale retail businesses.[46] And in Cleveland's Hough District and Chicago's West Side, which were transformed from ethnic ghettos into black ghettos after World War II, the percentages are probably even higher. Very few white merchants, as the blacks complain, reside in the ghettos either, and not many more are interested in the welfare and future of these communities. But few white merchants live and work in the same neighborhoods anywhere else, and, as militants are the first to point out, few black merchants are more involved. What is crucial about the ghetto merchants is not their color but their practices: put bluntly, most of them do exploit their consumers.

The price of food, clothing, hardware, and other everyday items (including housing, which is a special case and will be discussed elsewhere) is slightly higher in black ghettos (and, for that matter, in low-income neighborhoods generally). The quality is somewhat lower, too. The situation is even worse with regard to furniture, appliances, and other durable goods bought on installment plans (which, common thought to the contrary, the poor purchase as a means of what David Caplovitz aptly calls "compensatory consumption").[47] The poor, and particularly the black poor, have little or no credit. To acquire these goods they are forced to enter into a deviant market where door-to-door peddlers and high-pressure salesmen prevail upon consumers to overextend themselves and overcharge them in the process. In this way many blacks (as well as some whites) drift into permanent debt. Worse still, should the merchandise prove faulty, as it often does, the blacks are seldom aware of the legal remedies (which, in all fairness, are not very effective anyway). And should the blacks miss their payments, as they sometimes do, the finance companies repossess the goods, exact the remaining charges, and occasionally even garnishee the buyers' wages. The blacks, in Caplovitz's phrase, not only pay more; they also get less.[48]

Some ghetto merchants are unscrupulous: they feel little or no compunction about exploiting customers in order to market merchandise. To this end, as studies of black (and other low-income) communities in New York and other cities reveal, these merchants engage in a wide range of unethical practices. Among the most flagrant are the following. "Bait-ads," misleading advertisements offering furniture sets (which are either incomplete or badly run-down) at incredibly low prices. "Switch sales," sales techniques designed to persuade customers to buy much more expensive versions of the merchandise described in the "bait-ads." "Hidden costs," extra, and often exorbitant, costs effectively concealed from anyone but a lawyer by the complex wording of the installment contracts. "Substitute merchandise," inferior, and sometimes damaged, merchandise delivered in place of the merchandise selected in the stores.[49] Precisely how many ghetto merchants engage in one or another of these practices is not known, though probably a great many do. What is known is that these (and other closely related) practices contribute considerably to consumer exploitation in the ghettos.

Not all ghetto merchants are unscrupulous. But so precarious is their economic position that, with few exceptions, they too are obliged to charge higher prices, sell shoddier goods, and engage in other exploitative practices. Due to the long-standing reluctance of most regional and national chain stores to establish branches in the ghettos, most merchants there are small-scale businessmen with low credit ratings. They cannot buy in bulk to save on material costs; nor can they borrow money from reputable financial institutions except at very high, if not prohibitive, interest rates. Also, given the traditional unwillingness of underwriters to handle stores in the ghettos, the merchants cannot obtain fire and burglary insurance except at premiums so high as to be nearly extortionate. And the prices of space, labor, utilities, and miscellaneous items are not substantially lower, if lower at all, in black ghettos than in comparable white communities.[50] So long as these extra costs oblige the ghetto merchants to raise prices and lower quality to stay in business, the wholesalers, banks, insurance companies, and other external economic institutions share the responsibility for consumer exploitation.

If even scrupulous merchants engage in exploitative practices, why do most blacks still patronize them? The answer is that they have little or no choice. First of all, few blacks have the leisure, know-how, mobility, and confidence to take advantage of mercantile competition. They do not have the time to shop around and compare prices from one neighborhood to another; nor do they have the expertise to distinguish between genuine bargains and clever frauds. They are often isolated from the large downtown and suburban shopping centers; and they are sometimes reluctant (and, in view of their experience, understandably so) to shop outside the ghettos. Even more important, most blacks, and particularly unemployed and irregularly employed blacks, lack the money and credit to take advantage of marketing mechanisms. Their immediate demands are so pressing they cannot patiently wait for special sales; and their limited incomes are so uncertain they cannot slowly save for major expenditures. They cannot meet even the credit standards of the department stores and discount houses; nor can they borrow funds from reputable financial institutions at reasonable rates.[51] For these reasons most black consumers find the opportunities available to most white consumers well beyond their means.

Hence consumer exploitation is a function of the relative poverty and inadequate credit of the consumers and the unethical practices and high expenses of the merchants. Consumer exploitation is also more pervasive, poignant, and, if the riots are indicative, explosive in the black ghettos than anywhere else in urban America. It is more pervasive because nowhere else except in the rural South and the Appalachian hollows are consumers quite so impoverished and merchants quite so unscrupulous. It is more poignant because the least affluent, including the unemployed and the welfare recipients, are the most exploited—an increasingly common pattern in America. And it is more explosive because the merchants, and especially the large-scale and hard-goods merchants, are predominantly white. And though their practices are not necessarily any worse, their presence leads the blacks to define consumer exploitation in racial terms. And this combination of white merchants and exploitative practices in the black ghettos generates the intense resentment expressed through arson in the riots.

Only assault remains to be considered. By assault I mean attacking white passers-by, overturning automobiles, tossing bricks and stones, hurling Molotov cocktails, firing rifles at law enforcement officials, and engaging in the other violence directed at people as opposed to property. Somewhat less common than rioting, assault was considerably more complicated. It is one thing to grab a brick and, in a moment's anger, throw it at a passing car; it is quite another to take a rifle, find a protected spot, and shoot at a policeman. Each act reflects a different degree of disaffection; each conveys a different message to society; and, as the analysis of the arrest sheets reveals, each attracts a different sort of person.[52] But these complications should not be allowed to obscure one of the salient points of the riots. That is, that assault, like rioting, exhibited certain features which, on careful examination, clarify the motives of the rioters and illuminate their grievances and ideologies. Among the most noteworthy are a virulent strain of racism, a profound sense of territoriality, and a marked degree of restraint.

To say that assault manifested a virulent strain of racism is not to imply that all blacks treated all whites in the same way. Some blacks warned whites to stay away from the ghettos, others left them alone provided that blacks vouched for them, and still others went to the aid of whites. And though some blacks badly beat newspaper reporters, several others released them unharmed, after exacting promises that the journalists would tell the blacks' side of the story. The blacks also attacked passers-by with less anxiety than law enforcement officials; and they fought policemen with more ferocity than National Guardsmen and federal soldiers.[53] These differences aside, most blacks made little or no attempt to distinguish among the whites—to be white was to be guilty; their cry "Get Whitey!" was altogether indiscriminate—any white would do.[54] Ironically, so many riots erupted in the evening that most whites caught up in them were passers-by rather than merchants and others with a heavy stake in the ghettos. Hence black racism made Bedford-Stuyvesant, Hough, and Newark's Central Ward almost, though clearly not quite, as dangerous for whites as white racism once made East St. Louis, Chicago, and Washington for blacks.

Black racism is no less offensive than white racism, but, in view of the blacks' experience, it is more understandable. For three and a half centuries most whites have regarded blacks as blacks and not as fellow Americans or even, in some cases, as fellow men. And even today white racism, though intellectually and morally on the defensive, is fairly common, and not only in the rural South. It pervades the urban North too, particularly its trade unions, school systems, police departments, and real estate markets. Some time ago, as a result, the blacks, like other minority groups, absorbed (or perhaps adopted) the racist perceptions of white society. And until quite recently the blacks accepted the racist standards of white society, which relegated them to the bottom of the racial hierarchy.[55] This they no longer do, however. The nationalist message carried by Elijah Muhammad, Malcolm X, and Stokely Carmichael has permeated the ghettos. If black is good, the nationalists reason, white is evil: and, applying this reasoning, many blacks have concluded that, as one put it, " 'Whitey' is our only real enemy."[56] What is novel about black racism is not that it reflects the assumptions of white society but that it endorses the standards of black nationalism.

To claim that assault unleashed a profound sense of territoriality too, it is not enough to argue that the rioters did not roam outside the ghettos. After all, their principal targets, the police and the merchants, were accessible inside the ghettos, and the rioters' protective coverings, their numbers and anonymity, were not available elsewhere. Once the riots were under way, moreover, the police were quick, and increasingly so each year, to cordon off the ghettos, while the blacks, for their part, were apparently unwilling to attempt a break-through in order to attack peripheral targets.[57] Hence it is also necessary to point out that the rioters engaged in assault as a protest against the presence of whites in the ghettos. "Watcha doin' up in Harlem, White Britches?" a black youth asked a New York *Times* reporter; "Teach him to keep his ass out of Watts," several blacks cried as they beat a white motorist.[58] The rioters, the evidence suggests, resorted to assault not only to call attention to their grievances but also to even the score with the whites and drive them out of the ghettos.

And considering how few whites were shot in the riots, this probably holds true for the snipers too.

Narrowly construed, territoriality is not particularly admirable, but, again in view of the blacks' situation, it is certainly understandable. Ever since the great migration of the early twentieth century whites have rigorously excluded blacks from the greater part of urban America. Even today most builders, realtors, banks, insurance companies, and property owners are determined to reserve suburbia for whites. Meanwhile, white voters, in the name of personal freedom and property values, have rejected open housing in one community after another. Thus for blacks, and especially northern blacks, territoriality is nothing new.[59] What is new is that many blacks, far from protesting territoriality, are now preaching and even practicing it. If blacks must live in the ghettos, they reason, blacks must control the ghettos, their schools, houses, jobs, police, indeed all their institutions. Here is the ideology of self-determination, an ideology which stresses not apolitical separatism, not a black nation in Africa or a Muslim state in America, but rather black control of the ghettos.[60] And this ideology, more than anything else, has transformed the blacks' long-standing resentment of segregation into a profound sense of territoriality.

To say that assault displayed a marked degree of restraint too is not just to observe that the rioters attacked relatively few whites. Very few whites live in black ghettos, not many more work there, and most blacks did not riot in white neighborhoods. Moreover, the blacks did attack passers-by and law enforcement officials, and often with terrible brutality. For these whites (though not, of course, for the great majority safe in the suburbs) the situation was extremely dangerous. But even for them it was seldom fatal. Of the thousands of white civilians, policemen, guardsmen, and soldiers involved in the riots, very few were killed and even fewer were deliberately killed. Indeed, the number of whites killed in all the 1960s riots is lower than the number of blacks killed in the East St. Louis race riots a generation ago. The reason is fairly simple. In none of the recent riots, not even in the Los Angeles, Newark, and Detroit riots, did the blacks attempt to murder the whites, to frighten them, beat them, and injure them, yes, but to murder them, no. Nor did the blacks assault the whites in the recent riots with anything like the savagery with which the whites massacred the blacks in the race riots.[61]

The blacks' restraint, which is one of the few reassuring things about the riots, has three major implications. First, despite the tragic history of racial subordination and segregation in the United States, most blacks have not yet written the whites off as fellow Americans or fellow men. Second, despite the deprivations and indignities of ghetto life, most blacks have not yet reached the conclusion that white America and white Americans are beyond salvation. And third, despite the apocalyptic visions of the nationalists, most blacks have not yet accepted the proposition that blacks and whites cannot share the same moral community. In view of the long-standing tradition of interracial rioting in the United States,[62] this restraint is quite remarkable and highly impressive. This restraint has one other implication, too. If the mood of the ghettos is accurately reflected in the acts of the rioters—and I believe it is—the blacks' disaffection (though not their dissatisfaction) is probably somewhat less acute than is commonly thought.

But the riots made it quite clear that their disaffection is mounting rapidly. The blacks' patience is not inexhaustible, their confidence is not boundless, and, as one rioter said toward the end of the Los Angeles riots, "[We've] been holding out for a long time, a long time. Giving the white man a chance."[63] In view of this mounting disaffection, however, it is not clear how much longer whites can count on the ghetto's restraint. Nor, even conceding the exceptionally high level of tolerance for violence in the United States, is it clear how much longer blacks can count on the society's restraint. Restraint must be mutual, and, as the behavior of the New Jersey National Guard, in one case, and the Detroit rioters, in another, revealed, it is extremely difficult to sustain under riotous conditions.[64] In any event, the blacks, divided by an attraction to black nationalism and a commitment to American pluralism, are being pulled in one way by racism and territoriality and in another by restraint. And if the riots, and especially the assaults, are indicative, they are moving in an ominous direction.

Granted that the violence of the 1960s riots was a manifestation of the grievances of the black ghettos—and that the rioting, looting, arson, and assault were a function of racial discrimination, economic deprivation, consumer exploitation, and involuntary residential segregation—two additional questions must be raised. First, if it is true—and I think it is—that many other ethnic minorities have suffered these grievances at one time or another, why have only the blacks resorted to full-scale rioting? Second, if it is also true—and again I think it is—that the blacks were worse off in the 1930s, 1940s, and 1950s, why have they rioted for the first time in the 1960s? To phrase these questions somewhat differently, why have so many blacks protested in a manner unprecedented not only for other ethnic minorities but for themselves as well? Unfortunately, satisfactory answers cannot be offered at this point. The traditional histories of individual ghettos are extremely sketchy, and, what is worse, the comparative histories of ethnic minorities are scarcely under way.[65] But a few differences can be discerned, and some explanations can be suggested.

There is little doubt that many other ethnic minorities have suffered these grievances at one time or another. The Irish were discriminated against in Boston in the 1840s and 1850s; so were the Jews and Italians in New York in the 1890s and 1900s and the Mexicans and Japanese in Los Angeles in the 1910s and 1920s. The European immigrants were also depressed by chronic underemployment and extreme poverty in the nineteenth century; and the Mexicans, Puerto Ricans, and, in some cases, native Americans are not much better off in the twentieth. The European immigrants were, as Oscar Handlin has pointed out, exploited by ghetto merchants; and if the blacks are more deeply and widely caught in the installment economy today, so are most Americans whatever their background. Lastly, the Irish, Jews, and Italians were once confined, at least in part involuntarily, to run-down neighborhoods in the central cities; and so are the Mexicans and Puerto Ricans a generation or two later.[66] And yet of all these minority groups, only the blacks have resorted to widespread violent protest.

Although a satisfactory explanation must await further historical and sociological studies of American minority groups, a few differences can be observed at this time. One, the blacks have encountered more pervasive and prolonged racial discrimination than any other minority group; and they have probably been less adequately prepared, culturally and psychologically, to cope with it. Two, the blacks are better off today than the European immigrants were a generation or two ago, but so is everyone else; and, by the standard economic indicators, they are much worse off than the whites. Three, the blacks are more susceptible to consumer exploitation now than the European immigrants ever were; and, by virtue of the predominance of white merchants, they are more inclined to regard it as a racial issue. And four, unlike the Irish, Jews, Italians, and even the Mexicans and Puerto Ricans, the blacks (and not only the first-generation blacks) are segregated by a process which is essentially involuntary.[67] These differences do not fully explain why the blacks have engaged in full-scale rioting. But they clearly indicate several ways in which these grievances are more pronounced in the black ghettos now than they were in the ethnic ghettos.

Nor is there much doubt that the blacks were worse off in the 1930s, 1940s, and 1950s. Racial discrimination—whether de facto school segregation, "Jim Crow" public accommodations, restrictive real estate covenants, or colored job ceilings—was everywhere more comprehensive and systematic then. So was economic deprivation: whether measured by unemployment levels, occupational distribution, or overall earnings, the blacks were less well off, absolutely and relatively, in previous decades. Consumer exploitation was not as pervasive, if only because the installment economy was not as widespread; but otherwise the ghetto merchants, who were even more likely to be white a generation ago, were no more scrupulous. Finally, involuntary residential segregation was not only as common; it was also defended as desirable or at least inevitable by most whites and sanctioned and even promoted by most officials.[68] And yet most blacks, though far from passively accepting these conditions, did not resort to widespread rioting except in Harlem in 1935 and 1943.

Again, though a satisfactory explanation must await further studies of the black ghettos, a few observations can be made at this point. First, many blacks are more outraged now by racial discrimination because the expansion of civil rights in recent years has rendered the remaining abuses more visible and less tolerable. Second, many blacks are more frustrated by economic deprivation because the unprecedented prosperity of the economy since World War II has underscored the fact that they are not receiving their fair share. Third, many blacks are more infuriated by consumer exploitation because the extraordinary spread of the installment system in the last few decades has made the ghetto's dependence on white merchants more obvious and less acceptable. And fourth, many blacks are more incensed by involuntary residential segregation not only because they have been denied the right to live outside the ghettos but also because they have repudiated the ideology which deprives them of the choice.[69] Again, these observations do not fully explain why so many blacks have engaged in full-scale violent protest for the first time in the 1960s. But they do at least suggest several reasons why these grievances are more offensive than ever in the ghettos.

The reasons may be obscure, but the results are clear. The blacks, or at any rate a substantial minority of them, refuse to tolerate racial discrimination, economic deprivation, consumer exploitation, and involuntary residential segregation any longer. Instead they intend to call attention to their grievances, to share in the benefits of affluent America, to even the score with white merchants, and ultimately to gain control over their communities. They have long tried to do so through elections, demonstrations, education, training, and other conventional political and economic channels; and they will probably continue to do so. But the riots made it quite clear that where the blacks find these channels obstructed they will not be confined by them. Nor will they be bound by the fear of arrest, the concern for personal safety, the commitment to orderly social change, the trauma of white racism, and the other restraints on rioting in the United States.[70] Under these circumstances it is not remarkable that a significant minority of the blacks are now prepared, even determined, to resort to violence until their grievances are redressed.

What is remarkable is that thus far the rioters have been so restrained and selective. By restrained I mean that for all the rioting and assault, very few blacks attempted to kill white passers-by, policemen, or National Guardsmen. And by selective I mean that for all the looting and burning, even fewer sought to destroy banks, insurance companies, courthouses, and city halls. For all the violence and destruction, most blacks struck out exclusively against local policemen, ghetto merchants, and other obvious sources of their grievances. A few radicals aside, they did not renounce membership in American society; nor did they challenge its economic organization or political legitimacy. The rioters did not lack the opportunities, either. Although the police, National Guard, and, in some instances, federal soldiers cordoned off the ghettos and otherwise contained the rioters, their restraint and selectivity were essentially self-imposed. In other words, the violence was directed at the system's abuses and not the system itself because the rioters were trying to alert the society rather than overturn it.

Whether the blacks will remain restrained and selective—or whether they will arm themselves and murder whites, loot stores and burn buildings outside the ghettos, and, in effect, resort to rebellion rather than protest—is hard to tell. But if this course is to be avoided the responsibility lies not only with the blacks but also with the whites. It is incumbent upon the blacks to abide by the unwritten yet effective rule whereby American society tolerates the rioting precisely because it is restrained and selective. They must realize that terrorism will be met with repression and that the outcome will be worse for them than for anyone else. The whites, for their part, must recognize that in a democracy social justice is the fundamental precondition for public order (and not vice-versa). It is incumbent upon them to eliminate racial discrimination, economic deprivation, consumer exploitation, and involuntary residential segregation as quickly and as completely as possible. And not solely to prevent rioting by the blacks or even to preserve order in the ghettos but also to establish a closer relationship between the principles and practices of American democracy.

5: The Erosion of Restraint

It is one thing to be subjected to police malpractice, racial discrimination, economic deprivation, consumer exploitation, and residential segregation; it is another to defy policemen, join mobs, loot stores, burn buildings, and assault passers-by. It is, in other words, one thing to be aggrieved and another to riot. If this were not so, the United States would rarely enjoy public order; and yet, compared with many countries, the United States has been relatively free of collective violence.[1] And not only because it has achieved a degree of affluence and freedom which has kept most Americans reasonably satisfied. Many Irish, Italians, and other European immigrants were impoverished and victimized in the late nineteenth and early twentieth centuries; and many Mexicans, Puerto Ricans, and blacks are not much better off today. Many native Americans suffered too in times of economic depression.[2] The United States has also been relatively free of mass violence because it has developed certain restraints on rioting which have proven remarkably effective over the years.

Among the most important are the following. First, the concern for personal safety, the understandable reluctance to risk life and limb (and to permit relatives and friends to do so) in the face of the overwhelming opposition of the authorities. Second, the fear of arrest (and possible conviction and imprisonment), which is demeaning and expensive at the time and, as a simple arrest means a criminal record, burdensome later on. Third, the commitment to orderly social change, the profound conviction that necessary reforms can always be achieved through legitimate channels and that violent protest can never be justified as the only available recourse. Fourth, the trauma of white racism, a legacy of slavery, subordination, and segregation which has compelled the blacks to confine aggression to their own community rather than direct it at the outside society.[3] These restraints have usually prevented Americans, no matter how grave their grievances and how keen their resentment, from resorting to violent protest.

These restraints were not, it is true, fully operative at the beginning of the riots and for a short time thereafter. Few patrolmen came to the scene of the triggering incidents, and, as a rule, they left after arresting the suspect or otherwise resolving the problem. For this they cannot be blamed. No one, not the police and not even the blacks, knew which of the hundreds of triggering incidents would erupt into full-scale riots. Even where the police remained they lacked the manpower to do more than confine the rioting to the ghettos and call on the rioters to leave the streets. And where the police gathered in greater numbers they refrained from shooting into the crowds or taking other drastic measures against the rioters.[4] In view of the tension and confusion, their restraint was commendable. Nothing the rioters did warranted wholesale and indiscriminate slaughter. Not that the black rioters received anything like the passive support, not to mention the active cooperation, of the police that the white rioters received in 1917, 1919, and 1943.[5] The police, while restrained, were not sympathetic. But the black rioters, emboldened by a sense of camaraderie, jubilation, and accomplishment, did not face much danger early in the riots.

Once the rioting was well under way, however, the situation changed radically. Not only did the Mayors assign all available policemen to the ghettos, but the Governors also sent National Guardsmen into several cities, and the President even ordered federal soldiers into Detroit and Washington, D.C. In one city after another anywhere from one thousand to fifteen thousand policemen, Guardsmen, and soldiers swept through the burning streets of the black ghettos, chasing rioters and sometimes shooting at looters, arsonists, and snipers.[6] In the meantime, moderate leaders called on the rioters to return to their homes, arguing that they should work within the legit-imate channels to improve their position and that the riots would only serve to discredit their movement. Sympathetic whites seconded their appeals. And white officials, sympathetic or otherwise, branded the rioters as criminals or subversives, warned that the government would not reward lawlessness, and then suppressed the rioting.[7] By the peak and toward the end of the riots, the restraints on rioting were fully operative.

They were partially effective, too. Many blacks decided to with-draw from the rioting (and many others refused to participate at all) not because they were satisfied with ghetto conditions but because they were inhibited by society's restraints. A few examples should suffice. A teen-ager from south-central Los Angeles admitted, after some prodding, that during the 1965 riots his mother, terrified by the burning and shooting, locked him in the house. A young adult from Detroit's West Side, after a day of looting early in the 1967 riots, decided it was too dangerous and spent the next day watching tele-vision in his parents' apartment. An adult from New York's Harlem spoke out against the 1964 riots on the grounds that in the long run blacks, individually and collectively, would suffer the worst casual-ties.[8] Indeed, if the 1960s riots were simply a function of the ghetto's grievances, an overwhelming majority, and not just a substantial minority, of the blacks would probably have joined in the rioting. And they might well be rioting all the time.

Yet in spite of the dangers to life, limb, and freedom, the appeals of black leaders, and the criticisms of white officials, many blacks joined in the riots. According to a survey by Louis Harris and Asso-ciates, moreover, a substantial, and probably increasing, minority in-tend to riot in the future;[9] and according to another study by the University of Michigan's Survey Research Center, a majority now consider rioting a legitimate form of social protest.[10] The blacks are well aware of the consequences. Thousands have already been killed, injured, and arrested; thousands more have seen relatives and friends among the victims; and most blacks know that the authorities will not tolerate future rioting. Some blacks also realize that so many whites are so outraged by the riots that racism, in the guise of "law and order," is spreading over the nation. Thus if the blacks' past actions and future intentions are indicative, the restraints on rioting have been seriously undermined in the ghettos.

There are two common explanations. According to the McCone Commission, the rioting reflected the irrational despair of black riffraff and the irresponsible agitation of black leaders. This explanation has been adopted by many Americans. It is incorrect, however: for, as I have pointed out elsewhere, it misconstrues the composition of the rioters, misinterprets the position of the leaders, and, most important of all, underestimates the scope of the ghetto's grievances.[11] According to the Kerner Commission, the rioting reflected rather the black response to white racism.[12] This explanation, which is more sophisticated if less reassuring, does help account for the violence in the early stages of the riots. But it does not explain why, as the later stages of the riots clearly revealed, the restraints on rioting are less effective now than ever in the black ghettos.

If a more satisfactory explanation is to be found, it must start with the following assumption. That to riot in the face of extreme physical dangers and intense ideological pressures, as the blacks did in the 1960s, indicates not only that the grievances were intolerable but also that the restraints were ineffective. To argue that the riots were a function of ineffective restraints as well as intolerable grievances is not to deny that the grievances can generate conditions which may undermine the restraints. Indeed, this process has been under way for some time in the black ghettos.[13] It is rather to insist that it is necessary not only to identify the ghetto's grievances but also to determine how they have undermined the restraints on rioting and whether there are other conditions not yet considered which have further undermined these restraints. And to these ends it is essential to analyze why the concern for personal safety, the fear of arrest, the commitment to orderly social change, and the trauma of white racism have lost much of their effectiveness in the black ghettos.

The concern for personal safety is perhaps the most obvious restraint on rioting. To join in a riot—to jeer at the police, break into a store, burn down a building, beat up a passer-by, or simply stand in a crowd—is somewhat dangerous under any circumstances. The mobs are a hazard to life and limb; so, for that matter, are the rioters. To join in at the peak or toward the end of the 1960s riots was even more dangerous. The local police and (in several instances) the National Guard, armed with automatic rifles, tear gas, and occasionally even tanks, were aggressively patrolling the ghettos. Some policemen, enraged and exhausted, were determined to teach the rioters a lesson; and a few Guardsmen, young and inexperienced, were inclined to respond with more force than necessary.[14] The consequences were no less tragic for being predictable. Despite the commendable restraints of most law enforcement officials, the riots left roughly a couple of hundred dead and a few thousand injured. And aside from a small number of white passers-by, policemen, and Guardsmen, the overwhelming majority of the victims were blacks—rioters and spectators caught in the wrong place at the wrong time.

The blacks were well aware of these dangers. Although they did not expect to be killed or injured, they did not realize that the policemen and Guardsmen were prepared to kill and injure them. In view of the rumors which swept through the ghettos, greatly exaggerating the number of deaths and injuries, the blacks may even have overestimated the real danger.[15] Hence many who enjoyed the protective anonymity of the large crowds early in the riots later on concluded that the risks were too great and returned to their homes. But many others who dispersed in the face of the police and military regrouped in the less heavily patrolled portions of the ghettos and continued the rioting, looting, arson, and assault. And still others remained on the streets, refusing in spite of overwhelming force to back down from a confrontation until they were exhausted, arrested, injured, or, in a few cases, killed.[16] In time public order (or what passes for public order) was restored. By then, however, it was clear that the concern for personal safety is no longer a very effective restraint on rioting in the black ghettos.

The concern for personal safety is, and probably always has been, more profound among the middle class than among the lower and working classes. With certain noteworthy exceptions, these classes place high value on physical prowess and live in neighborhoods which, by virtue of poverty and density, are relatively dangerous. Violence is so integral a part of their lives that the lower and working classes accept it with greater equanimity than the middle class (except when it involves blacks, hippies, and, in their view, other deviants).[17] What is more, as a result of the civil rights movement and the Vietnam War, the concern for personal safety is probably less pronounced than ever among the middle class (or at any rate the young middle-class activists). As the demonstrations at the 1968 Democratic National Convention revealed, they are ready to disregard physical danger—though, interestingly enough, not as completely as European students.[18] Thus for Americans who share the attitudes of the lower and working classes or the commitments of the middle-class activists the concern for personal safety is not a very effective restraint on rioting.

For the blacks, however, the concern for personal safety is not very effective mainly because many of them have been hardened to the point of indifference by the continuous and haphazard violence of ghetto life. According to police statistics—which, though extremely unreliable, are confirmed on this point by personal impressions—the level of crime, and especially violent crime, is much higher there than anywhere else in urban America. According to the President's Crime Commission, black men are six times as likely as white men—and black women eight times as likely as white women and even four times as likely as white men—to be victims of a serious crime.[19] And according to historical and sociological studies, the predictability of crime, and especially violent crime, is much lower in the black ghettos today than in the ethnic ghettos a generation or two ago. The juvenile gangs are less purposive, the gangsters less well organized, and the deviants not only alcoholics and other unfortunate yet innocuous types but also drug addicts who resort to crime to support their habit.[20]

This analysis has not grappled with the complicated problems which have frustrated scholarly efforts to compare crime rates from one community to another and from one generation to the next. Nor has it dealt with the complex character of deviance in the ghettos, with, among other things, the erratic history of gangs, the intricate arrangements of criminals, and the adaptive behavior of deviants. But it has indicated why even ordinary law-abiding blacks find life in the ghettos very dangerous and why they have little control over their own and their families' physical well-being. Security is a matter of chance; and the odds are not good. It has also indicated why many blacks, and especially lower- and working-class blacks, have hardened themselves to all but the most serious crimes and outrageous attacks. For many blacks, then, the riots marked a dramatic intensification but not a fundamental discontinuity in their everyday experience.[21]

The high level and low predictability of violent crime in the ghettos is essentially a manifestation of economic deprivation and racial discrimination. Witness most accounts of ghetto life, which are filled with descriptions of blacks who turn to illegitimate enterprises because they find the ordinary avenues to success closed, assault friends and strangers alike because they cannot express their hostility toward whites, and resort to alcohol, narcotics, and other opiates to escape from their plight.[22] Economic deprivation and racial discrimination are not unique to black ghettos; nor are crime, violence, and deviance. They are known in other communities too, especially, though not exclusively, in low-income ethnic communities. But nowhere in urban America are these grievances so overwhelming and inextricable; and if the statistical and impressionistic evidence is reliable, nowhere are these symptoms so common.[23] If the riots are indicative, too, nowhere in urban America is this combination of grievances and symptoms so combustible as in the black ghettos.

The concern for personal safety has lost much of its effectiveness as a restraint on rioting for one other reason. Many blacks—like many young middle-class whites, but even more so—are ready, even determined, to disregard physical danger on essentially ideological grounds. They are prepared to risk life and limb in defense of race, dignity, manhood, and the other virtues of what Harold Isaacs has called "the new world of Negro Americans."[24] One black from south-central Los Angeles offered this explanation during the 1965 riots. "Everybody has to be willing to sacrifice something for what he believes in," he told reporters. "I'd be out of place, wouldn't I, if my race was out there fighting and I wasn't."[25] Many blacks, and particularly many young blacks, agree. For though they are not committed to violence—nor, it goes without saying, to nonviolence—they are committed to defending themselves (or, if need be, to meeting oppression with violence). The reasons can be considered later, but the implications should be pointed out here.

The concern for personal safety has discouraged many blacks from joining in the riots; but it has not discouraged many others, especially many blacks born and raised in the northern ghettos who reached maturity in the 1950s and 1960s. Nor, in all likelihood, will it do so in the years ahead. It is possible—though, in view of the conservative reaction under way in the country, only possible—that racial discrimination and economic deprivation will somehow be alleviated by government action and that as a result violent crime will be reduced in the black ghettos. But it is also possible—and, in view of the ideological currents prevailing in the ghettos today, even probable—that at the same time the increasing pride in blackness, dwindling fear of whites, and other conditions underlying black militancy will undermine the concern for personal safety anyway. And under these circumstances there is little reason to believe that this restraint will regain much, if any, of its effectiveness in the black ghettos in the foreseeable future.

The fear of arrest is probably the next most obvious restraint on rioting. To be arrested—to be picked up by the police, placed in a wagon, fingerprinted and photographed, and locked in a cell—is not only demeaning but also expensive, especially for low-income people who cannot take the time from work or find the money for bail. If the offense is serious and the evidence incriminating, the suspect is formally charged and tried and thereby subjected to additional losses of time, money, and dignity; if he is convicted and imprisoned, so much the worse. Whether convicted or not, however, the arrestee acquires a criminal record, which sets him apart from other citizens. Henceforth he is considered suspicious by the police, who are likely to detain and arrest him; and if they do he is deemed a recidivist by judicial and correctional authorities, who are likely to regard him as incorrigible. What is more, he is handicapped when applying for work and prevented from living in public housing.[26] And if Claude Brown's autobiographical account of life in Harlem, *Manchild in the Promised Land*, is reliable, the blacks are well aware of the implications of arrest, let alone conviction and imprisonment.[27]

At the peak and toward the end of the riots, if not earlier, the blacks were also aware that they might be arrested. By then the police were prepared to make as many arrests as necessary to restore order. To cite the figures from a few of the worst riots, they arrested roughly 300 in Cleveland (1966), 400 in Chicago (1966), 1500 in Newark (1967), 1600 in Milwaukee (1967), 4000 in Los Angeles (1965), 7200 in Detroit (1967), and 8000 in Washington, D.C. (1968).[28] The arrest statistics include a small number of blacks arrested for offenses unrelated to the riots and an even smaller number of whites involved in the rioting. But if they are otherwise accurate, roughly forty to fifty thousand were arrested in the riots. Moreover, according to a comparison of arrest statistics and personal interviews in Los Angeles, Newark, and Detroit, only around 20 per cent of the rioters were arrested. But one in five is no mean proportion, especially when the other four are watching.[29] All things considered, then, the fear of arrest is no longer a very effective restraint on rioting in the black ghettos.

The fear of arrest, too, is, and probably always has been, more powerful among the middle class than among the lower and working classes. Since they are more likely to engage in gambling and other illegal activities, an arrest is not quite so humiliating; nor, since they are less likely to aspire to careers in law and other professions closed to persons with a record, is it quite so detrimental.[30] The fear of arrest is also probably less powerful today than ever before among the middle class (or at any rate among middle-class youth). From their involvement in the civil rights movement, these youngsters learned that there are issues which warrant breaking the law; and from the resistance to the Vietnam War and the demonstrations at many major universities, they found that these issues are not exclusively in the South.[31] Provided that the cause is just, they view an arrest as an honor rather than a stigma. For Americans who share the attitudes of the lower and working classes or the commitments of the middle-class youth the fear of arrest is not a very effective restraint on rioting.

But for the blacks the fear of arrest is not very effective mainly because the great majority of them, or at least of the men, have already been arrested (if not convicted). According to the arrest sheets of the rioters, 39 per cent had prior records in Buffalo, 53 per cent in Detroit, 64 per cent in New Haven, 67 per cent in Atlanta, and 91 per cent in Dayton.[32] These figures may be appalling, but they are not exceptional. According to the President's Crime Commission, which has made the only estimate I know of, roughly 50 to 90 per cent of the black males in the urban ghettos have criminal records.[33] Overall 70 per cent is probably not an unreasonable estimate. And whether the actual figure is a trifle higher or lower is not particularly important because most of the remaining 30 per cent assume that they too will be arrested sooner or later and if not for rioting then for something else. For most black males life without an arrest is virtually inconceivable.

The high rate of arrest among blacks is partly a function of the high level of crime and violence in the ghettos, a situation which has already been discussed and is not worth repeating. But it is worth observing that, as most accounts of ghetto life reveal, the high level of deviance leads to frequent arrests (and occasional convictions and imprisonments). Ironically, this is one consequence of the professionalization of the police and the abolition of the double standard of law enforcement. It is also worth observing that this situation leads to continuous encounters with the police which result in even more arrests because so many blacks bait the police and otherwise deny their authority. Crime and violence are not of course sanctioned outside the black ghettos, though the police are somewhat more tolerant of offenders, and especially adolescent offenders, in white suburbs.[34] But nowhere in urban America is the level of deviance as high as in the black ghettos; and nowhere is the rate of arrest as high, either.

The high rate of arrest among blacks is also partly a function of the exceptional character of police practices in the ghettos. There the police, committed to controlling crime, yet unable to distinguish between the law-abiding and the lawless, employ preventive, as opposed to responsive, patrolling. In other words, they stop, search, and interrogate blacks passing by the scenes of recent crimes, milling on the streets, and otherwise behaving in an allegedly suspicious manner. Preventive patrolling may reduce the level of crime in the ghettos, but it also generates many unfortunate confrontations and culminates in many unwarranted arrests. And if the charges are dismissed the police defend their actions on the grounds that the suspects have probably committed other offenses for which they were not arrested. Preventive patrolling also encourages the police to assume a more casual attitude toward arrests in the ghettos, as if the blacks will be arrested sooner or later and as if the arrests will not make much difference anyway. As a young black said about the Los Angeles police: "It seemed like they figured they'd eventually have me in jail and wanted to save time."[35]

The situation would be bad enough under the most enlightened penal procedures, and in the United States these procedures are anything but enlightened. Here an arrest, and an arrest alone, means a criminal record. No account is taken of the disposition—whether the charge is dismissed or pressed, whether the verdict is innocent or guilty, and whether the sentence is suspended or imposed. Nor is any account taken of the age and background of the offender or the gravity and circumstances of the offense. According to a survey by the National Council on Crime and Delinquency, few Western European countries define a criminal record so broadly; and few disclose these records so readily.[36] Here too a criminal record is permanent. Regardless of the severity of the offense, the disposition of the charge, and the subsequent behavior of the offender, he carries a record for the rest of his life. Only in very special cases can it be expunged. In a country which presumes that a person is innocent until proven guilty, these procedures are plainly inconsistent with simple justice and common sense.

These procedures have a profound impact in the black ghettos. Since the vast majority of the men have been arrested, they are laboring under the stigma of a criminal record and will continue to do so whether or not they are arrested again. Hence the fear of conviction and imprisonment may deter some of them from joining in the riots, though only a very small proportion of the arrestees are imprisoned;[37] but the fear of arrest will not. Nor, in all likelihood, will it do so in the future. For none of the conditions underlying the high rate of arrest among blacks, not ghetto frustrations, police practices, or penal procedures, is likely to be alleviated in the years ahead. In the meantime the riots are leaving more blacks with criminal records and intensifying their dissatisfaction with ghetto conditions. Under these circumstances there is little reason to believe that the fear of arrest, and possible conviction and imprisonment, will regain much, if any, of its effectiveness in the black ghettos in the near future.

The commitment to orderly social change is probably the most powerful yet least obvious restraint on rioting. The most powerful because it is grounded on the profound conviction that in a democracy necessary reforms can always be achieved through legitimate channels and that violent protest can never be justified as the only available recourse. The least obvious because this conviction, unlike the concern for personal safety and the fear of arrest, is founded on assumptions about American society which have been so widely accepted for so long that they are rarely made explicit.[38] Thus to riot or otherwise engage in violent protest is to repudiate a quintessential component of American ideology. It is to proclaim that the legitimate channels are inoperative, that the existing institutions are unresponsive, and that violence is a legitimate, indeed an imperative, weapon in the struggle for social change. It is also to challenge assumptions about American society on which, as Louis Hartz has pointed out, most Americans have staked their claims to a distinctive civilization for almost two hundred years.[39]

Many blacks were aware of these implications. After all, if the long history of southern lynchings and northern race riots is indicative, no other minority group has suffered more severely from collective violence. Nor, if the recent history of the civil rights movement is indicative, has any other minority group so consistently based its demands for equality on the sanctity of the law. Indeed, it was on the basis of these considerations that the moderate black leaders appealed to the rioters to return to their homes.[40] The blacks were reminded of these implications time and again. Public officials and newspaper editors, warning that the rioting would alienate white moderates and strengthen white racists, insisted that public order was a prerequisite for social justice. So did the official commissions which investigated the Los Angeles, Newark, and Chicago riots.[41] And the response to these pronouncements clearly indicated that the commitment to orderly social change is no longer a very effective restraint on rioting in the black ghettos.

The commitment to orderly social change, too, is, and probably always has been, more pronounced among the middle class than the lower and working classes. These classes have repeatedly resorted to violence in order to discourage challenges to the status quo by racial, religious, and ethnic minorities; and they still do so, though, in all fairness, far less frequently.[42] The commitment to orderly social change is probably less powerful than ever among the middle class too, and not only among the young middle-class activists. The activists have lost confidence in the nation's ability to respond to their grievances, or, to be more specific, in its capacity to alleviate conditions in the black ghettos and extricate itself from the Vietnam War. But, in view of the recent rash of illegal strikes in New York and several other cities, so, on a more mundane level, have teachers and other public employees (and with much greater success).[43] For these reasons the commitment to orderly social change is not very effective among many Americans today.

But this restraint is even less effective among the blacks, and especially the young adults born and raised in the ghettos. Few Americans are more skeptical of claims that necessary reforms can be achieved through legitimate channels and that social justice can be attained without violent protest. According to a survey sponsored by the Kerner Commission, one of every three blacks thinks that they have made little progress and one of every five feels that they should turn to violence.[44] Nor are many Americans as inclined to engage in violence on a scale which dwarfs confrontations with university administrations and even strikes against public services. According to newspaper reports from the ghettos and public statements by militants, a few cadres of blacks even intend to resort to disruption and terrorism.[45] The reports and statements are open to question; and so, to a lesser extent, are the surveys. But what is not open to question is the conclusion that the blacks' confidence in the existing political channels has been rudely shaken in the recent past.

Underlying these developments is the sharp rise in black expectations.[46] This rise, which, as I pointed out earlier, goes back well into the twentieth century, has taken a whole new dimension since World War II. The blacks, and especially the young black adults born and raised in the ghettos who reached maturity in the 1950s and 1960s, have not only found hope for the future. That they have long had. Witness their long-standing interest in education, their traditional commitment to orderly social change, and, above all, their tremendous migration north. The blacks have also found new aspirations: in addition to voting rights, legal equality, and the other goals of the civil rights movement, they now demand decent jobs, quality schools, and proper housing. For these blacks the issue is not equality of opportunity but equality itself. The blacks have found new confidence, too: they sense that though the struggle is far from over the victory is for the first time in range—provided that they have the determination and courage to grasp it. For these blacks the time is propitious and the moment long overdue.

To realize, and also to symbolize, these new expectations, the blacks have engaged in a variety of appeals, boycotts, marches, pickets, petitions, and other forms of nonviolent protest. These demonstrations, which belong to a long, if not notably successful tradition, started in the South, first with the Montgomery bus boycott and then with the Greensboro sit-ins, and then spread to the North. Organized by S.C.L.C., C.O.R.E., S.N.C.C., and other civil rights groups, they were directed at discrimination in employment, housing, education, public accommodations, and police practices.[47] In south-central Los Angeles alone, one sociologist has estimated, the blacks held fully two hundred and fifty demonstrations in the two years immediately preceding the 1965 riots.[48] This figure is not extravagant; nor is Los Angeles exceptional. The blacks have probably organized even more protests, and certainly more dramatic ones, in New York, Chicago, Cleveland, and, what with the 1963 March and 1968 Resurrection City, Washington, D.C. With a few exceptions, their tactics have been peaceful and their goals moderate. Yet, according to many moderate leaders, these protests have had relatively little impact on daily life in the black ghettos.[49]

There has been progress in recent years, probably more than at any time since Emancipation; but by almost any standards this progress has been highly uneven. Civil rights, narrowly construed, are better established; but job opportunities are badly lagging, school facilities are woefully inadequate, and housing segregation is, if anything, on the increase. Middle-class (and especially college-educated) blacks have made impressive advances, and so, on a more modest scale, have southern blacks; but lower- and working-class blacks have not done nearly as well. Hence whatever progress has been won shows up quite clearly in Englewood, Crenshaw, and the other black suburbs, but less clearly, if at all, in Bedford-Stuyvesant, Watts, and the other urban ghettos.[50] And if the battle over school decentralization in New York City is indicative, nonviolent protest may be even less effective in the upcoming struggle for institutional change.

In any event, by evaluating their position in terms of frustrations rather than achievements, the blacks have begun questioning the efficacy of the existing political channels; and from there it is but a short step to repudiating the commitment to orderly social change.

Not all blacks, perhaps not even most, reject this commitment; but certainly a great many do. Or at any rate enough so that a large minority has resorted to violent protest and an even larger minority, which has not done so, sympathizes with the rioters and regards rioting as a legitimate form of protest. They will probably continue to do so in the years ahead, too: for there is little likelihood that the blacks will reduce their expectations or that American society will change rapidly enough to satisfy them. As a result of the controversy over community control of the schools, police, and other urban institutions there may even be a hardening of positions. And under these circumstances there is little reason to expect that the commitment to orderly social change will regain much, if any, of its effectiveness as in the black ghettos in the foreseeable future.

The trauma of white racism is the only restraint on rioting peculiar to the blacks. It reflects not the common concerns, fears, and commitments of most Americans but the unique adjustment of most blacks to two centuries of slavery and one of subordination and segregation. This trauma, which is too intricate to be unraveled here, has two striking features. First, from the very outset white racism placed the blacks, and especially southern blacks, in such a vulnerable position that their lives depended on their ability to conceal or otherwise contain their aggression. To rebel, retaliate, resist, or even to protest, was, as the long and grim record of southern lynchings and northern race riots reveals, to open themselves and their families to terrible danger.[51] So terrible that, as a few novelists and psychiatrists have observed, black women spared no effort to channel the aggression of their husbands and sons toward the family and away from the outside society.[52] What is crucial is not whether, as Stanley Elkins has argued, the blacks internalized their passivity and transmitted it from one generation to another, but that down through the early twentieth century they could not strike out at the whites without putting their lives at stake.[53]

Second, at the same time white racism imposed on the blacks, and again especially southern blacks, its perceptions, which was bad enough, and its standards, which was even worse. By these perceptions blacks were at once childish and sensual, lazy and aggressive, and docile and dangerous; and by these standards white was lovelier than black, Anglo-Saxon culture better than African, and the Caucasian superior to the Negro. Down through the early twentieth century white racism thereby relegated the blacks to the bottom of the racial hierarchy, leaving them very low in self-esteem and equally high in self-hatred. And from this position the blacks saw one another as suitable objects for their hostility and frustration.[54] Hence white racism simultaneously prevented the blacks from directing their aggression at the whites (and at society itself) and encouraged them to direct it at other blacks. Not all the blacks of course, but apparently enough so that until quite recently the trauma of white racism was an effective restraint on rioting in the ghettos.

Let there be no misunderstanding. The blacks have not directed their aggression exclusively at one another. To the contrary, as Kenneth Stampp has pointed out, slaves often stole from their masters, destroyed their equipment, burned their buildings, ran away from their plantations, and even attacked their overseers.[55] And since Emancipation the blacks, and especially northern blacks, have intermittently baited and defied the whites, engaged them in gang warfare, and even assaulted and killed them.[56] Nevertheless, the blacks have directed their aggression mainly at one another. The extremely high level of violent crime in the ghettos is indicative; so is the evidence that the overwhelming majority of the victims are black. The blacks have commonly masked their aggression toward the whites, too. The sullen glance of the adults and the insolent slouch of the juveniles are typical; so are the cocky stance of the hipsters and the mock deference of the boppers.[57] Except for such incidents as the abortive uprisings of Denmark Vesey and Nat Turner, the limited resistance in the Detroit race riot of 1943, and the sporadic disorders in Harlem in 1935 and 1943, the blacks have rarely struck out at the whites.

What made the 1960s riots unprecedented was that in spite of the overwhelming opposition of American society—and in spite of the efforts of the local police and National Guard and the appeals of public officials and newspaper editors—the blacks did strike out at the whites (and did so in the open and as a group). The implications of these actions are momentous. The blacks' adjustment to subordination and segregation has apparently assumed a whole new dimension: rather than conceal or otherwise contain their aggression, or direct it almost exclusively at one another, the blacks are now directing it at whites too. This change does more than just indicate that the blacks have undergone a remarkable transformation in the recent past. It also indicates that the influence of white racism is on the wane in modern America: it can no longer place the blacks in the extremely vulnerable position which immobilized them vis-à-vis the whites, nor can it any longer impose on them the profound sense of inferiority which alienated them from one another.

White racism is on the wane for two main reasons. First, so many blacks have left the South in the last half century that today around one of every two, as opposed to roughly one of every ten in 1900, lives in the North. There the etiquette of race relations is, and always has been, more casual; there are far fewer racial taboos, and there is much greater tolerance for deviants. There, too, the whites (including the second- and third-generation whites) are not as inclined to enforce the rules with violence; nor are the law enforcement officials.[58] What is more, approximately three of every four northern blacks have settled (or, more accurately, have been forced to settle) in the ghettos. And they derive from these rigorously segregated and heavily congested communities a degree of security from racial attacks which is unheard of in the South. They do encounter white racism; they cannot possibly avoid it. But in the northern ghettos, as opposed to the southern hamlets, white racism is expressed less through violence, or even the threat of violence, than through highly impersonal, often strictly bureaucratic, arrangements.[59]

Second, racism, as an ideology, is very much on the defensive today: discredited by scientists, denounced by theologians, and forsaken by politicians, it has no claim to authority left. The national reaction to Nazi Germany undermined it before and during World War II; and the ideological competition of Soviet Communism did so through the Cold War.[60] Hence white racism is losing its impact not only because it runs counter to the American creed—that has been true for well over a century—but also because it has lost its credibility. Few whites preach it. And, what with the emergence of independent nations in Africa and the eloquence of black nationalists in America, even fewer blacks believe it.[61] So, to a degree inconceivable a decade ago, the blacks refuse to see themselves through white perceptions or judge themselves by white standards. What forms their own perceptions and standards will take is uncertain. But surely they will not relegate the blacks to the bottom of the racial hierarchy, nor designate them as suitable objects for their aggression.

Underlying the waning influence of white racism in modern America, then, are profound demographic and ideological changes which have been under way for roughly two generations. The non-violent demonstrations of the 1950s and the violent protests of the 1960s are but two of their more recent, if more noteworthy, manifestations. These changes have not yet run their course. But they have already liberated many blacks, first from the southerners, then from the whites, and, in the process, from themselves. The blacks have thereby gained additional options; violent protest is one and community control another. Although these options have limits, these limits are established not so much by racial taboos as by national ideology (and, above all, by the commitment to orderly social change). And they are enforced not by vigilante groups bent on maintaining the racial status quo but by police and military forces committed to preserving public order.[62] The importance of these distinctions can hardly be exaggerated: it is still dangerous for blacks to disregard these limits, but it is no longer traumatic.

To extend the analogy, the trauma of white racism is healing. It has not yet fully healed, especially in the rural South, where many blacks still find themselves in extremely vulnerable positions and others still view themselves as somewhat inferior. But it has healed enough so that many blacks (and especially northern blacks) are quite capable of directing their aggression at whites as well as blacks. Hence the trauma of white racism cannot prevent a substantial minority of blacks from joining in riots; nor, in all likelihood, will it be able to do so in the years ahead. If, as seems likely, the blacks continue to leave the countryside for the cities and to settle in the ghettos, they will probably be even less vulnerable to white intimidation. And if, as also seems likely, the blacks continue to feel greater racial pride, more self-esteem and less self-hatred, they will probably be even less susceptible to white ideology. And under these circumstances there is little reason to expect that the trauma of white racism will regain much, if any, of its effectiveness in the black ghettos in the near future.

Assuming that the concern for personal safety, the fear of arrest, the commitment to orderly social change, and the trauma of white racism are no longer very effective restraints on rioting in the black ghettos, two additional questions must be raised. First, if it is true—and I believe it is—that many of the conditions undermining these restraints were present in other ethnic ghettos, why have these restraints only lost their effectiveness in the black ghettos? Second, if it is also true—and again I believe it is—that many of these conditions were present in the black ghettos in the 1930s, 1940s, and 1950s, why have these restraints lost their effectiveness there for the first time in the 1960s? To put it another way, why are the restraints on rioting which have operated so well in the United States no longer very effective in the black ghettos? Definitive answers cannot be offered at this point because, as I have observed earlier, the traditional histories and comparative studies of America's minority communities leave much to be desired.[63] But certain broad differences can be discerned, and a few tentative conclusions offered.

Although many of the conditions undermining the restraints on rioting were present in other ethnic ghettos, these conditions are more acute in the black ghettos. The level of crime, and especially violent crime, was very high in the ethnic ghettos. Juvenile gangs, racketeers, and assorted deviants made everyday life precarious for the Irish, Italians, and Jews at the turn of the century and for the Puerto Ricans and Mexicans two generations later. But whether or not the level of crime is higher in the black ghettos—and, for various reasons, it is hard, if not impossible, to tell—the predictability of crime is probably lower there.[64] The rate of arrest, which, so far as I know, has never been precisely computed, was fairly high in the ethnic ghettos. Deviant activity was quite common; and so was intense conflict between the police and the newcomers. But the rate of arrest is probably—though, as relevant statistics are not readily available, only probably—higher in the black ghettos; there crime and deviance are at least as frequent, and police patrols are even more thorough.[65]

The disparity between expectations and achievements was also rather sharp in the ethnic ghettos. The pace of economic and social progress was not always rapid and even; nor was the efficacy of the normal political channels always apparent. But this disparity is probably—though, again in the absence of comparable indicators, only probably—sharper in the black ghettos; there not only are expectations at least as high and achievements at least as erratic, but, perhaps more important, awareness of the discrepancies is much greater.[66] These differences do not fully explain why the concern for personal safety, the fear of arrest, and the commitment to orderly social change have only lost their effectiveness in the black ghettos. But they do at least suggest a few reasons why the conditions undermining these restraints are more acute there than in the ethnic ghettos.

What is more, though many of these conditions were present in the black ghettos in the 1930s, 1940s, and 1950s, they are more acute there in the 1960s. The level of crime, and especially violent crime, was very high in the past; and, in view of the double standard of law enforcement, the danger to life and limb was extremely great. But whether or not the level of crime is higher in the black ghettos at present—and here too it is extremely difficult to say—the level of haphazard crime is probably higher; and, notwithstanding a single standard of law enforcement, the precariousness of everyday life is probably greater.[67] Also, if the historical accounts of ghetto life are reliable—if, as they indicate, deviant activity was common and hostility between police and blacks intense—the rate of arrest was once fairly high there. But the rate of arrest is probably higher now not only because the level of crime and deviance is exceedingly high but also because the police have instituted preventive patrolling.[68]

The disparity between expectations and achievements was also rather sharp in the black ghettos in the past, though it fluctuated from one decade to another and from one region to the next. But this disparity is probably even sharper now because the residents have made considerable, though not consistent, progress and gained greater awareness of their deprivation.[69] The repudiation of white racism has been under way for well over a generation in the black ghettos too. But this repudiation has reached a peak in the 1960s with the coming of age of the second-generation northern blacks who are less vulnerable to white intimidation and less susceptible to white ideology.[70] Again, these differences do not fully explain why the concern for personal safety, the fear of arrest, the commitment to orderly social change, and the trauma of white racism have lost their effectiveness in the black ghettos for the first time in the 1960s. But they do at least suggest reasons why the conditions undermining these restraints are more acute there now than in the past.

The reasons may be somewhat obscure, but the results are clear enough. The blacks—or at any rate a substantial and fairly representative minority of them—will no longer be bound by the customary restraints on rioting. Nor will they be moved by the opposition of American society, whether expressed through the appeals of white officials and black moderates or the threats of the police and National Guard. Unless their grievances are alleviated, they will protest, nonviolently, when appropriate, and violently, if need be; and if this means rioting, so be it. The authorities can restore order. They can summon the police and, if necessary, the National Guard and federal troops; and they have more than enough men and weapons at their disposal. But the authorities cannot prevent the blacks from rioting in the first place. In other words, the customary restraints on rioting have lost so much of their effectiveness in the black ghettos that the authorities can do nothing more than suppress rioting there. And then only with paramilitary and military forces.

The gravity of the situation should not be exaggerated. The restraints on rioting, particularly the concern for personal safety and the commitment to orderly social change, are still effective among a small (though probably dwindling) majority of blacks. And these restraints are still fairly effective even though the authorities have not attempted to enhance their efficacy by resorting to indiscriminate retaliation and indefinite incarceration. Also, though these restraints are no longer very effective in preventing rioting, they are still quite effective in preventing disruption, terrorism, and other more serious forms of violence. And, as the recent histories of Algeria, Vietnam, and France reveal, this is no mean accomplishment. In other words, very few blacks are so indifferent to personal safety and so disillusioned with orderly social change that they are prepared to engage in the types of violence which would certainly provoke massive repression and probably cost them their lives and their nation its liberty.

But neither should the gravity of the situation be underestimated. The restraints on rioting, particularly the fear of arrest and the trauma of white racism, are no longer effective among a substantial, representative, and growing minority of blacks. These restraints are less effective among ordinary blacks than among white activists; and they are less effective in typical ghettos than on university campuses. For better or worse, the blacks have a capacity to engage in violence which is unparalleled in modern America. If the demonstrations at the Democratic National Convention and, more recently, at San

Francisco State University are indicative, the white activists may well intensify their violence in the future. But until they do it is fair to conclude that the restraints on rioting have been more seriously undermined in the black ghettos than anywhere else in American society and that unless major efforts are made to reverse current trends they will be even further undermined in the years ahead.

6: The Moderates' Dilemma

The riots placed the moderate black leaders in an extremely difficult position. As blacks, they not only shared a unique history with the rioters but also suffered many of the same grievances and resented many of the same injustices. Moreover, they had been subjected to countless beatings and jailings in the South and endless harassment and intimidation in the North in the long struggle against subordination and segregation. Now that thousands of ordinary blacks were defying the police and National Guard and risking arrest, injury, and death to deliver their protest, many moderate leaders strongly sympathized with them. A few, by their own admission, were even tempted to join in the rioting. The rioters, for their part, encouraged the moderates to do so and, as the experience of Mervyn Dymally, a popular assemblyman from south-central Los Angeles, reveals, regarded their response as a test of their loyalty. Walking in the ghetto during the 1965 riots, Dymally was approached by a young rioter and asked, "Who you with?" "I'm with you, man," the assemblyman replied. "Then here's a rock, baby—throw it," the youth ordered.[1] Dymally, quite upset by the incident, refused.

So did the other leaders, if only figuratively. For they were moderates as well as blacks, personally and professionally committed to nonviolent protest, orderly social change, and the existing institutional structure. They enjoyed close ties with the N.A.A.C.P., S.C.L.C., Urban League, and other civil rights organizations which shared these commitments. And they feared that the rioting would undermine the tactics, strategies, and ideology of the civil rights movement. What is more, the moderates were confident that the

129

blacks could overcome subordination and segregation by working within the available channels. And to this end they maintained cordial relations with white liberals, on whom they depended heavily for financial and political support. Thus they also feared that the rioting would embarrass their friends, comfort their enemies, and discredit their movement.[2] The competition of Stokely Carmichael and other militants, on the one hand, and the campaigns of Barry Goldwater and George Wallace, on the other, heightened these anxieties too. For good reasons, then, the moderates could not support the riots.

But they could not ignore them either. They were leaders as well as moderates; they belonged with their people, leading them if possible, following them if need be, but with them in any event. Moreover, the riots suggested that they were leaders without followers.[3] By resorting to violent protest instead of abiding by the commitment to orderly social change, the rioters were repudiating the moderates' tactics and strategies. And by exploiting the rioting to demonstrate the futility of working within the existing institutional structure, the militants were challenging the moderates' ideology. Hence the riots cost the moderate leaders much of their credibility in both the black ghettos, which was bad enough, and the white communities, which for some was even worse. For the whites would not long recognize the moderates as leaders if, as the riots indicated, the rank-and-file would no longer follow them. From the perspective of the moderate leaders, the riots raised severe doubts not only about the value of their past work and future hopes but also about their claims to leadership in the ghettos.

If they could not support or ignore the riots, what could the moderates do? They could protest the conditions which gave rise to the riots and criticize the society which tolerated these conditions. They could warn that the blacks would riot again unless the authorities acted to alleviate the ghetto's grievances. They could urge the local police and the National Guard to exercise the utmost restraint in handling the rioters. And they could issue statements, offer testimony, and otherwise explain the rioting to white America. The moderates could do these things; and most of them did so.[4] But from the very outset they realized that, in view of their problems as moderates and leaders, these activities were inadequate. Thus, far from organizing, instigating, or encouraging the riots, as the McCone Commission and other conservative critics charged, the moderates vigorously and unequivocally opposed them. They also attempted to prevent the rioting and, when necessary, to restrain the rioters.[5] By doing so they staked their prestige on their ability to maintain order in the ghettos, knowing full well that if they failed their position, already seriously weakened by the rioting, would be even further undermined.

The moderates were first tested in the Harlem riots of 1964, which erupted a few days after a white policeman shot and killed a black teen-ager. Following the funeral service, a crowd of angry blacks gathered in the streets. Bayard Rustin, associate of the Reverend Martin Luther King, Jr., and director of the A. Philip Randolph Foundation, climbed aboard a sound truck and urged the crowd to disperse. "We know that there has been an injustice done," he shouted. "The thing that we need to do most is to respect this woman whose son was shot." The crowd shouted back, "Uncle Tom." "I'm prepared to be a Tom if it's the only way I can save women and children from being shot down in the streets," Rustin replied, "and if you're not willing to do the same, you're fools." The crowd ignored him.[6] Having organized a quarter of a million Americans who marched on Washington in 1963, Rustin could not persuade a few hundred blacks to clear the streets of Harlem a year later. Nor could James Farmer, chairman of C.O.R.E., Cecil Moore, president of the Philadelphia N.A.A.C.P., and the other moderates who also attempted to prevent rioting and restrain rioters in New York, Rochester, and Philadelphia that summer.[7]

Other moderates—among them, Wendell Collins, vice-chairman of Los Angeles C.O.R.E., the Reverend Hartford H. Brookins of the United Civil Rights Committee, John A. Buggs of the Los Angeles County Human Relations Commission, and Congressman Augustus F. Hawkins—could not maintain order in south-central Los Angeles the next summer.[8] They worked long and hard all year to confine protest to nonviolent channels. And when the rioting erupted in August they called public meetings, spoke on radio and television, negotiated with police officials and youth leaders, and otherwise implored the residents to stay off the streets; they even appealed directly to the rioters, often at great personal risk. But most of them were ignored. And one—Dick Gregory, a well-known entertainer and civil rights activist, who had defied sheriffs and klansmen in the Deep South and was now performing outside Los Angeles—was shot in the leg when he pleaded with the rioters to remove the women and children from the streets. And though it was scant consolation to Gregory, other moderates were unable to prevent rioting or restrain rioters in Chicago, Omaha, and a dozen other cities in the summer of 1966.[9]

Nor were still other moderates, including Oliver Lofton of the Newark Legal Services Project and Congressman John Conyers, Jr., of Detroit, more successful in Newark, Detroit, and scores of other cities the following summer.[10] Their courage was commendable, but their impact was negligible. The Detroit riots so dismayed the moderate black establishment that shortly afterwards Dr. King, Roy Wilkins of the N.A.A.C.P., Whitney Young of the Urban League, and a few others issued a statement denouncing the rioters.[11] The whites applauded their statement. But, in view of the rioting which erupted in Washington, Baltimore, Chicago, and a hundred other cities after the assassination of Dr. King in April 1968, it is clear that the blacks did not heed it.[12] Thus, far from preventing the rioting or restraining the rioters, the moderate leaders watched in despair as the riots broke out in one community after another and raged until the local police, National Guard, or federal soldiers occupied the ghettos. By their own standards the moderates wholly failed in their attempt to maintain order.[13]

The task was very difficult. Many blacks so resented the ghetto's conditions and rejected the society's restraints that the moderates could not have said or done anything to prevent them from rioting.

And if the moderates could not confine the protest to nonviolent channels in the first place, how could they possibly restrain the rioters afterwards? Also, the rioting was so dispersed that the moderates could only plead with a few rioters at a time; and they were not inclined to listen to, much less to heed, these pleas anyway. But the task was not impossible. The histories of other ethnic minorities reveal that effective leadership can help inhibit rioting; so do the experiences of black gangs in Chicago and other cities. Also, nearly all the riots started sometime in the evening, ended in the early morning, and then started again, if at all, sometime the next evening. The moderates had the opportunity to appeal to their followers not only during the rioting, a most inauspicious time, but also during the relatively orderly period in between.[14] All things considered, the moderates' failure reflects the profound weakness of their leadership in the ghettos.

On the surface this situation is a bit perplexing. Many moderates, especially the late Martin Luther King, have possessed the charisma to arouse tremendous enthusiasm among people and transform personal adulation into political loyalty. Many have embodied courage, commitment, self-sacrifice, and other values which not only reflect a flattering image to whites but present a reassuring portrait to blacks themselves. And many, including Senator Edward Brooke, Supreme Court Justice Thurgood Marshall, and former Secretary of Housing and Urban Development Robert C. Weaver, have attained positions which confer status on the group. Most important of all, many moderate leaders have articulated black grievances so eloquently that the authorities have been obliged to pay attention to the ghetto's plight.[15] On a deeper level, however, this situation is not so perplexing. Although the moderates have protested the ghetto's grievances, they have not remedied them. The moderates have not, in a word, produced, or at any rate produced enough so that, in the opinion of the rank-and-file, they deserve strong and sustained support.

The moderates have long fought subordination and segregation. They have carried to the Supreme Court a host of landmark cases challenging southern nominating conventions, restrictive real estate covenants, and segregated school systems. They have also exerted constant pressure on local, state, and federal authorities in support of fair employment practices, integrated public accommodations, and open housing legislation. They have even engaged in sit-ins, boycotts, demonstrations, and civil disobedience to protest discriminatory activities by unions, corporations, and government agencies.[16] The moderates have won a fair share of these fights, too. These victories have not only upgraded the blacks' occupational distribution, increased their per capita income, enhanced their educational achievements, and improved their housing facilities. They have also restricted de jure segregation to the rural South, contested de facto segregation in the urban North, and encouraged successive administrations to affirm an integrated society as a national goal. And these victories, as Oscar Handlin has pointed out, have curtailed subordination and segregation during the past two or three decades.[17]

But the moderates have also lost a great many of these fights. They could not prevent the repeal of California's open housing act by a coalition of real estate interests, conservative organizations, and white homeowners. Nor could they compel the desegregation of New York City's school system in the face of the bureaucratic inertia, not to say the outright opposition, of the Board of Education. And in spite of countless well-documented complaints to the U. S. Civil Rights Commission, they could not eradicate racial discrimination in the building trades.[18] In other words, the moderates have not brought about equality and integration. Racial discrimination is, as the Kerner Commission found, quite common; and residential segregation is, if anything, on the increase. Economic deprivation, whether measured by unemployment level, per capita income, or occupational distribution, is rampant in the ghettos; and so is consumer exploitation.[19] Despite marked progress in the recent past the disparity between black expectations and achievements has not yet been fully overcome.

Hence the moderates have won too few victories—or, as Whitney Young recently observed, too few "tangible, concrete victories"[20]—and suffered too many defeats. Not that they are entirely responsible for this record: much progress toward equality and integration was sponsored by others, and many strongholds of subordination and segregation were beyond their power. But in the absence of anyone else the moderates are held accountable. And so their defeats over open housing, school desegregation, police review boards, and other controversial measures have undermined their tactics, strategies, and ideology. Few leaders, no matter how charismatic and eloquent, can survive so many defeats with their prestige unimpaired and their position wholly intact. And if the apathetic reception accorded Martin Luther King in the Chicago ghetto just before his assassination is indicative,[21] the moderates are not exceptions. Hence they are caught in a desperate predicament. They cannot strengthen their position without obtaining rank-and-file support, but they cannot obtain its support without producing, which they have not yet done.

At the core of the moderates' predicament are several formidable constraints. The blacks are a minority, a highly visible and heavily concentrated minority, but a minority just the same and, vis-à-vis the whites, a fairly small minority, too. They cannot elect more than a few candidates of their own; nor can they influence an election unless the outcome is very close (and, as the 1968 presidential race showed, not always then). They are a majority in a few cities and will soon be a majority in many others. But even there they are subject to the decisions of metropolitan, regional, state, and federal authorities which are mainly responsive to white constituents.[22] The blacks are also a relatively impoverished, ill-educated, and un-organized minority. They do not work as often, earn as much, and advance as high as whites; nor do they control enough business to redress the inequities. They are not well informed about the system, nor confident in its flexibility; and they are hard pressed to mobilize against bureaucratic indifference and irresponsibility.[23] For these reasons the moderates are left with no alternative but to work with the whites.

Violence as Protest

But the whites have a long tradition of racism. This tradition, which has been thoroughly described by Gunnar Myrdal and other scholars, extends well back into the colonial period. And though it has been on the wane for well over a generation, it is, as the Kerner Commission reported, still fairly common today. Or at any rate common enough to impose severe limits on black demands which threaten (or appear to threaten) white notions about the good community and the secure society. Witness the referenda on California's open housing law in 1964 and New York City's police review board in 1966.[24] The white community has a strong trend toward institutional rigidity, too. This trend, which reflects the bureaucratization of the police, schools, welfare, and other urban institutions, started in the early twentieth century. And since then it has rendered these institutions so unresponsive that they place other limits on black demands for better services and greater participation. Here was one lesson of the recent (and as yet unsettled) struggle over school decentralization in New York City.[25]

These constraints would be formidable under ordinary conditions; and conditions today are anything but ordinary. The blacks' expectations are rising much faster than their achievements; and the moderates, far from being praised for the obvious advances, are blamed for the remaining disparities. They are caught on a treadmill; they do everything possible to move ahead, only to end up in the same place, if not further behind. What is more, black demands are no longer centered on voting rights and other relatively noncontroversial issues but on community control and other extremely sensitive issues in which northern whites and white institutions have an enormous stake. This combination of progress and frustration has encouraged black militants to compete for the allegiance of the rank-and-file, too. And this competition, which will be dealt with later on, has severely undermined the moderates' position in the black community. Under these circumstances the moderates cannot produce enough to gain the support of the rank-and-file and strengthen their leadership in the ghettos.

These constraints are not unique to the blacks, however. The Irish,

136

Italians, Poles, and Jews were minorities in the late nineteenth century, and extremely impoverished, ill-educated (though not unorganized) minorities too. So were the Mexicans, Japanese, and Puerto Ricans a generation later. Also, these groups were long subjected to racism or nativism and ignored for a while by many urban institutions. Racial discrimination and administrative rigidity are nothing new to American cities.[26] Nonetheless, if the historical and sociological accounts of these ethnic minorities are reliable, somehow their leaders often overcame the constraints which have stymied the black leaders.[27] Hence the profound weakness of the moderates has another dimension. And that is, just as the moderates do not enjoy rank-and-file support because they have not produced enough, so they have not produced enough because they do not enjoy rank-and-file support. In which case an attempt to find out why is very much in order.

One starting point is the class structure of the black ghetto. Most moderate leaders are middle-class, if only because the middle class has the time, money, and ability to head organizations, raise funds, and handle the other chores of leadership. And most rank-and-file blacks are lower and working class. This arrangement was fairly common in other ethnic communities; and, if the experiences of the Irish, Italians, and other European immigrants are indicative, it is not necessarily deleterious. But the experience of the blacks is another matter. Notwithstanding a deep and abiding affection for many middle-class leaders as individuals, many lower- and working-class blacks have a deep-seated distrust of them as a group. As one Rochester N.A.A.C.P. official admitted shortly after the 1964 riots, "Very few of us (that is, moderate leaders) are considered one of our own in these ghetto communities."[28] Hence class antagonism isolates the middle class from the lower and working classes and thereby deprives moderate leadership of rank-and-file support.

The lower and working classes' distrust of the middle class is not altogether unwarranted, a point first made by E. Franklin Frazier and recently confirmed by other social scientists.[29] Not that the middle class has been completely indifferent to the problems of the lower and working classes. On the contrary, it has devoted considerable energy to enhancing the position of blacks whatever their class; the N.A.A.C.P.'s challenges to segregated schools are a case in point, and so are the Urban League's training programs. Nor that the middle-class efforts have completely failed to alleviate lower- and working-class grievances. On the contrary, they have markedly weakened subordination and segregation in recent decades; the application of fair employment practices to the civil service is one example, and the abandonment of the double standard of law enforcement is another. But most middle-class blacks have not shown the same concern for lower- and working-class blacks that most middle-class Italians and Jews showed for lower- and working-class Italians and Jews two generations ago.[30] Or at any rate not until quite recently, a situation which is rapidly changing and, in view of the attitudes of black college students, will probably change even faster in the future.

There are two main reasons why. To begin with, middle-class blacks have different interests than lower- and working-class blacks. To apply James Q. Wilson's distinction, the middle class is primarily interested in its status—that is, in its relations with the white community and especially in the integration of the schools and neighborhoods. And the lower and working classes are primarily interested in their welfare—that is, in the tangible conditions of ghetto life and particularly in the provision of decent accommodations and adequate services.[31] Hence middle-class blacks are often at odds with lower- and working-class blacks. To cite one example, many middle-class blacks opposed construction of a public housing project on Chicago's South Side, which would have materially increased the lower and working classes' rental market, on the grounds that it would have perpetuated residential segregation.[32] This distinction should not be carried too far. Middle-class blacks are interested in welfare, and lower- and working-class blacks are interested in status; and often status and welfare are inextricably connected. But this distinction does help explain why middle-class blacks have not shown a keen concern for the lower and working classes.

Even more important, middle-class blacks have felt a weaker attachment to the black ghettos than middle-class immigrants felt to the ethnic ghettos a half century ago. Unlike many middle-class Italians, who remained in their neighborhoods unless forced to move by massive migration (the Puerto Rican influx into New York's East Harlem) or government action (the urban renewal of Boston's West End), many middle-class blacks have left the ghettos physically. And unlike many middle-class Jews, who stayed active on New York's Lower East Side even after moving away to Manhattan's Upper West Side, the East Bronx, or Brooklyn's Williamsburg and Boro Park districts, many middle-class blacks have left the ghettos spiritually.[33] These differences should not be carried too far either. Many middle-class blacks are prevented from moving out of the ghettos by racial discrimination, and many others, especially entrepreneurs and professionals, are deeply involved in the ghettos; some middle-class Italians and Jews fled the ghettos at the first opportunity too. But these differences also help explain why middle-class blacks have not shown a keen concern for the lower and working classes.

Middle-class blacks have left the ghettos physically because the streets are dangerous, the schools are inadequate, and, above all, the housing is inferior. This inferiority has been so thoroughly documented elsewhere that it requires only a brief summary here. No matter when the ghettos were developed—Harlem in the 1900s, Chicago's South Side in the 1920s, or south-central Los Angeles in the 1940s—the houses are worse off there than in the adjacent white communities. And no matter how the ghettos were developed— apartments and tenements in Harlem, two-family houses on Chicago's South Side, and single-family dwellings in south-central Los Angeles—the houses are more crowded there.[34] What is more, ghetto housing is anything but cheap; most blacks pay much more than their accommodations are worth (and much more than their incomes can support). The whole matter was concisely summed up by one demographer in the 1950s: "non-white householders, both renters and owners," he wrote, "obtained a poorer quality of housing than did whites at all levels of rent or value, in all regions of the country."[35] And this disparity has not decreased since then.

Middle-class blacks have also left the ghettos spiritually, not only detaching themselves from the lower and working classes, a common practice among middle-class Americans whatever their color, but also dissociating themselves from the ghetto itself. The ghetto is for them, as the plantation was for their fathers, the embodiment of the blacks' appalling position in American society, the symbol, as it were, of their subordination and segregation.[36] The middle-class blacks have thus forsaken the ghetto as part of a long-standing campaign to overcome this position and its attendant disabilities and frustrations. This stigma is not perceived in the same way in every ghetto. There is a pride of place in Harlem unmatched on Chicago's South Side and until recently virtually nonexistent in Newark's Central Ward, Cleveland's Hough district, and south-central Los Angeles.[37] Nonetheless, it is (or, in any case, it has been) so rare as to be remarkable for middle-class blacks to remain in the ghettos and devote their energy to resolving its problems. Within or without the ghetto, the middle class is not of it; and for this reason it does not enjoy rank-and-file support.

Underlying the inferiority of ghetto housing and the stigma of ghetto life is the system of residential segregation. It is not necessary, in view of Karl and Alma Taeuber's exhaustive research, to belabor the point that the system is widespread: suffice it to say that it extends to every major city in the country.[38] But it is worth stressing, even at the risk of simplification, that it is involuntary. Unlike the Irish, Italians, Jews, and other European immigrants, the blacks have not chosen to live as a group: they have not chosen, period; they have been compelled to reside together. And the consequences have been both unfortunate and inevitable. So long as the blacks have been denied equal access to the metropolitan real estate market and so long as they have been unable to move freely if dissatisfied with their housing, they have been confined to substandard, overcrowded, and overpriced accommodations. Also, so long as the blacks have lived in ghettos because no alternatives were available and so long as they have regarded them as places of confinement, they have perceived them as symbols of subordination and segregation.[39]

Involuntary residential segregation, which cannot be discussed at length here, is essentially a manifestation of an integral feature of the American concept of the good community, namely, racial homogeneity.[40] By this standard an integrated community is an undesirable community. Moreover, as Charles Abrams and Robert Weaver have pointed out, this conviction has been embodied in restrictive covenants, implemented by real estate interests, supported by banks and insurance companies, and sanctioned by local authorities. These institutions have fully adjusted to the preferences of white America. What is worse, this conviction has been underwritten by the federal government and, in particular, by the Federal Housing Administration, the Public Housing Administration, and the Urban Renewal Administration.[41] This indictment could be extended much further. But rather than do so it is enough to conclude that, besides imposing obvious burdens on the blacks, involuntary residential segregation has also intensified the conflict between the middle class and lower and working classes. And thus it has seriously, if indirectly, undermined the position of the moderate leaders.

Another starting point is the political organization of the black ghetto. After all, some middle-class blacks have stayed in the ghetto and promoted its welfare; and, in view of the recent upsurge of racial solidarity, many others may join them in the future. Some middle-class blacks have also pressed for community control of public schools and other programs on which their interests and the lower and working classes' interests coincide. But even under these circumstances the moderate leaders have found it extremely difficult to mobilize the rank-and-file and transform common concern into strong support.[42] And their difficulties suggest that the black community is not as well organized today as the Irish, Italian, and Jewish communities were a generation or two ago. Accordingly political disorganization not only leaves the moderates hard pressed to tap whatever middle-class commitment and lower- and working-class trust remain; it also undermines their claims to leadership. And to analyze this constraint it is essential to look more closely at the voluntary associations in the black ghetto.

Voluntary associations are the nonprofit and nongovernmental fraternal, benevolent, religious, cultural, civic, commercial, and political groups which have characterized American society ever since the early nineteenth century. These associations, as Oscar Handlin has pointed out, have probably played a more prominent role in the United States than in most other countries.[43] And nowhere in the United States have they played a more prominent role than in the lives of the millions of newcomers excluded from middle-class native-American society on the grounds of race, religion, and national origins. The voluntary associations not only assimilated the immigrants, tied them to one another, protected the weak against misfortune, promoted the aspirations of the ambitious, and generated and educated their leaders. They also mobilized the newcomers by organizing them into constituencies which could be counted on to vote, picket, strike, and thereby demonstrate to the outside society that they stood solidly behind their leaders.[44] Hence the political organization of the ethnic communities depended largely on the cohesion of their voluntary associations.

Although there is not enough statistical data to make precise comparisons, there is ample impressionistic evidence to suggest that the voluntary associations in the black ghettos are less cohesive today than their counterparts in the ethnic ghettos were two generations ago. The situation is not essentially a function of poverty. Although the blacks are so poor and work, if at all, so long and hard that they cannot devote much money and energy to associational activities, they are no poorer now than the European immigrants were in the past; nor do they—or the whites—work as hard or as long.[45] This situation is not essentially a function of residential mobility either. If the tremendous turnover in the ghetto schools in indicative, the blacks apparently move very often inside the ghettos; and in the process they join groups only to drop out afterwards and join others more conveniently located. And though very little is known about the residential mobility of ethnic minorities in the late nineteenth and early twentieth centuries, the Irish, Italians, and Poles (if not the Jews) probably did not change address quite so frequently.[46] Thus the stable membership vital for effective organization is rare in black associations.

But even if the blacks moved less often their associations would labor under serious handicaps. Unlike the Italians, Poles, and Jews, the blacks lack a separate language, a traditional culture, and, by virtue of two centuries of slavery, an interrupted history. They have viewed themselves through the eyes of whites for so long that until fairly recently they have not taken much pride in their uniqueness. Nor, by reason of their dependence on whites and their commitment to integration, have they relied on indigenous organizations as widely as other newcomers.[47] The country has recently changed in ways which have undermined voluntary associations, too. Public authority and private enterprise have assumed responsibility to safeguard individuals against unemployment, illness, accident, and death. The mass media, and especially television, have supplanted the newspapers, theaters, and other cultural organizations based on ethnicity. And many civic and commercial groups, once tied to distinct neighborhoods, have been reorganized on a city-wide (if not wider) basis.[48] Their primary functions thus fulfilled, the voluntary associations do not generate leaders, mobilize constituents, or serve their other secondary functions too well today.

Of all voluntary associations one merits special attention, namely, the political machine. The machine, a voluntary association which attempts to acquire power by exchanging material inducements for political loyalty, emerged as a special feature of American life in the early nineteenth century. And for well over a century, and even longer in certain cities, it thrived by rendering invaluable services to local entrepreneurs, aspiring politicians, and, more pertinent here, European immigrants. The machine introduced the newcomers into the political system and linked them with it. It served as the mechanism through which they expressed their feelings, improved their positions, learned about the system, consolidated a constituency, and, if luck was with them, assumed political power.[49] This was not a smooth process; most minority groups struggled hard to wrest power from their predecessors: the Irish and Germans from the native Americans and a generation later the Italians, Poles, and Jews from the Irish and Germans. Whatever the outcome, however, the political machine facilitated the organization of the ethnic communities.

Although there is not enough statistical data to make precise comparisons here either, there is ample impressionistic evidence to suggest that the political machine has been much less effective in the black community. Unlike the Italians, Poles, and Jews, the blacks are not just one minority among many; except in the handful of cities with large numbers of Mexicans and Puerto Ricans, the blacks are the minority. They are a very special minority, too. They have accumulated many grievances which cannot be alleviated simply by providing a few jobs, improving a few services, and redistributing a few political favors. They have also intensified many anxieties among the Irish, Italians, Poles, Jews, and other minority groups which are the major constituents of the machine. Hence the blacks' demands strike the machine as excessive, the machine's responses strike the blacks as trivial, and in the meantime the disparity between demands and responses increases.[50] The blacks do not have much leverage over the machine, either. Not only are many black politicians willing to tailor their positions to the machine's interests, but most ordinary blacks are inclined to vote Democratic anyway.

What is more, the machine has lost much of its strength over the past two generations. By virtue of a reform movement which started in the progressive era, extended through the New Deal, and maintained momentum thereafter, municipal government has been centralized, professionalized, and bureaucratized. In the process power has been transferred from elected officials to civil servants, from municipal agencies to public authorities, and from neighborhoods and cities to the states and federal government. Hence the machine has many fewer material inducements at its disposal.[51] Meanwhile, many European immigrants have entered the middle class; and the middle-class ethos which underlies municipal reform has spread throughout metropolitan America. In the process few persons have been left dependent on the machine for essential services and even fewer are prepared to exchange political loyalty for material inducements (or at any rate for modest inducements). Thus the machine has a much smaller constituency at its command.[52] For these reasons the machine cannot organize the blacks as effectively as it once organized the Irish, Italians, Poles, and Jews.

In the absence of cohesive voluntary associations and effective political machines, the moderate black leaders have attempted to organize the community through the N.A.A.C.P. and other protest organizations. But this approach has not worked very well. With very few exceptions, these organizations have so faithfully reflected the frustrations and aspirations of the middle class that they have not attracted the lower and working classes, much less gained their support.[53] In other words, the moderates have failed to create the organizations without which it is (or at least it has been) virtually impossible to mobilize the rank-and-file. This failure has had a profound impact. It has seriously undermined the moderates' position not only in the black community but also in the white community (which measures black leadership partly by the rank-and-file backing). Their predicament is self-perpetuating. If the moderates cannot gain rank-and-file support, they cannot shape the white authorities' response; and if they cannot do that, if, in effect, they cannot produce, they cannot gain rank-and-file support.

Class conflict and political disorganization would be severe constraints under ordinary conditions. And conditions are anything but ordinary today in the black ghettos. In particular, a small but rapidly growing group of militants is subjecting the moderates to exceedingly sharp competition. Militant competition is nothing new in the black community. Witness the tremendous enthusiasm generated among the lower and working classes by the Garveyites in the 1920s and the Muslims in the 1950s. But militant competition was less strenuous in the past. Neither the Garveyites, who sought an independent nation in Africa, nor the Muslims, who desired a separate state in America, directly challenged the moderates' pre-eminence in the mundane matters of ghetto life.[54] Not until the late 1950s and early 1960s, with the emergence of Malcolm X and other nationalist leaders, the transformation of S.N.C.C. and other civil rights organizations, and the formulation of community control and other black power ideologies, did the militants enter into direct competition with the moderates.

The militants have joined the struggle on several fronts. They have appealed not only for rank-and-file support, their primary objective, but also for the middle-class loyalty. To this end the militants have challenged the moderates' tactics, strategies, and goals. They have questioned the efficacy of nonviolent protest, the feasibility of orderly social change, and the practicability, indeed the desirability, of integration; and they have raised grave doubts about the ideological assumptions underlying the moderates' past work and future hopes.[55] The militants have made major gains in the struggle. They have attracted considerable rank-and-file support, weakened long-term middle-class allegiances, and even subverted the moderates' dwindling confidence; indeed, some moderates have already modified their positions to reduce the militants' pressures.[56] Also, by presuming to speak (and, for that matter, by speaking) for the rank-and-file, the militants have undermined the moderates' standing in the white community.

What accounts for the militants' success? To begin with, many militants, notably Malcolm X and Stokely Carmichael, have, by virtue of great charisma, attained a rapport with the lower and working classes probably unmatched since the time of Marcus Garvey and Father Divine. Many militants have also articulated the grievances of their people in a forthright and eloquent way; they have said what others have felt but could not say, and they have brought into the open what others have long kept hidden.[57] These achievements alone would have won the militants a following in the ghetto. But the moderates have not lacked charismatic figures either, and not only the late Martin Luther King, but also James Farmer and Bayard Rustin. Nor have the moderates failed to articulate the grievances of their people; Dr. King's indictments of subordination and segregation are as forthright and eloquent as any protests in the nation's history.[58] The militants have won a large following not just because they are charismatic and eloquent but also because they are in close touch with the upcoming generation and its emerging ideology.

By the upcoming generation I mean the several million blacks who were born and bred in the northern ghettos and reached maturity in the late 1950s and early 1960s. These blacks differ markedly from their fathers. They are young, profoundly idealistic and extremely impatient; they are appalled by hypocrisy and outraged by compromise. They are northerners who have spent little, if any, time in the South; they measure the ghettos not by the southern countryside but by the northern suburbs. They are materialistic and nationalistic, deeply influenced by American standards and at the same time exceptionally conscious of their racial heritage.[59] For them the ghetto's conditions are conclusive proof that the moderates' tactics are ineffective, their strategies irrelevant, and their goals misguided. For them only the militants, who are intransigent vis-à-vis white society and committed to black autonomy, are capable of providing adequate leadership. This convergence of the postwar generation, the children of the ghetto, and the nationalist leadership, so charismatic and eloquent, accounts for much of the militants' success.

The militants also enjoy three special advantages which give them a keen competitive edge over the moderates. First, they are free of the financial, political, and organizational responsibilities which weigh heavily on the moderates. They are not accountable to white politicians and philanthropists who have long given the moderates votes, funds, and other aid. Nor are they dependent on black professionals, civil servants, and businessmen who have a great stake in the existing institutional structure. In other words, the militants are responsible to a different constituency than the moderates. They can appeal to blacks, and especially to lower- and working-class blacks, in the most blunt and extreme fashion without fear of external reaction. They can even point to serious criticism by liberals and civil rights groups as evidence of the society's racism and the moderate's treason. And if the speeches of Malcolm X and the other nationalist leaders are indicative, the militants have exploited this opportunity with great effectiveness.[60]

Second, the militants are more newsworthy than the moderates. They are colorful and sometimes sensational; their statements make splendid copy for newspapers, and their activities superb footage for television. Who but the militants openly threaten whites, repeatedly lead protests, publicly defend rioters, and continually warn of a racial apocalypse? The moderates, by contrast, are drab; they dress conservatively, speak quietly, and spend their time in deliberations, negotiations, and other critical but essentially colorless affairs. Incidentally, the mass media may well reflect its audience's preferences: the militants do offer a rationale for the liberal's guilt, the conservative's prejudice, and the radical's aspiration. In any event, except for the late Martin Luther King, Jr., the moderates have not gained comparable access to the mass media. And by covering the militants so thoroughly, the media have not only reinforced their position in the black ghettos but also raised doubts in the white community about who actually speaks for the blacks.[61]

Third, the militants are not required to produce as much as the moderates. They are expected to articulate the ghetto's grievances, not to alleviate them: to criticize the white authorities, not to deal with them; to enhance the group's respect, not to resolve its problems. They are allowed to leave the moderates the tedious tasks of drafting, defending, and lobbying for legislation, designing and implementing programs, and guiding cases through the courts. It is an enviable position, which is particularly well suited to dissident leaders and equally bothersome to established leaders; but it is not a position which the militants can count on indefinitely. By virtue of their success, the militants will in time be obliged to transform their rhetoric into proposals, to devise, sponsor, execute, and, if need be, revise programs. School decentralization is an early (if not highly auspicious) example; and, in view of the alleged receptivity of the Nixon Administration, black capitalism may well be another.[62] But thus far this advantage has, in conjunction with the others, given the militants a keen competitive edge over the moderates.

Hence the moderates cannot compete with the militants on their terms. They are burdened with too many responsibilities, handicapped by too little exposure, and overwhelmed by unrealistic expectations. The moderates are not in close touch with the upcoming generation either; nor are they in strong sympathy with its nationalist ideology. They have lost their most charismatic and eloquent figure, and they have failed to attract the most promising black youth to his position. And in light of the sharp exchanges between Roy Wilkins and black undergraduates at Brandeis and other universities, they will probably meet with even less success in the near future.[63] Hence the moderates can only compete with the militants on their own terms. From their long involvement and many victories in the civil rights struggle they have not only won affection and admiration in the black ghettos. They have also acquired expertise in legislative and judicial affairs, secured access to white officials, and gained organizational and financial backing. But there is a rub. The moderates cannot compete effectively without producing; and thus far they have not produced enough to gain rank-and-file support.

Whether the moderates will do better in the future is hard to say. Many imponderables are involved, including the policies of government authorities, the sentiments of whites, and the attitudes of middle-class blacks. Moreover, many traditional values and beliefs are undergoing intense scrutiny nowadays, especially in the black ghettos; and so are the assumptions underlying them. Remarkably little is known about power relations in the black ghettos, too; and, according to well-informed blacks, these relations are now in a state of unprecedented flux. And, if these difficulties are not enough to

raise grave doubts about predictions of future trends, it is worth re-
calling that apparently no one predicted the eruption of the 1960s
riots. Notwithstanding these difficulties, a few observations can be
made about the above-mentioned constraints—minority status, class
conflict, political disorganization, and militant competition—that
may illuminate the prospects of the moderate leaders.

From a national perspective, the blacks will remain a minority
(and, vis-à-vis the whites, a relatively small, impoverished and ill-
educated minority) in the foreseeable future. From a local perspective, however, the situation appears quite different. According to the
Kerner Commission, which relied on 1965 population estimates,
the blacks are already a majority in one of the country's thirty largest
cities (Washington, D.C.). They are also 40 per cent or more in
four others (Newark, Atlanta, New Orleans, and Memphis) and 30
per cent or more in another five (Baltimore, St. Louis, Cleveland,
Detroit, and Philadelphia).[64] The black population is growing
rapidly in most cities, too. According to *U. S. News and World Report*, the blacks will probably be a majority in eight of the country's
largest cities in 2000 (New York, Chicago, Philadelphia, Detroit,
Baltimore, Cleveland, and St. Louis, as well as Washington). And
even in the two others (Los Angeles and Houston) they will be a
substantial minority.[65] It may take the blacks awhile to transform
numerical majorities into political majorities. But it is only a matter
of time before they elect black mayors and councilmen and gain control of the nation's cities.

But control is one thing, and power is another. And given the
trends toward centralization, professionalization, and bureaucratization, it is likely that by the time the blacks gain control of city hall,
power will be lodged elsewhere. Municipal departments, long the
preserves of second- and third-generation ethnic groups, already enjoy considerable autonomy; and they will strongly resist any intru-
sions by elected officials, especially black ones. Also, metropolitan,
state, and federal authorities already make crucial decisions about
transportation, education, and other municipal services; and they will
probably expand their influence in the future.[66] If Richard Cloward

and Frances Piven are correct, other obstacles may well be in the offing too. Federal authorities may sponsor movements for metropolitan government, a progressive panacea which failed to win popular approval a generation ago, to head off black control of cities. They may also encourage large-scale corporate enterprise to undertake ghetto programs which will further remove elected officials from vital decisions.[67] And these trends will probably separate formal control and effective power in most cities before the blacks take over.

By then most cities may not be worth taking over anyway. As a result of civil service and other progressive reforms, black officials will not have many jobs at their disposal; indeed, civil service is already a major source of employment, if mainly low-level employment, for the blacks. Nor, in view of the possibility that private enterprises will move out of the cities and thereby reduce employment and revenue, will black officials have the option of raising property taxes to create additional jobs. As a result of the influx of lower-class blacks, the exodus of middle-class whites, and the inequitable tax arrangements, black officials will also find their municipalities verging on bankruptcy. And they will be hard pressed to maintain, much less improve, schools, hospitals, and other public services which are dreadful in black communities and not much better in white ones.[68] This vision is perhaps unduly pessimistic. If the blacks acquire effective power, they will certainly create a few jobs, improve a few services, and alleviate a few of the ghetto's other grievances. But they will probably not do a great deal more.

And unless the blacks overcome the internal constraints which sorely weaken their position vis-à-vis the whites they will probably do a good deal less. The prospects are not altogether promising. In view of the middle class's heightened concern for the lower and working classes, class conflict will probably be reduced somewhat in the years ahead. The distinction between status and welfare will not disappear immediately; nor will the stigma produced by involuntary residential segregation. And the lower and working classes will not immediately disavow the long, deep, and, in large part, justified distrust of the middle class. Nonetheless, the recent upsurge of racial pride is drawing blacks of all classes closer together now than at any time since Emancipation. Witness the remarkable transformation of black undergraduates, predominantly middle class in background and middle or upper middle class in prospects.[69] It is not clear that this situation is permanent. But it is clear that a sizable and rapidly growing number of middle-class blacks now see themselves less and less as middle class and more and more as blacks.

In view of the blacks' heightened sense of community, political disorganization will probably be slightly mitigated in the years ahead too. The voluntary associations will not be more cohesive; nor will the political machines be more effective. Unless there are radical (and, at the moment, unanticipated) changes in American society, these institutions will be, if anything, even weaker. And community action programs, sponsored by antipoverty and other federal legislation, may possibly inhibit organizational efforts by undermining municipal government.[70] Nevertheless, the recent upsurge of racial pride is also generating an organizational base in the ghettos, and not only for the militants. Specific grievances, especially consumer exploitation and welfare regulations, supply the rationale for black organizations; but racial identification provides the binding for their members. Here may be the basis for the institutional mechanisms conspicuously absent in the black ghettos and yet absolutely indispensable for political mobilization.

Under normal circumstances both developments would materially strengthen the position of the moderates. But circumstances, as I pointed out earlier, are not normal in the black ghettos. Militant competition is already intense and, if current trends continue, will probably intensify in the years ahead. If the militants remain in close touch with the upcoming generation, they will gain additional rank-and-file support too. And if they manage to avoid institutional responsibilities, attract the mass media, and yet escape the pressure to produce, they will further undermine the moderates' position. In which case the militants will be as well, or even better, prepared to exploit a reduction of class conflict and political disorganization than the moderates. And if, as a result, the moderates cannot compete effectively with the militants on their own terms, they have only two options. Either they can compete with the militants on their terms, which, as I have already observed, is hopeless: or they can change their tactics, strategies, and goals to accommodate the militants, which, from their viewpoint, is self-defeating. In either case the moderates' prospects are not very promising.

So the familiar, if poignant, scenario will probably be played out again in the near future. The moderates will vigorously and unequivocally oppose the rioting; they will also attempt to prevent the riots and, when necessary, to restrain the rioters. Their appeal will be eloquent, their reasoning persuasive, and their behavior courageous; and the white community will praise their commitment and responsibility. But it will not make much difference: the moderates do not command enough loyalty among the rank-and-file to confine protest to nonviolent channels or to restrain violent protest. Hence moderate leadership will be ineffective as a restraint on rioting in the foreseeable future. The militants themselves may attempt to head off the rioting; they have already done so in a few cities, and with occasional success. But they do not have a great stake in maintaining public order, nor do they have a good reason to risk their prestige on so hazardous an enterprise. In any event, the moderates will probably exert as little influence over the course of the riots in the near future as they have in the recent past.

7: Liberalism at an Impasse

The riots placed the nation's elected leaders in an extremely difficult position. So difficult that on July 27, 1967, in the wake of the Detroit riots, President Johnson appointed a commission to inquire into the recent disorders and proclaimed July 30 a National Day of Prayer. To the commission, known as the National Advisory Commission on Civil Disorders or, after its chairman, Governor Otto Kerner of Illinois, as the Kerner Commission, Johnson named two senators, two congressmen, and seven prominent citizens.[1] Nine were whites, and two were blacks; but all were moderates. Two days later the President instructed the commissioners to consider three main questions: "What happened? Why did it happen? What can be done to prevent it from happening again and again?" Promising the commissioners the full cooperation of the federal government and urging them to disregard the conventional wisdom, the President asked for an interim report within seven months and a final report within a year.[2] The next day the President and his family led a perplexed nation in prayer. All things considered, it was a typically American response and, in view of the record of previous riot commissions, not a particularly auspicious one.

But the Kerner Commission was not a typical riot commission. Unlike its predecessors—the Chicago Commission on Race Relations (1919), the Mayor's Commission on Conditions in Harlem (1935), and, among others, the Governor's Commission on the Los Angeles Riots (1965)—the Kerner Commission was a national commission. It held an unprecedented mandate, a mandate, as Governor Kerner put it, "to probe into the soul of America."[3] The commissioners also represented several vital sectors of American society, including, in addition to Congress, corporate business, organized labor, the blacks, the police, and the cities. Few of the commissioners depended on presidential favors; and one of them, John V. Lindsay, Mayor of New York City and vice-chairman of the commission, had presidential ambitions. Also, by announcing the appointments on nationwide television and discussing them at his next press conference, President Johnson ensured the Kerner Commission much wider initial exposure than any other riot commission. And in light of the great public concern aroused by the riots, the commission was assured extensive coverage by the mass media in the months ahead. If the commissioners, evenly divided between liberals and conservatives and Democrats and Republicans, could agree on a report, it would command widespread attention.

The commission began work on August 1. For three months the commissioners received testimony from elected and appointed officials, moderate and militant blacks, social scientists, police chiefs, and concerned citizens; they also visited the ghettos of Newark, Detroit, and a few other cities. In the meantime David Ginsburg, a long-time Washington attorney and sometime public servant who was Johnson's choice as Executive-Director, created a staff by borrowing federal officials, recruiting full-time lawyers and scholars, and employing part-time consultants. The staff assembled teams to analyze the riots and examine the ghettos and authorized the scholars and consultants to conduct surveys, collect information, and prepare papers on such varied topics as riot participation, black history, ghetto sociology, and judicial practices. The staff, as Michael Lipsky and David J. Olson have pointed out, had trouble securing adequate funds, attracting first-rate personnel, and coordinating research projects; and the commissioners, for their part, had difficulty reaching agreement on controversial issues.[4] But after a while, as draft after draft was reviewed and revised, a consensus emerged; and on February 29, 1968, the commission, which had earlier shelved plans for an interim report, released its final report.

Put briefly, the Kerner Commission found that the riots, far from being an organized conspiracy or a revolutionary uprising, were a violent reaction against ghetto conditions. It also found that white society has not only created and perpetuated the black ghetto, but has also condoned, without fully understanding, the terrible grievances there. From these findings the commission concluded that the riots were essentially a function of white racism (and in the report's sharp phrase, a reflection of the movement toward "two societies, one black, one white—separate and unequal").[5] Notwithstanding this indictment, the commission repudiated rioting as a legitimate recourse, arguing that disruption and disorder would not lead to social justice and that American society could not tolerate coercion or violence. To maintain order it recommended not blind repression nor abject capitulation but rather a massive financial commitment by the government combined with a profound personal commitment by its citizens. Declaring that its recommendations rated the highest priority on policy and the largest claim on conscience, the Kerner Commission warned that nothing less could reverse the movement toward two societies.[6]

The report, as expected, commanded widespread attention. The press covered it at length; so did the other media; and the public purchased more than a million copies of the paperback edition (which, by special arrangement, appeared at the same time as the government version). The report warranted this attention, and for at least three reasons other than the obvious one that moderate presidential commissions do not normally issue severe indictments of white racism. First, the report, which ran over four hundred pages in the government version and fully six hundred pages in the paperback edition, was the most thorough analysis of racial unrest since the Chicago Commission on Race Relation's study of the 1919 riots. Second, the report, which examined the status of the blacks, the formation of the ghettos, and, among many other things, the patterns of racial protest, was the most comprehensive account of race relations since Gunnar Myrdal's *An American Dilemma*. And third, what with its recommendations on police, employment, education, welfare, housing, and other problems, the report was at once the most elaborate blueprint for public policy and the most promising approach to public order available.[7] All in all, it was an important document and, by the standards of American riot commissions, an impressive one.

The report also received a favorable response. Martin Luther King, Jr., Floyd McKissick, Whitney Young, and, though with considerably less enthusiasm, H. Rap Brown praised it for acknowledging the terrible consequences of white racism. And Mayors Carl Stokes of Cleveland, Jerome P. Cavanagh of Detroit, Hugh J. Addonizio of Newark, and Samuel W. Yorty of Los Angeles defended it for proposing additional federal funding. Many Protestant, Catholic, and Jewish organizations endorsed the report too; and so did thirty-six liberal congressmen from New York City and a few other urban areas.[8] Most citizens commended the report not so much for its specific findings or tangible recommendations, about which they knew little, but for its obvious concern, its admirable morality, and, above all, its profound sense of urgency. Perhaps Tom Wicker of the New York *Times* sensed most acutely why the report struck a responsive chord in so many liberal Americans. "Reading it is an ugly experience," he observed,[9] "but one that brings, finally, something like the relief of beginning. What had to be said has been said at last, and by representatives of that white, moderate, responsible America that, alone, needed to say it."

The report did not escape criticism entirely. Congressmen F. Edward Hebert of Louisiana and Albert Watson of South Carolina criticized its emphasis on white racism as administration propaganda; and Congressmen William B. Widnall of New Jersey and George H. Mahon of Texas dismissed its proposal for increased appropriations as altogether impractical. President Johnson refused comment for the first four days—while, on his behalf, Vice-President Hubert H. Humphrey challenged the report for ignoring the administration's accomplishments and questioned its conclusion that the United States is moving toward two societies—and only then grudgingly commended the commission for its work. Former Vice-President Richard M. Nixon protested that the report blamed everyone except the rioters; and along the same line the *National Review* contended that the report, by recommending domestic reform instead of effective repression, would heighten the probability of future rioting.[10] But though some of the critics spoke for responsible citizens and raised relevant issues, their comments lacked the precision and direction which might have undermined the favorable response to the report and compelled other Americans to look more closely at it.

Aside from Gary Marx and a few other scholars, then, few Americans have subjected the report to careful scrutiny.[11] Nor, in all probability, will many others do so in the foreseeable future. The widespread protest against the Vietnam War has diverted social criticism from domestic policies to foreign affairs and military appropriations. The intermittent outbreaks of black terrorism have channeled official concern from questions of reform to problems of repression. And the recurrent uprisings at the nation's universities have distracted many Americans from the issues raised by the 1960s' riots. This situation, though understandable, is most unfortunate. For the report, while not, as the New York *Times* observed, "a major turning point in the history of the nation," epitomized the liberal response to the riots and embodied the liberal approach to the ghettos. Better than any other report, better than the report on the Newark riots and better by far than the report on the Los Angeles riots, it posed the question whether liberalism has the capacity to resolve the racial crisis.[12] And if for no other reason than to consider this question an evaluation of the Kerner Commission report is worth while.

It was fairly easy for the commission to choose between a liberal and a conservative interpretation. Most of the commissioners (including the chairman, vice-chairman, and most of the more influential and knowledgeable commissioners) were, broadly defined, liberals. So were most of the staff and the consultants. What is more, virtually everyone on the commission knew (or, after a while, learned) that the basic assumptions of a conservative interpretation, namely, the outside agitator theory and the riffraff theory, were already partially discredited. The outside agitator theory, which blamed the rioting on irresponsible extremists and in particular left-wing radicals and black militants, was at odds with the reports of the F.B.I., C.I.A., and other investigative agencies and the findings of the commission's field teams. The riffraff theory, which traced the rioting to a small and unrepresentative minority of unemployed, ill-educated, and uprooted blacks, was incompatible with survey research reported by social scientists and arrest statistics compiled by police and correctional authorities.[13] And the commission, to its credit, sponsored the studies which further discredited these misleading assumptions.[14]

But it was much harder for the commission to devise a consistent liberal interpretation. For, as Allan Silver has shrewdly pointed out, the commission was caught in the same bind as the Chicago Commission on Race Relations, the Mayor's Commission on Conditions in Harlem, and other liberal riot commissions. Although the commission was committed to racial equality, it was also committed to public order; and though it was appalled by ghetto conditions, it was also appalled by violent uprisings. From the very outset, then, its overriding objective was to reconcile these conflicting convictions —or, in other words, to retain sympathy for the rioters without conferring legitimacy on the riots. To this end the commission, much like other riot commissions, adopted the perspective of what Professor Silver aptly calls "diagnostic sociology," a perspective from which collective violence appears the inevitable response, as opposed to the deliberate choice, of an oppressed group.[15] By so doing the commission viewed the riots as reactions rather than protests, the rioters as victims rather than demonstrators, and racial unrest as a manifestation of problems which can be resolved within the existing institutional structure.

Given this perspective, the commission's interpretations fall neatly into place. At the core of the riots, the commission argued, are racial discrimination, economic deprivation, family disorganization, personal insecurity, consumer exploitation, residential segregation, and the blacks' other grievances. Combined with the black migration from the South and the white exodus from the city, these conditions have created a situation of exceptional degradation in the black ghetto and unprecedented disorder in the entire society. Underlying this situation, the commission insisted, is white racism. Also, by virtue of inadequate communication in the cities, ineffective organization of local government, and inequitable representation of the ghettos, many blacks find it hard to redress grievances in legitimate ways. And by virtue of the rising expectations of the blacks, the increasing legitimacy of violent action, and the growing influence of the militants, many blacks tend to regard violence as a feasible alternative. Under these circumstances a minor incident or a series of minor incidents, often involving the police or other visible symbols of white authority, can easily trigger full-scale rioting in the black ghettos.[16]

This was a formidable interpretation of the riots. It was much more sophisticated than the McCone Commission's conception of the Los Angeles riots and the Cuyahoga County Grand Jury's perception of the Cleveland riots, two well-known documents with a conservative viewpoint. And it was far more elaborate than the explanation of the Governor's Commission on the Newark riots, the Chicago Riot Study Committee, and the other official commissions with a liberal perspective.[17] This was a plausible interpretation of the riots, too. The findings were not sharply inconsistent with available information on the ghettos: by any criteria unemployment rates are excessive, educational practices defective, welfare regulations humiliating, and housing facilities dreadful. Nor were the conclusions wholly inconsistent with available information on the riots: the blacks' grievances and frustrations are closely related to the recent violence, and white racism is inextricably connected with ghetto conditions.[18] Given the sensitivity of the topic, the prominence of the commissioners, and the impatience of the public, this was no mean accomplishment.

But it is one thing to be plausible and another to be credible, one thing to offer an explanation and another to prove it. And here, as Gary Marx has observed, the report left a good deal to be desired.[19] By classifying the riots simply as "major," "serious," and "minor," the report overlooked the specific differences and general similarities which might have revealed the critical patterns. By separating the accounts of the riots from the analysis of the ghettos, the report failed to describe how the ghetto's grievances and frustrations combined to precipitate the violence. And by applying its main concepts too broadly, the report neglected to document (though ample documentation was available) how white racism has engendered black grievances and frustration. This critique could be extended to the report's desultory and sometimes misinformed surveys of black history and racial protest and to its mistaken impression of the riot's impact on the black ghettos and white suburbs. Rather than do so, it is enough to point out that these criticisms (which probably reflect the commission's haste and deserve the scholar's understanding) do not prove that the report was wrong. Only that its findings cannot always be taken at face value.

Other criticisms are more damaging. Consider the report's approach to the ghetto's grievances. In line with its conviction that at the core of the rioting are racial discrimination and many other grievances, the commission attempted to discern and measure black discontent. To this end it analyzed twelve hundred interviews conducted soon after the disorders (and sponsored two public opinion surveys which were finished afterwards).[20] What is objectionable about this approach is not the technique but rather the presumption that the grievances could be found just by interviewing the blacks. Had the commission looked more closely at the riots, and particularly the violent acts and precise targets, it might have uncovered rather different grievances with rather different intensities. And these findings might have persuaded the commission to reconsider its position that ghetto grievances were a reflection less of misguided policy than of widespread apathy. To do so, however, the commission would have been obliged to acknowledge a direct relationship between violence and grievances. And though there is much evidence to support this position, the commission could not subscribe to it without regarding the riots as protests and the rioters as demonstrators.

Consider next the report's treatment of the blacks' frustration. In

line with its conviction that many blacks find it hard to redress grievances in legitimate ways, the commission attempted to locate the
source of the blacks' powerlessness. To this end it reviewed the hearings, field reports, and academic papers, examined the recent histories
of the stricken cities, and surveyed black attitudes toward local government. From these studies it concluded that the blacks' frustration
is essentially a function of inadequate communication, ineffective
organization, and inequitable representation.[21] What is objectionable about this treatment is not so much the conclusion as the implication that these barriers are accidental or technical. Had the
commission studied the evidence more carefully, it would have
learned that these barriers are intentional and political. They are
employed by individuals and organizations, including ethnic minorities and municipal bureaucracies, to prevent blacks from influencing
decisions. But the commission could not accept this idea without ad-
mitting the possibility that the racial problem cannot be resolved
within the existing institutional structure.

Consider also the report's concept of white racism. Although the
commission shied away from a precise definition, it applied this concept in two misguided ways: first, as if all whites, regardless of age,
class, or region, are racist, and racist to the same degree; second, as if
individual prejudice rather than institutional rigidity is the major
reason for racial inequality in urban America.[22] According to recent
studies of prejudice, the first application is plainly wrong. It is also
misleading: for as Hannah Arendt has shrewdly observed in *The New
York Review of Books*, "Where all are guilty, no one is; confessions of
collective guilt are always the best possible safeguard against the
discovery of the actual culprits."[23] The second application is misleading too. Not only is individual prejudice on the wane and institutional rigidity on the rise nowadays, but, even more important,
rigid institutions have a more pervasive and deleterious effect on the
everyday life of the ordinary black today than do prejudiced individuals.[24] But the commission could not incorporate these objections
without seriously undermining the credibility of its interpretations.

These criticisms raise doubts about the validity of the recommendations. For the commission drew from its interpretations the conclusion that American society could not prevent future rioting by resorting to outright repression or abject capitulation. Nor by pursuing present policies, which would perpetuate subordination and segregation and probably culminate in black rioting, white retaliation, and a police state. And not by yielding to separatist pressures to enrich the ghetto and abandon integration, which would culminate in affluent suburbs, impoverished ghettos, and permanent inferiority for blacks. Rather the commission insisted that American society could prevent future rioting only by adopting a forthright policy to enrich the ghetto and at the same time encourage integration. To this end the commission recommended large-scale and long-term private and public programs to alleviate ghetto grievances, reduce black frustration, and eliminate white racism. Only by implementing these programs, the commission warned, could American society halt the movement toward two societies and, in the report's resounding peroration, end the violence "not only in the streets of the ghetto but also in the lives of people."[25]

This was an admirable approach to racial unrest. Few responsible Americans would challenge the commission's conviction that American society cannot maintain public order by resorting to outright repression or by pursuing present policies. Nor would many responsible Americans challenge the commission's conclusion that American society must alleviate ghetto grievances, reduce black frustrations, and eliminate white racism. This was an ambitious blueprint for public policy, too. The commission took advantage of its special mandate to recommend policies not only to the states, the cities, and their respective bureaucracies, which many riot commissions had already done, but also to the Congress, the President, and the American people. And whatever the immediate problem, whether employment, education, welfare, housing, or law enforcement, the report proposed not only broad national programs, which was what most public officials probably expected, but also specific legislative action.[26] Given the tight schedule imposed on the commission, the sharp divisions among the commissioners, and the popular demand for law and order, this was quite an accomplishment.

But it is one thing to be admirable and another to be relevant, one thing to be ambitious and another to be feasible. And thus the recommendations must be subjected to more careful scrutiny. To alleviate the ghetto's grievances the commission recommended that the authorities increase employment by expanding training programs, consolidating recruitment activities, creating additional jobs, developing impoverished regions, and encouraging ghetto enterprise. Improve education by attracting first-rate teachers, developing new curricula, reducing class size, offering supplementary services, and reinforcing preschool and college-preparatory programs. Reform welfare by setting minimal benefits, increasing the federal government's share, eliminating residency and other onerous requirements, and providing due process and other legal safeguards. Upgrade housing by granting low-interest loans to builders, enlarging rent-supplement funds, amending building codes, diversifying public housing, reorienting urban renewal, and expanding the model cities program.[27] These recommendations, which epitomize the liberal approach to domestic problems, suggest how strongly the commission believed that the ghetto's grievances were a reflection of the nation's apathy, which required new will not new programs.

But if the ghetto's grievances are also a reflection of misguided policy, these programs are of questionable value. In view of the costs of the Vietnam War, the demands of the defense establishment, and the conservative reaction in the country, it is highly unlikely that the authorities will pass the legislation or appropriate the funds.[28] Even if the money is made available these programs may increase employment, improve education, reform welfare, and upgrade housing a bit, though job training, head start, A.F.D.C., and public housing have not exactly been unqualified successes. They may even enlarge the welfare state enough so that, in terms of income, housing, health, and other vital services, the public sector will provide for depressed blacks what the private (or quasi-private) sector provides for affluent whites. But these programs will not affect the inequitable distribution of wealth which underlies the ghetto's grievances; this requires not minor changes in existing programs or modest extensions of welfare capitalism[29] but drastic changes in income distribution. By failing to include an effective mechanism for redistribution, these programs will probably not alleviate the ghetto's grievances.

The commission realized that, in view of the likelihood that ghetto grievances will be a severe problem in the immediate future, other recommendations had to be devised to reduce the blacks' frustration. And to this end it recommended that the authorities open channels of communication by organizing Neighborhood Action Task Forces, joint community-government agencies which would discuss and redress neighborhood grievances. Enhance governmental efficiency by establishing Neighborhood City Halls, which would institutionalize the task forces, and Multi-Service Centers, which would expedite the delivery of health, welfare, legal assistance, and other municipal services. Increase ghetto representation by appointing blacks to high-level policy posts, employing them at all levels of local government, curtailing at large representation on city councils, and encouraging participation by representative community organizations.[30] These recommendations, which were probably modeled on the Lindsay administration's response to black militancy in New York City, reveal how strongly the commission believed that the blacks' frustration was essentially a technical problem. And one which did not require radical institutional changes.

But if the blacks' frustration is essentially a political problem, the commission's recommendations are beside the point. Neighborhood task forces and city halls may give blacks a greater sense of participation, and multiservice centers may provide them a more convenient arrangement for acquiring public services. Black civil servants and community organizations may also wrest occasional concessions from mayors and other officeholders whose political futures are closely tied to public order in the ghetto. But these programs will not end the bureaucratic irresponsibility which underlies the blacks' frustration.[31] This requires not only adequate communication, efficient organization, and equitable representation but also a redistribution of political power, which is under way in many cities, and a transformation of urban institutions, which is meeting furious resistance in the same cities.[32] About these issues the commission said virtually nothing. Thus by neglecting to include an effective mechanism for participation, its programs will not reduce the blacks' frustration; and by raising their expectations, they may even increase it.

The commission also realized that these programs will not eliminate white racism, that, if anything, white racism might eliminate these programs. Hence it recommended that the authorities remove racial barriers to employment by extending federal antidiscrimination legislation to government agencies, granting the F.E.P.C. strong cease and desist powers, and supplying the E.E.O.C. additional staff and resources. Curtail de facto school segregation by providing financial bonuses to integrated school systems, creating exemplary schools and educational parks, opposing racial discrimination by school boards, and, if necessary, cutting off federal funds to segregated school districts. Abolish racial restrictions on housing by enacting a national, comprehensive, and enforceable open occupancy law for private (and not only federally assisted private) housing and, by financial inducements, rent supplements, and direct construction, enlarge the stock of low-income housing in the suburbs.[33] These recommendations, which extend the civil rights legislation of the Kennedy and Johnson administrations, suggest how widely the commission assumed that the major reason for racial inequality was individual prejudice, which could be effectively controlled by federal antidiscrimination legislation.

But if the major reason for racial inequality is institutional rigidity, these recommendations are wide of the mark. Fair employment practices may remove certain barriers to employment, but, if the E.E.O.C. reports are a reliable indicator, they will not guarantee equal opportunity to blacks. Legislative action may prompt a good many schemes to eliminate de facto school segregation, but, in the face of bureaucratic procrastination, it will not generate very many integrated schools. Open occupancy laws may inconvenience realtors and property owners, but, if recent studies are an accurate guide, they will not inhibit residential segregation.[34] To put it bluntly, federal antidiscrimination legislation may benefit some blacks, and especially middle-class blacks, but, no matter how strong and thorough, it will not end racial inequality. For if individual prejudice once made blacks inferior, institutional rigidity, notably in the police, schools, welfare, housing, and other institutions, now keeps them so. And not only because of racial antipathy, a serious problem to be sure, but also because of the centralization, professionalization, and bureaucratization of these institutions.[35] About which the report made no recommendations.

These criticisms not only undermine confidence in the report; they also raise the possibility that by holding to its liberal assumptions the commission might have overlooked more relevant and feasible approaches to the ghetto's problems. Doubtless the black militants thought so. They regarded the disorders not as riots but as rebellions and racial unrest as a manifestation of problems which cannot be resolved within the existing institutional structure,[36] a position the commission casually dismissed. Now the militants' interpretations are probably not worth extended analysis: a thorough examination of the riots, and especially the violent acts and precise targets, leaves little doubt that they were protests, even highly articulate protests, but not rebellions.[37] But the militants' recommendations are another matter: a careful examination of the commission's recommendations leaves a good deal of doubt that the ghetto's problems can be resolved within the existing institutional structure. And if only to determine whether the commission overlooked a more promising approach an evaluation of black power is in order.

According to the commission, black power is an outgrowth of two closely related developments. First, the failure of civil rights legislation and nonviolent direct action to overcome segregation in the rural South and subordination in the urban North. And second, the resurgence of racial pride among blacks of all regions and particularly among the upcoming generation of blacks in the northern ghettos. The commission conceded that black power does more than simply reflect the blacks' growing alienation from white America. It also expresses the increasing pressure for black autonomy, ranging from economic self-sufficiency and independent political action to retaliatory violence, and underlies the demand for community control of schools, police, welfare, housing, and other urban institutions. But the commission also contended that black power is nothing but a modern version of the nationalist (or separatist), as opposed to the assimilationist (or integrationist) tradition, of black protest. An old program encased in a new rhetoric—or, as the report put it, "old wine in new bottles"—black power is a revival of the "separate but equal" notion, a retreat from racial integration, a victory for white racism, and a defeat for black equality.[38]

Much can be said for the commission's indictment. Black power does belong to the nationalist tradition of black protest which extends beyond Elijah Muhammed, Marcus Garvey, and Booker T. Washington well into the ante-bellum period. It emerges out of the disintegration of the civil rights movement of the 1950s and 1960s much like the Atlanta Compromise developed out of the breakdown of the Civil War reconstruction in the 1870s and 1880s. Its ideology of racial solidarity, self-reliance, and autonomy is a variation on traditional nationalist themes; and so is its program of economic self-sufficiency, independent political action, and retaliatory violence.[39] Black power also reflects the revival of the "separate but equal" notion. It expresses an increasing disparity between expectations and achievements and a growing frustration with the assimilationist approach to ghetto problems. It regards racial integration as irrelevant and, in view of white attitudes, impossible; and it considers white racism, individual and institutional, ineradicable.[40] And in view of the blacks' economic and political position, it is possible that black power will, as the commission argued, rationalize segregation and subordination in urban America.

But more can be said against the commission's indictment. The militants' conviction that integration and equality are not the same thing is plausible; and so is its belief that at this moment the concern for integration may set back the struggle for equality. It is open to question whether, as the commission argued, integration is a prerequisite for equality. The militants' contention that community control of the ghetto (and not an extension of welfare capitalism or an appeal to white conscience) is the only relevant program for equality is defensible too. It may well be that, as the militants contend, participation is a prerequisite for redistribution.[41] From this perspective the militants' demand for community control is fundamentally different from the Garveyites' quest for an independent African nation and the Muslims' demand for a separate American state. It is more realistic and yet more radical; it is, above all, more political. So much so that, notwithstanding the militants' revolutionary rhetoric and military posture, there is little doubt that with the emergence of community control black nationalism has come of age politically.[42] And if, as the commission suggested, this is "old wine," it is heady stuff.

What is vital then is not so much the resurgence of black nationalism, which the commission briefly considered, as the emphasis on community control, which the commission completely ignored.[43] And though a full explanation cannot be offered here, a few reasons can be suggested. Much like the Garveyite, Muslim, and other nationalist movements, community control is a manifestation of, among other things, the persistence of subordination and segregation. It is a reflection of the failure (or at any rate the partial failure) of the strategy pursued by the N.A.A.C.P. and other civil rights groups down through the twentieth century. What sets community control apart is the character of the upcoming generation of blacks. Born in northern cities two generations after Booker T. Washington, it is, on the one hand, too sophisticated for a Marcus Garvey and, on the other hand, too secular for an Elijah Muhammed. And raised in black ghettos during and after World War II, it regards them, not a separate American state or an independent African country, as the blacks' rightful communities. This generation has thus developed an exceptionally strong sense of territoriality; it is convinced that the blacks must (and, for that matter, should and can) work out their destiny in the ghetto.[44]

This generation has also been greatly influenced by the colonial analogy, the idea that blacks are a colonial people, whites a colonial oppressor, and ghettos colonies. This analogy first appeared in the 1920s, though it was applied by white radicals to the rural South and not by black radicals to the urban North; but it generated very little enthusiasm. And it did not reappear until the early 1960s, first in the speeches of Malcolm X and other black nationalists and then in the studies of Kenneth Clark and other black scholars. By now, however, the colonial analogy is essential to the thinking of militant spokesmen and influential in the ideology of moderate leaders.[45] Precisely why it has been so widely accepted is hard to say; for by most objective considerations the colonial analogy has little applicability to the ghetto (and even less to the society as a whole).[46] No doubt the emergence of independent African nations, the legacy of Frantz Fanon and Che Guevara, and the occupation of black ghettos by white police have all played prominent roles. In any event, the colonial analogy has tremendous implications: for if it is true, or even if it is believed to be true, the blacks cannot improve their status without overthrowing the whites.

This is no mean aspiration. It is manifestly impossible on the national level: there the blacks are a minority, and a relatively impoverished and unorganized minority, which commands extremely little political and economic, not to mention military, power. On the local level, however, the prospects are somewhat brighter: besides being an overwhelming majority in the ghettos, the blacks are also a substantial minority, if not an outright majority, in many central cities.[47] For this reason the militants have assigned the highest priority to gaining control of the schools, police, welfare, housing, and other institutions which administer everyday life in the ghetto. The blacks can gain control, the militants claim, but only if, like the Irish, Italians, Jews, and other ethnic minorities, they concentrate, not dissipate, their strength and work as a cohesive group, not as disparate individuals. If they succeed the militants propose to make these institutions more responsive to the schoolchildren, civilians, welfare recipients, and tenants who use them than, as is now the case, to the professionals and bureaucrats who run them.[48] For the militants, as for a growing segment of the upcoming generation, this version of black power is extremely compelling.

The reasons may be vague, but the implications are clear. Community control rejects the Kerner Commission's distinction between grievances and frustration; it insists that they are inextricably connected and that, if anything, grievances are a function of frustration. It argues that integration is irrelevant and, even more important, that meaningful participation is a prerequisite for effective redistribution. Community control also rejects the commission's commitment to the existing institutional structure; it demands a thorough overhaul of welfare capitalism (and particularly the institutions which administer it). It insists that the centralization, professionalization, and bureaucratization of urban institutions be halted, if not reversed. Hence community control repudiates the progressive view of local government which has prevailed since the turn of the century and the liberal notion of federal authority which has prevailed since the start of the New Deal. And it calls instead for a return to public authority which emphasizes administrative decentralization, citizen participation, and political responsibility.

Community control will probably intensify racial solidarity, enhance black self-esteem, stimulate ghetto enterprise, encourage community organization, and provide other intangible benefits. But whether it will alleviate the ghetto's grievances and reduce the blacks' frustration—whether it will prove a relevant and feasible approach to the group's tangible problems—is a moot point. And at its heart are two questions. First, will community control generate a more equitable distribution of income; will it ensure the blacks a greater share of the nation's wealth? Second, will community control generate a more responsive attitude by municipal institutions; will it afford the blacks a greater voice in the city's policies? In other words, will community control prove an effective mechanism for redistribution and participation? A definitive answer cannot be offered at this point. There are few precedents, and even fewer clear ones; what is more, there are many imponderables, among them, the attitude of the black community, the reaction of the white community, and the response of the national administration. But a few general observations can be made, and some tentative conclusions can be drawn.

According to the black militants, the economic sources of the group's problems are twofold: first, unlike the Irish, Italians, Jews, and other European immigrants, the blacks own only a small fraction of the community's business; and second, like many underdeveloped countries in Africa, Asia, and Latin America, the ghettos contain too little commerce and industry for their population.[49] This situation holds down the number of jobs, particularly rewarding and responsible jobs, keeps up the price of goods, especially durable goods, and channels the flow of capital from the ghettos to the outside society. To remedy this situation the militants recommend that the blacks take control of existing ghetto enterprises and, through community development corporations or other corporate (or quasi-governmental) mechanisms, open additional commercial and industrial enterprises. These enterprises will create additional jobs, enlarge available opportunities, reduce the cost (and improve the quality) of goods, and divert the flow of capital back into the community. In this way, the militants insist, community control will generate a more equitable distribution of income and ensure the blacks a greater share of the nation's wealth.[50]

The blacks can probably take control of many existing enterprises. Many white businessmen are willing, even anxious, to sell their holdings; their investments, not to speak of their lives, are exceedingly precarious nowadays. A few blacks have worked for these businessmen in high-level positions and acquired the expertise and experience to manage ongoing enterprises. And a few government agencies and private institutions are prepared to supply these entrepreneurs capital and credit to underwrite the transfer (though thus far only on a small scale).[51] The blacks can probably open some additional commercial and industrial enterprises, too. Black merchants enjoy a built-in demand for consumer goods, especially appliances, clothing, foodstuffs, and furniture, which, with intelligent management, might prove profitable. Black industrialists, by contrast, enter a market where the demand is much greater, but the competition much keener, the expense much larger, and, as a result, the risks much higher. Given the cooperation of public authority and private enterprise, however, even the industrialists might break even at the start and prosper after a while.[52]

But these measures alone will not generate a more equitable distribution of income and ensure the blacks a greater share of the nation's wealth. The blacks cannot repeat the patterns of other minority groups. Ghetto commerce and industry is only one source of black employment; and in view of the marked expansion of corporate enterprise and government activity, it is probably not the most promising.[53] Nor can the ghettos imitate the policies of the underdeveloped countries. Without a heavy and long-term subsidy, ghetto enterprises must compete in a national (and even an international) economy where, in terms of raw materials, labor supplies, and other economic factors, they have few, if any, competitive edges.[54] Hence community control may well benefit a few blacks; but under present conditions it cannot create jobs for all (or even most) unemployed blacks, nor provide more rewarding and responsible jobs for very many underemployed blacks. Unless accompanied by a vigorous assault on the racial, educational, legal, and other artificial barriers to employment outside the ghettos, it will have relatively little impact on the blacks' economic position in the foreseeable future.

According to the militants, the political source of the group's problems is that the blacks have little control over the schools, police, welfare, health, housing, and other institutions which administer everyday life in the ghetto. Hence these institutions operate less efficiently and more arbitrarily there than anywhere else (and in view of the standards elsewhere, this is inefficient and arbitrary indeed) and, by means of bureaucratic procrastination, systematically divert, subvert, and otherwise frustrate reform.[55] To remedy this situation the militants propose that these institutions—starting with the schools and the police and extending to welfare, health, and housing—be organized according to existing neighborhoods and placed under local control. This will not only make them more efficient and less arbitrary but will also render them responsive to citizens rather than bureaucrats, sensitive to clients rather than professionals, and, in the final analysis, responsible to the black community rather than the white society. In this way, the black militants conclude, community control will generate a more responsive attitude by municipal institutions and afford the blacks a greater voice in the city's policies.[56]

Community control would not work out so smoothly. The municipal institutions are subject to political influence and administrative regulation at the local, state, and federal levels which would limit the blacks' discretion. Also, in light of the sharp divisions within the black community, one faction or another would probably exploit local control in order to reward its supporters and weaken its opponents. Besides, control is worth little unless imaginative schemes are designed (and adequate funds appropriated) to educate children, protect citizens, and deliver other services to ghetto dwellers.[57] But community control might be an improvement over the existing system. At the very least these institutions would probably listen more attentively to the blacks' proposals, respond more sympathetically to their grievances, and labor more actively for their loyalties. If the recent experience of the Ocean Hill-Brownsville school district is indicative—which, in all candor, it may not be—community control would probably attract more dedicated public servants, too. And, most important of all, it might possibly provide an administrative mechanism which would encourage public servants to devise better ways to serve their clients.[58]

But community control has stirred up so much opposition among whites that it will probably not be implemented (or at any rate not as the militants envision it). This opposition is not led by the second- and third-generation ethnic groups which, by virtue of their own insecurity, have little sympathy for the blacks' aspirations; so long as the blacks stay out of their neighborhoods and schools the ethnics care little about what they do in the ghettos.[59] Rather, as the struggles over community control of the Washington, D.C., police and the New York City schools indicate, this opposition is led by the public employee unions and the municipal bureaucracies which have the greatest stake in maintaining the status quo.[60] These organizations are supported, on the one hand, by business (and, to a lesser degree, labor) interests, which are firmly committed to centralization, and, on the other hand, by liberal groups, which are just as firmly committed to professionalization and bureaucratization.[61] In other words, the demand for community control runs counter to the major trends in urban government and to the individuals and organizations which stand to lose most, professionally, financially, and otherwise, by their reversal. And at the moment their opposition is insurmountable.

Hence community control is not as promising an approach to ghetto problems as the black militants argue. As a device for redistribution, it may be feasible, but it is probably not adequate (or at any rate not without radical changes in the American economy which are inconceivable in the foreseeable future). And as a device for participation, it may be adequate, but it is probably not feasible (or at any rate not until the blacks gain control of the cities, which will not happen for at least another generation). But community control is not as trivial an approach to ghetto problems as the Kerner Commission concluded. Among other things, it emphasizes the connections between institutional rigidity and racial injustice and thereby serves as a valuable corrective to the commission's focus on individual prejudice. It also questions the conventional wisdom about the relationship between integration and equality and, even more noteworthy, about the relationship between redistribution and participation. And for these reasons alone the Kerner Commission should have given community control (and black power) a more extensive hearing and more thorough evaluation.

But the commission could not do so without reconsidering its fundamental principles, namely, the integrationist approach to race relations, the progressive view of local government, the liberal version of welfare capitalism, and the traditional commitment to the existing institutional structure. It could not do so without contemplating whether integration is the prerequisite for equality or, as the militants contend, integration is irrelevant to equality (and, if anything, equality is a prerequisite for integration). Whether the centralization, professionalization, and bureaucratization, of municipal institutions has enhanced social justice or, as the militants argue, perpetuated racial subordination and segregation. Whether distribution and participation are two fundamentally different issues or, as the militants claim, equitable distribution is inconceivable without effective participation. And whether the racial troubles can be resolved within the existing institutional structure or, as the militants declare, community control is the only relevant and feasible approach to ghetto problems. In other words, the commission could not give community control due consideration without inquiring into the conventional wisdom of American liberalism.

And this the commission could not do. The staff, which was composed mainly of lawyers, did not have the expertise; and it was too busy scheduling hearings, organizing studies, and finding consultants. The consultants, for their part, did not have the time to examine any but the most obvious matters; and even so they had difficulty completing their work on time. What is more, the commission was sharply (and, if newspaper reports can be trusted, evenly) divided between a liberal and a conservative faction.[62] And the liberals, among whom were the chairman, the vice-chairman, and the black commissioners, did not have the inclination to do so—and with good reason. For they could not inquire into the conventional wisdom of American liberalism without raising several perplexing questions about American society and their interpretation of it. Questions about the relationship between integration and equality, the economic and political sources of social mobility, the relationship between progressive reform and social justice, and the applicability of

177

welfare capitalism.[63] These questions would have compelled the liberals to focus the study not on the black ghetto but on the entire society—and to view it in institutional terms. And this they would not do.

It would not have made much difference anyway; the conservatives, among whom were the spokesmen for business and labor and both congressmen, would probably not have gone along. And their influence was formidable. On several modest proposals, the press reported, the liberals won by a six to five margin, with Atlanta Police Chief Herbert Jenkins casting the decisive vote. And on a few controversial proposals, including one recommending a guaranteed national income, the liberals yielded in the face of the conservatives' vigorous opposition.[64] Conceivably the liberals could have pushed harder; they were better informed about the issues, better known to the public, and better qualified to answer criticism. But the liberals knew that in the course of the deliberations the conservatives had lost on several critical votes and made several crucial concessions. They also knew that the report which emerged closely followed their interpretation of the riots and recommendations for the ghettos. And they realized that by pushing harder they might win a few more points but in the process would irreparably divide the commission. Under the circumstances the risk was too great.

For these reasons the report is at once impressive and disappointing. Impressive because it is the most thorough analysis of racial unrest since *The Negro in Chicago*, the most comprehensive account of race relations since *An American Dilemma*, and the most promising approach to public order available. Disappointing because it does not advance our understanding of the racial problem much beyond the point where these classics left it and because it does not view the questions of distribution and participation in a contemporary context.[65] In other words, the report has much to say, which is no small accomplishment, but little to say which is new. And if the ghetto riots have made anything clear, it is that something new is desperately needed. It was commendable for the commission to discredit conservative assumptions; but it was not enough for it simply to repeat liberal assumptions, particularly in view of the evidence that these assumptions can no longer be regarded as axiomatic. This may be too much to expect of a presidential commission. But the Kerner Commission had a splendid opportunity to free our conceptions of the racial problem from the ideas of the 1940s and 1950s and to re-examine them in the context of the 1960s; and it failed to do so.

The commission's failure should be placed in proper perspective, however. According to recent public opinion surveys, 45 per cent of the whites, as opposed to 10 per cent of the blacks, consider outside agitation a major cause of the riots; and 71 per cent of the whites, as opposed to 37 per cent of the blacks, regard the riots as part of an organized effort. Only one white in five believes that many blacks are discriminated against by employers, roughly two in five concede that they are mistreated by landlords and policemen, and fully three in five are convinced that the blacks' worst disadvantages are due mainly to themselves. True, 58 per cent of the whites hold that the federal government should create jobs, 59 per cent that it should upgrade housing, and 78 per cent that it should promote education; 66 per cent would favor a program to reach these goals, and 53 per cent would pay slightly higher taxes to finance it. But 68 per cent of the whites, as opposed to 47 per cent of the blacks, think that arsonists should be shot; and 62 per cent of the whites, as opposed to 27 per cent of the blacks, think that looters should be shot too (though all but a few whites would leave the shooting to the authorities). And fully 41 per cent of the whites recommend repressive measures to prevent future riots.[66]

According to another poll conducted by the *Congressional Quarterly*, which was answered by 268 congressmen, 16 governors, and 130 mayors, the nation's elected officials are not very well informed either. Asked to evaluate a few reasons for the riots, 69 per cent of the congressmen attached great importance to joblessness and idleness, especially among young blacks. But only 42 per cent so viewed neglect by state and local government, 27 per cent poor police-community relations, and 26 per cent white indifference to black needs. And fully 47 per cent attached great importance to black irresponsibility, 46 per cent to nationalist agitators, 33 per cent to recent Supreme Court decisions, and 20 per cent to Communist influence. Asked also to evaluate various proposals to prevent riots, 74 per cent of the congressmen attached great importance to state and local efforts and 66 per cent to private activity. But only 26 per cent so viewed a federally financed "Marshall Plan" for the cities. And fully 73 per cent attached great importance to traditional church and family values, 61 per cent to stiffer penalties for rioters and agitators, and 54 per cent to larger and better paid police departments.[67] The governors gave similar, if somewhat more perceptive, answers; and the mayors offered, if anything, less sophisticated opinions.[68]

If these figures are indicative, the nation as a whole has little inclination to think hard about the riots and even less to do much about the ghettos. And the polls are not the only signs. Witness the election of conservative mayors in Minneapolis, Los Angeles, and other cities. Witness also the emasculation of school decentralization by the New York State Legislature and the adoption of anti-riot legislation by the Congress. And witness the Nixon Administration's procrastination over school desegregation (which has drawn a vigorous protest from Roy Wilkins).[69] It is too early to tell whether, as C. Vann Woodward has suggested, the country is undergoing a reaction to the civil rights movement of the 1950s and 1960s similar to the reaction it underwent to the Civil War reconstruction of the 1860s and 1870s.[70] Surely the current generation of blacks will not accept it with the same passivity as its grandfathers. But it is not too early to say that in the foreseeable future few whites will show much sympathy for violent protest and few elected officials will look with much favor on militant demands.

All things considered, the Kerner Commission did a good, but not exemplary, job. As I have observed, its approach to ghetto grievances, its treatment of black frustration, and its concept of white racism leave a good deal to be desired. And so do its recommendations to extend welfare capitalism, increase citizen participation, and restrain individual prejudice without changing the existing institutional structure. Its casual dismissal of community control and black power, not to speak of more radical proposals for social change, is particularly disappointing. But in light of the public opinion polls, the Kerner Commission did a better job than the country deserves. It offered a comprehensive and plausible interpretation of the riots when it might have explained them away as the product of outside agitators and irresponsible riffraff. It also offered elaborate and reasonable recommendations for the ghettos when it might have written them off with vague phrases about private enterprise and local initiative. And had it abandoned its liberal perspective and submitted a more original interpretation and more radical recommendations, it would probably have been rejected outright by most Americans.

Epilogue

A year after the Kerner Commission issued its report Urban America and the Urban Coalition made a survey of the country's response to the commission's recommendations and the racial crisis. They called it *One Year Later*. The survey found a few minor improvements. Employment and income had increased somewhat in the black ghettos; school desegregation had proceeded ahead in a few small and medium-size cities; and fair housing legislation had gained passage in the Congress. But otherwise the survey found little change. Poverty was pervasive in the ghetto, job discrimination was widespread outside, and the hard-core unemployed were untouched by nationwide prosperity; nothing was done to reform the welfare system either. Federal implementation of school desegregation was lagging; so were local efforts to improve education; and the ghetto schools, racked by the controversies over decentralization, were failing the children. Congress had not appropriated adequate funds to implement the 1968 Housing Act (or to enforce its open housing provisions); housing rehabilitation had not fulfilled its promise, and model cities had not yet had much impact. In sum, the survey concluded, the country has not made "a serious start toward the changes in national priorities, programs, and institutions advocated by the Commission."[1]

Nor, in all likelihood, will it do so in the foreseeable future. The Nixon Administration is more concerned about the profits of defense industries than the survival of ghetto residents; witness its positions on the antiballistic missile and welfare reform. The Congress is reluctant to deal with the conditions underlying the ghetto's grievances; and in view of the character of the House of Representatives, it is probably just as well. The Supreme Court may assume a more passive role under its new Chief Justice; and besides, the problems plaguing the black ghettos are not particularly susceptible to judicial solution.[2] Prospects are highly inauspicious on the local level, too. The municipal bureaucracies and public employee unions are hostile to black demands; and they can count on substantial support among middle-class liberals as well as working-class conservatives. To aggravate this situation several capable mayors, notably Jerome P. Cavanagh of Detroit, have retired, and several others, including John V. Lindsay of New York, have barely won re-election. So even if the Kerner Commission's recommendations would assure the blacks a greater share of the national wealth and a greater voice in local decisions, which is highly unlikely, they would probably not be implemented.[3]

Turning from conditions to attitudes, the survey found a few reassuring signs. Few blacks were prepared to follow militant leaders toward separatism and violence; and many whites were moved by the commission's report and the assassination of Dr. Martin Luther King, Jr. But otherwise the survey found the situation extremely ominous. The militants were exerting increasing influence in the ghettos, particularly among the young blacks who are growing more and more proud of their racial heritage. At the same time pressure for "law and order" was undermining sympathy for domestic reform among whites; and white resistance to black demands was gaining momentum virtually everywhere. White and black perceptions of civil disorders (which have recently erupted not only in the ghettos but also, on a smaller scale, in the universities and high schools) have become increasingly divergent. And despite the virtual halt in black migration, the segregation of the races has not diminished; nor, in spite of (or perhaps because of) these patterns, have the authorities changed the prevailing policy of drift. All in all, Urban America and the Urban Coalition concluded, the country is "a year closer to being two societies, black and white, increasingly separate and scarcely less unequal."[4]

And, in all probability, it will be even closer two years, five years, or ten years later. The blacks and particularly the upcoming generation of blacks born and raised in the northern ghettos who reached maturity in the 1950s and 1960s will not settle for token concessions; they are determined to eliminate the ghetto's grievances. They intend to carry this struggle not only to the Capitol but to city hall and the ghetto, not only to corporations but to unions, and not only to politicians but to policemen, teachers, caseworkers, highway engineers, and other civil servants.[5] In the process the blacks will probably antagonize many working-class, first- and second-generation whites who believe that the blacks are demanding (and, even worse, receiving) too much too soon—and at their expense. And if, as appears likely, the blacks insist on community control, they will probably alienate many middle-class, native-American whites who are strongly committed to the centralization, professionalization, and bureaucratization of urban institutions.[6] To put it bluntly, a return to the relative harmony of the civil rights movement of the late 1950s is out of the question: for better or worse, racial confrontation is probably inevitable in the foreseeable future.

But whether riots are also inevitable is another issue. Indeed, some observers have insisted that the 1960s riots, as exemplified by the Los Angeles, Newark, and Detroit riots, have already run their course. Much can be said in favor of this position. By most measures, the intensity of the riots has declined since the Washington and Chicago riots of spring 1968 (and possibly even the Newark and Detroit riots of summer 1967). Also, most ghettos have already experienced riots; and, if it turns out that no ghetto will suffer more than one major riot, the number of riots may decrease too.[7] What is more, many blacks have realized that blacks, not whites, suffer the worst personal casualties (though not the most property damage) in the disorders. And many militants have decided that the group's interests can best be advanced by encouraging self-help, pressing for community control, and avoiding violent confrontations. And, as if this were not enough, the police, National Guard, and federal troops have devised fairly sophisticated and highly effective riot-control tactics over the past few years.[8] From this perspective, the 1960s riots are a transitory, if highly dramatic, episode in the history of American race relations.

But much can be said against this position. Although none of the 1969 riots matched the Washington and Chicago riots of 1968, none of the 1966 riots equaled the Los Angeles riots of 1965; and yet the Newark and Detroit riots erupted in 1967 anyway. One relatively quiet summer does not make a long-term trend. Also, though few ghettos have experienced more than one major riot, many ghettos, notably Chicago's West Side and south-central Los Angeles, have suffered several riots of varying intensity. And the pressures which generated the early riots are building up again. If the public opinion polls are reliable, a large segment of the black community believes that the disorders were beneficial and an even larger segment holds that they are inevitable. A significant minority intends to join in them, too.[9] Also, thus far very few militants have gained the loyalties or formed the organizations which would enable them to head off future rioting in the ghettos. Besides, not all the militants are determined to avoid confrontation. And, notwithstanding improved riot-control tactics, neither the police, the National Guard nor the federal troops can keep the ghetto under full-time surveillance. They can contain the riots, but they cannot prevent them. Hence the blacks will probably resort to violent protest in the years ahead.

Whether they will also resort to disruption and terrorism is another matter. From time to time over the past few years the country has been warned that cadres of blacks are planning to block highways and subways, poison water supplies, dynamite banks and department stores, and ambush white patrolmen. These warnings have been issued by black militants, seeking to strengthen their bargaining position vis-à-vis white authorities, and by law enforcement officials, trying to legitimize repressive legislation and increased appropriations.[10] Moreover, a few developments have enhanced the credibility of these warnings. Some militant organizations, including the Revolutionary Action Movement, have taken the stance that only through disruption and terrorism can the blacks overcome white racism. Many ordinary blacks, and especially young blacks in the northern ghettos, have expressed doubts that American society will respond to non-violent protest. And according to Brandeis University's Lemberg Center for the Study of Violence, scattered incidents of disruption and terrorism have occurred recently in several large cities.[11] If these warnings are accurate, insurrectionary activity will supplant violent protest in the black ghettos in the near future.

But these warnings are probably premature. Very few blacks have engaged in disruption or terrorism; and, though obviously no one can be certain, not many more are planning to do so. Besides, most militant organizations are not cohesive enough to maintain the secrecy essential for these activities. Very few blacks are so disaffected with American society that they are ready to offer the militants the tacit support that the Algerians gave the F.L.N. And without this support guerrilla tactics are, as Che Guevara found out in Bolivia, all but hopeless. What is more, the whites are not so divided in their loyalties that the authorities would be prevented from vigorously suppressing disruption or terrorism. In the face of these activities virtually all whites would quickly rally to the support of the government. Lastly, most black militants apparently realize that, as Barrington Moore, Jr., recently observed, the United States is not in a revolutionary (or even a prerevolutionary) situation.[12] It is hard to tell how long the realization will restrain them. But it is safe to say that the blacks will probably not resort to disruption and terrorism in the near future—or at any rate not unless they are driven to it.

Shortly after the 1967 riots it seemed that they might be. Throughout the country local, state, and federal law enforcement officials were, in the phrase of *Esquire* reporter Gary Wills, "arming for armageddon." The F.B.I., I.D.A., and other government (or quasi-government) agencies were designing contingency plans and devising riot-control tactics; so were local police departments, National Guard units, and regular army divisions. To the benefit of General Ordnance and other weapons manufacturers, the police and the military were also building up arsenals of carbines, submachine guns, bazookas, tanks, helicopters, and MACE and teaching their personnel how to use them. Moreover, local, state, and federal intelligence units were compiling dossiers on thousands of black militants and placing H. Rap Brown and other conspicuous militant leaders under exceedingly close surveillance. And in the meantime white civilians were not only buying guns and rifles in record numbers in Los Angeles, Detroit, and Chicago but also forming vigilante organizations in the ethnic neighborhoods of Newark. Everywhere, it seemed, the authorities were drawing the line very tightly—indeed so tightly that after completing a survey of the racial crisis Wills wrote a book predicting a second civil war.[13]

Events took a different course, however. The official response to the Washington, Baltimore, Chicago, and other riots which followed the assassination of Martin Luther King in the spring of 1968 was exceptionally quick, tightly disciplined, and admirably restrained. The authorities restored order in most of these cities with relatively few casualties and relatively little resentment—a far cry from the performance of the Newark police or the Michigan National Guard in the 1967 riots.[14] Apparently the Kerner Commission deserves a good deal of the credit. In response to testimony by Cyrus R. Vance, President Johnson's personal emissary to the Detroit riots, the commission persuaded the President to call a conference of mayors, city managers, and police chiefs to discuss the problem of riot control. The Justice Department and International Association of Chiefs of Police jointly sponsored it. At the meetings, held later in the year, the commission and the administration prevailed upon local authorities to adopt the policies of prior planning, professional supervision, and deliberate restraint recommended in the appendix to the commission's report.[15] The authorities rapidly implemented these policies, successfully employed them in the spring disorders, and presumably will do so in any future riots.

These policies suggest that the nation—or at any rate its public officials—has learned a few valuable things about the 1960s riots. One, that the riots are not revolutionary uprisings against American society but violent protests against its abuses; hence it is incumbent upon the authorities to avoid resorting to overwhelming and indiscriminate force at all costs. Two, that violent protest can best be understood not in terms of a simple dichotomy between violence and nonviolence but in terms of a political continuum ranging from apathy, at one end, to insurrectionary activity, at the other. And three, that the country can survive riots, even riots on the scale of the Los Angeles and Detroit riots; but it cannot survive disruption, terrorism, or guerrilla warfare, at least not as a pluralistic democracy under civilian rule. By following the Kerner Commission's guidelines the authorities signaled to the blacks that though they could not riot with impunity they could riot and that they need not turn to more serious and less visible forms of violence. And by so doing the authorities honored the unwritten rule (the internal morality, so to speak) of the riots, which is that violent protest and official repression are tolerable only so long as they are restrained and selective.

But, in light of the white reaction in Chicago and a few other cities to the official response to the 1968 riots, it is not clear whether the local authorities will be restrained in the near future. Nor, in view of the increasing militancy of the upcoming generation of blacks, and particularly the black teen-agers, is it clear whether the militant blacks will be restrained in the years ahead. Hence the situation is, to say the least, quite precarious; and, in all likelihood, it will remain so until American society responds to the protest delivered in the 1960s riots. The authorities must not only design sophisticated riot-control tactics; they must also provide the blacks with a greater share of the nation's wealth and a greater voice in the city's decisions. For, in the final analysis, the problem is less the 1960s riots than the black ghettos and less the black ghettos than the American society (and especially its existing institutional arrangements). Indeed, a redistribution of national income or increase in black participation will, as I have already pointed out, require fundamental changes in America's political and economic institutions. And thus far the American people have displayed little understanding of this problem and even less determination to resolve it.

Appendix

WHITE ON BLACK

On August 11, 1965, a white California highway patrolman arrested a young black for drunken driving in south-central Los Angeles (commonly known as Watts). A scuffle involving the youth, his mother, and the patrolman followed, attracting a large crowd which was further incited by the arrival of the local police. From about eight that evening to one the next morning, mobs stoned passing automobiles, assaulted white motorists, and threatened a police command post. On August 12, after a tumultuous meeting called by the Los Angeles County Human Relations Commission, the rioting, accompanied by looting, arson, and assault, spread through the ghetto. At great personal risk many moderate black leaders, some from Los Angeles and others of national renown, pleaded with the rioters to end the violence, but to little avail. The next day the disorder was so widespread that Los Angeles Police Chief William Parker asked California Lieutenant Governor Glenn Anderson (standing in for vacationing Governor Edmund Brown) to order in the National Guard. Rioters and Guardsmen besieged Watts that evening, and after Anderson imposed a curfew the authorities slowly suppressed the nation's worst racial riots in a generation. On August 15—with thirty-four dead, over a thousand injured, and almost four thousand arrested, six hundred buildings damaged, and twenty to forty million dollars in property destroyed—order was restored.[1]

Four days later Governor Brown (by then returned to California) appointed a commission consisting of six whites and two blacks and headed by John A. McCone, a prominent industrialist and former director of the C.I.A., to make "an objective and dispassionate study of the Los Angeles riots." Brown instructed the commission to "prepare an accurate chronology and description of the riots . . . probe deeply the immediate and underlying causes of the riots . . . [and] develop recommendations for action designed to prevent a recurrence of these tragic disorders." The commission, which was allocated $250,000, hired twenty-nine staff members, sixteen clerks and secretaries, and twenty-six consultants, and then launched its investigation. It heard seventy-nine witnesses, including Governor Brown and his advisers, local politicians, police administrators, civil libertarians, teachers, black spokesmen, and Watts residents; its staff members interviewed several hundred persons, including ninety arrested during the riots, and its consultants questioned another ten thousand people. Working at an extremely, perhaps unduly, rapid pace, the commission completed its investigation in three months. And on December 2, 1965, it presented its interpretations and recommendations in an eighty-six page report entitled *Violence in the City— an End or a Beginning?*[2]

Put bluntly, *Violence in the City* claimed that the rioters were marginal people and the riots meaningless outbursts. The rioters were marginal people because they were a small and unrepresentative fraction of the black population, namely, the unemployed, ill-educated, juvenile, delinquent, and uprooted. What provoked them to riot were not conditions endemic to black ghettos (i.e., police harassment and consumer exploitation), but rather problems peculiar to immigrant groups (i.e., insufficient skills and inferior education) and irresponsible agitation by black leaders. Also, the riots were meaningless outbursts not simply because there was no connection between the blacks' grievances and their violence, but also because the rioting was unwarranted. Watts, for all its inadequacies, is not a slum—

its streets are wide and clean, and its houses are detached one- and two-story dwellings; nor are its residents subject to racial discrimination—to the contrary, they enjoy full legal and political equality.[3] Thus, to prevent a repetition of rioting in south-central Los Angeles, *Violence in the City* concluded, requires that police-civilian relations be improved, unemployment reduced, education upgraded, and civil rights protests suppressed.

Less than two months later the California Advisory Committee to the United States Civil Rights Commission challenged the McCone Commission's findings. Shortly thereafter Bayard Rustin, the civil rights spokesman, Robert Blauner, a Berkeley sociologist, and Harry Scoble, a U.C.L.A. political scientist, criticized the report too.[4] Notwithstanding a few differences, these critics agreed on the following points. First, that a much larger and more representative segment of the ghetto populace than the McCone Commission estimated joined the rioting and that many others who did not participate supported the rioters. Second, that the blacks rioted because they could no longer passively accept conditions in the ghetto and not because they were unprepared for urban life or because their leaders were contemptuous of law and order. Third, that the rioting, and especially the looting and burning, were articulate protests against genuine grievances and as such meaningful responses to ghetto conditions. Fourth, that Watts is, by any physical or psychological criteria, a slum, in which blacks are rigorously and involuntarily segregated. Hence, to maintain public order in Los Angeles, these critics countered, demands fundamental changes not only in the black ghetto but in the white metropolis as well.

The controversy between the McCone Commission and its critics was resolved late in 1966 when the U.C.L.A. Institute of Government and Public Affairs completed a survey of the Los Angeles riots for the U. S. Office of Economic Opportunity and I finished a report on the 1960s riots for the President's Commission on Law Enforcement and Administration of Justice.[5] Together these studies left little doubt that the McCone Commission completely misunderstood the character and implications of the Los Angeles riots. Yet as the McCone Commission archives were inaccessible for several months after the investigation, none of the critics (nor, for other reasons, either of the studies) made it clear why the commission failed. Accordingly it was not until the summer of 1966, when the archives—which consist of the report, a chronology of the rioting, twelve volumes of staff interviews, and two volumes of consultants' papers—were deposited in the California State Library in Sacramento and the University of California Library in Los Angeles, that it was possible to reconstruct the commission's investigation and to discern where and why it went wrong.

The archives indicate that the investigation failed for more profound reasons than the critics presumed. To begin with the most obvious explanation, the commission was unduly hasty in its work. The schedule, which allowed only slightly more than three months for the investigation,[6] was exceedingly tight and the pace excessively rapid. And the commission presented an extremely sketchy report, a document much less impressive than the exhaustive study of the Chicago riots of 1919 and even the modest account of the Harlem riots of 1935.[7] But during the three months available, a careful reading of the report, hearings, interviews, and consultants' papers reveals, the McCone Commission collected enough information for a satisfactory explanation of the rioting. And so completely did the commissioners ignore or misintrepret this information that there is no reason to believe that if given three years rather than three months they would have prepared a better report.

To turn to another obvious explanation, the commission was not inclined to probe deeply into the riots anyway.[8] Governor Brown, who was gravely concerned about his political future (with good cause, it turned out), knew that the riots were an explosive issue. Hence he appointed an impeccably conservative commission. In addition to McCone, who, by virtue of his prestige, dominated the deliberations, it consisted of a prominent attorney, the chairman of the Pacific Mutual Life Insurance Company, the president of Loyola University, the dean of the U.C.L.A. Medical School, and a former president of the California League of Women Voters (the six whites) as well as a Los Angeles judge and a Presbyterian pastor (the two blacks). Except for the blacks, who were anything but militant and exerted little influence anyway, the commissioners were representative of California's establishment. This was hardly auspicious because blue-ribbon commissions in the United States, unlike royal commissions in Great Britain, have as a rule sought political, as opposed to literal, truth.[9] And the McCone Commission was no exception.

There is, however, a more crucial explanation for the commission's failure. The commissioners were not altogether unsympathetic to the plight of the south-central ghetto, nor were they unintelligent or irresponsible. But they were mainly upper-middle-class whites who brought to their task assorted preconceptions about violence, law enforcement, ghettos and slums which they shared with others of their class and race. These preconceptions filtered the testimony and other information received by the commission and enabled it to draw conclusions based on the flimsiest material while ignoring more substantial but less reassuring data. They thereby prevented the commission from perceptively analyzing the evidence and correctly interpreting the riots. Hence a reconsideration of the investigation is worth while not only because *Violence in the City* is the official statement on the Los Angeles riots but also because the McCone Commission's fiasco sharply illuminates why most whites have not understood the 1960s riots.

At the outset of the investigation the commission reached the conclusion that only 10,000, or approximately 2 per cent, of Los Angeles County's 650,000 blacks joined the rioting. Moreover, the rioters were not representative of the black community; they were the unemployed, ill-educated, delinquent, juvenile, and uprooted—in short, the riffraff.[10] The overwhelming majority of blacks, the commission implied, were law-abiding, that is, nonriotous; doubtless they disapproved of the disturbances. The riffraff theory, it should be noted, was not formulated for the first time by the McCone Commission.

It had been adopted a year earlier by Paul Screvane, Acting Mayor of New York City, and Nelson Rockefeller, Governor of New York State, in order to explain the Harlem, Bedford-Stuyvesant, and Rochester riots.[11] Nevertheless, for the McCone Commission (as well as for the Brown administration and most white Californians) the conclusion that the riffraff was primarily responsible for the riots was highly reassuring.

For if the rioters were only a small group of unemployed, ill-educated, delinquent, juvenile, and uprooted blacks, the Los Angeles riots were less serious than would otherwise be the case. It follows that the rioting was not only peripheral to the issue of black-white relations, but also a manifestation of problems of poverty, which is alterable, rather than race, which is immutable. It also follows that the riots reflected not so much the social problems in the ghettos as the personal disabilities of the newcomers. It follows further that the violent acts, the looting, arson, and assault, were not expressions of legitimate grievances, that they were, in the commission's words, "formless, quite senseless," and, by implication, meaningless.[12] Hence future riots could be prevented in south-central Los Angeles merely by elevating the riffraff without transforming the ghetto—without, in effect, radically changing greater Los Angeles or seriously inconveniencing its white majority.

Given the profound implications of the riffraff theory, its foundations should have been based on solid evidence. Yet little evidence, solid or otherwise, is contained in *Violence in the City*. For all its hearings, interviews, and consultants, the McCone Commission made no surveys of riot participation. Instead, it derived its estimate that only 2 per cent of the blacks rioted from the impressions of Mayor Samuel Yorty, Police Chief Parker, and other officials who had good reason to minimize the extent of participation.[13] What is more, the commission based its conclusion that the rioters were the riffraff on nothing more than a breakdown of the persons arrested during the rioting according to age, prior criminal record, and place of birth. It did not present the comparable statistics for the south-central ghetto which would have shown that the number of juveniles, criminals, and newcomers involved was not disproportionately large.[14] Nor did it compile any data about employment rates and educational levels. Finally, the commission offered no proof that the great majority of blacks disapproved of the rioting and even ignored the testimony of many middle-class blacks who did not riot but fully sympathized with the rioters.[15]

Why then, in the absence of corroborating evidence, did the McCone Commission adopt the riffraff theory? The answer, I believe, can be traced to its conviction that no matter how grave the grievances, there are no legitimate grounds for violent protest—a conviction, shared by most whites and, until recently, most blacks, which reflects the nation's traditional confidence in orderly social change.[16] To have accepted, indeed, even to have raised, the possibility that a substantial and representative segment of the blacks participated in the riots would have compelled the commission to draw either of two conclusions. One, that the deterioration of the south-central ghetto has destroyed the prospect for gradual progress and provided the justification for violent protest; the other, that even if the commission does not believe that the situation is so desperate a large number of ordinary blacks do. Neither conclusion could have been reconciled with the commission's commitment to orderly (and extremely limited) social change. And to have accepted either would have obliged the commissioners to re-examine a fundamental feature of the ideology of their class, race, and country. Not surprisingly, they were disinclined to do so.

The riffraff theory is wrong, however. On the basis of statistical and other data now available, the commission's estimate that only 10,000, or approximately 2 per cent, of Los Angeles County's 650,-000 blacks participated in the riots is wholly farfetched. For to claim that only 10,000 rioted when almost 4000 were arrested is to presume that the police apprehended fully 40 per cent of the rioters, a presumption which, as Harry Scoble has pointed out, is inconsistent with firsthand descriptions of the rioting.[17] Indeed, recent surveys conducted by David O. Sears, a U.C.L.A. political scientist, and John F. Kraft, Inc., an opinion research organization, reveal that the

figure is at least 20,000 and perhaps as high as 50,000.[18] Of the 650,-
000 blacks then living in Los Angeles County, moreover, no more
than 450,000 resided in the curfew area; and of these roughly 180,000
—namely, children under ten and adults over sixty—did not participate in the rioting.[19] Thus, of the potential rioters (the male and
female adolescents and young and middle-age adults)—and the Mc-
Cone Commission notwithstanding, potential rioters, not total
population, is the appropriate base on which to compute riot participation—a substantial minority joined in the riots.

Arrest data and survey research also refute the McCone Commission's conclusion that the rioters were the unemployed, ill-educated,
delinquent, juvenile, and uprooted. The commission's profile is not
internally consistent—a study prepared for the Area Redevelopment
Administration by the U.C.L.A. Institute of Industrial Relations
reveals that the newcomers tend to be better educated and more
regularly employed than the older residents.[20] Nor is it otherwise
accurate. Young adults and not minors made up the large majority
of the arrestees; that most of them had prior records reflects not
so much their criminality as the high incidence of arrest in the
ghetto. Evidence about educational achievement suggests that the
rioters were, if anything, slightly better educated than their peers;
so, survey research indicates, were their parents. And data on residence and employment, also based on arrest records, show that the
great majority of the rioters had lived in Los Angeles for at least five
years and were currently employed. For these reasons the U.C.L.A.
Institute of Government and Public Affairs concluded that the rioters
were very much in "the mainstream of modern Negro urban life."[21]

Recent public opinion surveys also contradict the McCone Commission's implication that an overwhelming proportion of the blacks
disapproved of the riots. Not only did a substantial and representative minority participate in the rioting, but many others who did
not riot sympathized with the rioters.[22] Nor did attitudes in the
ghetto change later. Whereas a small majority of blacks interviewed
after the rioting expressed confidence in nonviolence, nearly as many
believed that the riots had improved the blacks' position. Also, many

who disapproved of the rioting gave as their reason that blacks not whites, suffered most of the personal injuries. Asked what impact the riots had on them, a slight majority answered that they felt more pride, a large minority reported no change, and almost none said that they felt less pride.[23] Contrary to the McCone Commission's findings, then, the Los Angeles riots were made by a large minority of the potential rioters, typical of the young adult population, which received widespread support within the ghetto.

This conclusion has very different, but no less profound, implications than the riffraff theory. If the rioters were a substantial and representative minority, sympathetically regarded by the black community, the riots were clearly of the utmost importance. They were not only central to the issue of black-white relations but also manifestations of problems of race even more than class. Indeed, there is considerable evidence that working- and middle-class blacks resent the indignities of ghetto life more than lower-class blacks do. The rioting also reflected social problems endemic to black ghettos rather than personal disabilities peculiar to immigrant groups (or, as Bayard Rustin put it, the unpreparedness not of the newcomers but of the cities). And the violent acts were expressions of genuine grievances and as such meaningful protests. If these implications are valid, future riots can be prevented only by transforming the south-central ghetto, not simply by elevating the riffraff—a recommendation which is highly irresponsible when exploited, as it was by the McCone Commission, to obscure the ghetto's legitimate grievances.

The riots made it quite clear that many blacks in the south-central ghetto regard the conduct of the local police as one of these grievances. The incident which precipitated the rioting—a routine and, were it not for what followed, trivial arrest for drunken driving—is otherwise incomprehensible. Why else did hundreds of blacks gather at the site of the arrest, shout abuse at the patrolmen, attempt to free the prisoners, and hurl bricks at the police cars? Why else did

many blacks believe the wild rumors that the patrolmen were mis-
treating other blacks which swiftly spread through the ghetto? Why
else did the arrival of police reinforcements attract a thousand blacks
to the scene and transform the crowd into a mob? And why else did
the rioters later vent their hostility against local patrolmen and not,
with some exceptions, against National Guardsmen?[24] So overwhelming is the evidence that even the McCone Commission realized
that police action has an incendiary effect in the south-central ghetto
that it has nowhere else in Los Angeles. And for this reason the commission spent many of its sessions investigating the blacks' resentment of the police.

Several middle-class blacks conceded at these sessions that many
blacks are resentful of the police because of their earlier experience
in the South. But, they insisted, even in Los Angeles blacks are victims of brutality and harassment so often that their resentment is
justified. These witnesses also admitted that for the patrolmen who
work there (as for the people who live there) the south-central
ghetto is a very dangerous place. Even so, they pointed out, blacks
are convinced, and with good reason, that the police enforce the law
less rigorously in their community than elsewhere in Los Angeles.[25]
It is, Assemblyman Mervyn M. Dymally told the commission, because
blacks have "generally expected the worst from the police and generally received it"[26] that they resent them so. To ease this resentment Dymally and the other black witnesses urged the commission
to recommend that brutality and harassment be eliminated, law enforcement tightened, and a civilian review board established.

The Los Angeles Police Department spokesmen, Chief Parker,
John Ferraro, president of the Board of Police Commissioners, and
Mayor Yorty, replied that these charges were altogether unfounded.
Indeed, to Parker they were manifestations of the dwindling respect
for law and order in the United States and attempts to undermine
the effectiveness of law enforcement in Los Angeles. Police brutality
is extremely uncommon, they argued, police harassment is deplored
and discouraged, and a single standard of law enforcement is maintained everywhere in Los Angeles. The blacks' resentment, they

claimed, is due to their past mistreatment in the South and present maladjustment in the North, and not to the conduct of the police in the ghetto. Blacks vent their hostility toward patrolmen not as patrolmen but as representatives of white society and white authority; the police are the recipients, not the source, of black resentment. Past practices aside, the police department's spokesmen assured the Commission, Los Angeles' blacks have no genuine grievances against the police; and no major departmental reforms are necessary.[27]

The McCone Commission endorsed the police department's position.[28] It dismissed the charges of brutality and harassment, ignored the allegations of inadequate law enforcement, and concluded that the problem of police-community relations was a problem not of misconduct but of misunderstanding. To alleviate this misunderstanding the commission recommended that the police department's complaint procedure be revised. But it rejected demands for a civilian review board—on the grounds that such boards have not worked well in two other cities (both of which were unnamed) and that they tend to demoralize patrolmen (though black, not police, morale was the issue)—and proposed instead the creation of an "inspector general" under the jurisdiction of the chief of police. It also recommended the professionalization of the Board of Police Commissioners, the nonsalaried agency which has ultimate responsibility for the police force, and the expansion of the police department's current community relations program.[29]

To reach these conclusions was no mean task. The McCone Commission had to do more than just reject the testimony of many middle-class blacks. It also had to disregard the affidavits and other evidence submitted by the Southern California chapter of the American Civil Liberties Union substantiating the allegations of police misconduct and to ignore the statement of one Los Angeles policeman who reluctantly admitted that most white patrolmen cannot distinguish between law-abiding and lawless blacks.[30] And it had to accept unqualifiedly the testimony of Chief Parker, a man whose antipathy to the civil rights movement was exceeded only by his devotion to the Los Angeles police, whose professional views were ex-

tremely conservative even for a conservative profession, and whose
personal behavior at the commission's hearings bordered on the
paranoid.[31] That the McCone Commission—or, more accurately,
Chairman McCone, for the other commissioners deferred to him on
the problem of police-community relations—overcame these obstacles
without the benefit of any surveys or other data refuting the blacks'
complaints or supporting the department's replies is indeed remarkable.

What is even more remarkable is that McCone had already resolved this problem by the start of the investigation. Questioning
George Slaff of the American Civil Liberties Union, to whom he was
inexcusably rude,[32] McCone remarked that as C.I.A. director he
had found that in all recent domestic riots and overseas insurrections
the issue of police brutality was raised in order to destroy effective
law enforcement. This tactic is reprehensible, he explained, because
society is held together by respect for law, and respect for law is
maintained by effective law enforcement, an assertion which reap-
peared almost verbatim in *Violence in the City*,[33] even though Slaff
and others challenged its fundamental premise at the hearings. If
brutality is admitted, McCone reasoned, authority will be undermined, law will be disregarded, society will be disrupted, and, in the
words of the report, "chaos might easily result"—a prospect for which
the commission was unwilling to assume responsibility. That effective
law enforcement is only one source of respect for law, that respect
for law is only one basis for public order, and that society is not
simply a collection of predatory individuals and groups, McCone did
not realize. Given his preconceptions and the other commissioners'
deference, the commission could not have reached any other conclusions.

These conclusions are untenable, however, not only because they
are inconsistent with the testimony and evidence offered by black
witnesses and Civil Liberties Union spokesmen, but also because
they are contradicted by two independent surveys of police conduct
in the south-central ghetto subsequently prepared by the Kraft organization and U.C.L.A. psychologist Walter J. Raine. These surveys

reveal that most blacks, middle class as well as lower class and law-abiding as well as lawless, have suffered brutality or harassment at one time or another.[34] These surveys also indicate that few blacks believe that they receive adequate police protection, a belief supported by the crime statistics Chief Parker submitted to the McCone Commission. Hence, without analyzing the blacks' complaints or the patrolmen's conduct at this point, it is possible to define brutality, harassment, and inadequate protection as the primary problems underlying resentment of the police which triggered the Los Angeles riots.

These problems are problems of substance, not misunderstanding, which the commission's recommendations do little to alleviate. Professionalization of the Board of Police Commissioners is irrelevant because it is not intrinsically related to the questions of brutality, harassment, and inadequate police protection in the ghetto. Establishment of an "inspector general," as opposed to a civilian review board, is valueless because the blacks will not place much trust in any police official, no matter how impressive his title. And expansion of the police department's community relations program is at best beneficial and at worst, if exploited, as it was by the McCone Commission, to avoid the real issue, misguided. That issue is to provide south-central Los Angeles with the same law enforcement as the rest of the metropolis, a policy which would reduce brutality and harassment and at the same time enhance police protection. This is not easy, politically or otherwise. But if the relationship between police and blacks in Los Angeles is to be improved so that routine incidents do not trigger terrible confrontations in the future it is imperative.

The McCone Commission did not do much better in its investigation of the other reasons underlying the riots. That there were other reasons no one, not the commission and not its critics, seriously doubted. Although only a thousand blacks gathered at the scene of the triggering incident, thousands more, few of whom had witnessed the initial arrest, subsequently joined in the rioting. Night after night, for almost a week, they left their homes and, with a camaraderie and jubilation usually reserved for festive occasions, thronged the streets. There they not only attacked patrolmen (flinging bricks and Molotov cocktails and occasionally firing rifles from the rooftops), but also assaulted white passers-by and looted and burned neighborhood stores.[35] These actions transformed a minor disturbance into a full-scale riot. This transformation was not inevitable, however: there are too many instances in which bands of Americans, often adolescent members of ethnic minorities, challenged police authority without provoking widespread disorder for this to be so.[36] But neither was it accidental. It was rather a violent manifestation of the fact that the blacks resent other conditions in the south-central ghetto just as keenly as they resent police misconduct. To discern these conditions, and to recommend action to remedy them, was the McCone Commission's principal responsibility.

To this end the commission received from its witnesses and consultants sixteen volumes of testimony and reports which, for all their inconsistencies, made certain points quite clear. First, that in addition to police misconduct the crucial problems of Los Angeles' blacks, and not only its lower-class blacks, are economic deprivation, consumer exploitation, inadequate accommodations, and racial discrimination. Second, that these problems are deeply rooted in the conditions of ghetto life, especially in the high rates of unemployment, extreme risks of business enterprise, rigid patterns of residential segregation, and the profound weakness of moderate leadership. Third, that the rioters were so selective in their violence that, with few exceptions, they looted and burned only white-owned stores which charged outrageous prices, sold inferior goods, and applied extortionate credit arrangements.[37]

But for the McCone Commission it was one thing to receive information and quite another to accept it. A few examples illustrate this difference. Jeffrey Nugent and Michael DePrano, University of Southern California economists, suggested that the rioting was generated by the disparity between the black's educational achievements and his employment opportunities.[38] An imaginative hypothesis, but one incompatible with the riffraff theory, it was completely ignored by the commission. Paul Schrade, a United Automobile Workers official, argued that unemployment in the ghetto is due primarily to job shortages in greater Los Angeles, an assertion which contradicts the assumption that individual disabilities, not social conditions, provoked the rioting.[39] McCone sharply dissented, claiming that the problem is a function of insufficient training, and the commission adopted his position. Thomas Reddin, deputy chief of the Los Angeles Police Department, testified that the theft and arson were directed at unscrupulous white merchants.[40] His testimony ran counter to the presumption that the rioting was meaningless, and, though confirmed by half a dozen witnesses, it too was disregarded by the commission.

Rejecting this and other evidence inconsistent with its preconceptions, the McCone Commission found three main reasons for the riots (other than police-community misunderstanding and irresponsible black leadership): excessive unemployment, inferior education, and inadequate transportation. Jobless blacks cannot attain a decent standard of living, the commission argued, nor can they assume responsibility for their families. Hence their self-esteem wanes, and their community ties erode; welfare, which feeds their children, intensifies their dependency. Training black workers to compete in the labor market is one solution. Also, the commission insisted, black youngsters cannot understand what is taught in the schools because they are culturally deprived. Nor can the schools help; they have insufficient equipment and a limited curriculum, too few experienced teachers and too many double sessions. To educate the black students so that they can be trained for skilled employment is another solution. Finally, the commission contended, the blacks are sorely inconvenienced as workers and students because the ghetto is isolated from Los Angeles. In a metropolis which lacks adequate mass transit facilities only 14 per cent of the families in south-central Los Angeles, as opposed to over 50 per cent in Los Angeles County, own automobiles. Improving transportation to facilitate movement in and out of the ghetto is yet another solution.[41]

The McCone Commission's recommendations are also consistent with its preconceptions. To reduce unemployment it proposed that government, business, and labor create a job training and placement center in south-central Los Angeles, that federal and state authorities insure due advantage is taken of available training programs and job opportunities, and that the California legislature require employers and unions to disclose the racial composition of their employees and members. To upgrade education it urged that a permanent pre-school program be established in the ghetto to assist three-year-olds to develop the skills required to learn to read and write, and that certain elementary and junior high schools there, designated "emergency schools," be authorized to set up literacy programs with classes limited to twenty-two students and special services provided by supplementary personnel. To improve transportation it recommended that all transit companies in greater Los Angeles be consolidated with the Southern California Rapid Transit District, and that public authority subsidize the district to expand service in the ghetto[42]—a recommendation partially implemented when the U. S. Department of Housing and Urban Development granted $2.7 million for the district in May 1966.[43]

These recommendations are unsatisfactory, however. Unemployment in south-central Los Angeles—which, by the U. S. Census Bureau's conservative estimate, exceeds 10 per cent—is very high. But inadequate training is only one among many reasons for unemployment, and unemployment is only one among many economic problems in the ghetto.[44] About these reasons—job shortage, racial discrimination, and criminal records—and these problems—irregular employment and inadequate wages—the McCone Commission said virtually nothing. Education in the ghetto—where, according to commission consultant Kenneth A. Martyn, students in all subjects and at all grades score extremely low—is inferior, too. But approximately one black in four who graduates from high school cannot find employment anyway, and many others must settle for menial jobs.[45]

To urge blacks to acquire an education under these conditions, as the McCone Commission did, is unfair and perhaps even unsafe. Lastly, mass transit is awful in south-central Los Angeles as well as in greater Los Angeles. But according to a 1965 census, fully 65 per cent of the families in the ghetto, and not, as reported by the McCone Commission, only 14 per cent, own one or more cars.[46] The south-central ghetto is isolated, but not for reasons as simple and reassuring as dreadful bus service.

The McCone Commission's findings are particularly incomplete with regard to consumer exploitation and racial discrimination. The commission admitted that many witnesses charged that white merchants systematically exploit black consumers in south-central Los Angeles. But it insisted that low-income consumers are at a disadvantage everywhere, not only in the ghetto, and denied that there was a correlation between consumer exploitation and looting and burning.[47] To relieve consumer exploitation it recommended establishment of educational programs and expansion of legal services. The commission's findings do not withstand careful scrutiny, however. Consumer exploitation is a function of race as well as poverty, of customers without credit, high-risk businesses, and merchants without scruples. The correlation between rioting (and especially arson) and consumer exploitation is imperfect, but, the archives reveal, convincing just the same.[48] And the commission's recommendations are inadequate because if implemented they would not increase consumer credit, reduce business risks, or curtail mercantile cupidity in south-central Los Angeles.

If the McCone Commission minimized consumer exploitation it ignored racial discrimination. For this the witnesses were not to blame. One after another, and sometimes with great eloquence, they spoke of discrimination. They testified that it started when the blacks first migrated to southern California at the turn of the century and still persists today, fully fifty years and half a million blacks later. They also testified that most whites, not only patrolmen, politicians, realtors, and merchants, treat most blacks as unworthy, undesirable, and even inferior.[49] Yet their testimony, which, while subjective, was quite restrained, made no impact on the McCone Commission—and for good reason. The commission could not concede that resentment of racial discrimination (as well as economic deprivation and consumer exploitation) was justified, or that assaults on white passers-by and looting and burning of neighborhood stores were manifestations of these grievances, without abandoning its preconceptions about the riots. Hence the McCone Commission failed to discover the conditions underlying the riots and to devise recommendations which might prevent future rioting.

The McCone Commission also failed to explain why the customary restraints on rioting were inoperative in the south-central ghetto. To be sure, it did devote a large part of its limited time to investigate the ineffectiveness of the external restraints, namely, paramilitary and military power. It questioned Chief Parker, Lieutenant Governor Anderson, and Lieutenant General Roderic Hill, Commander of the California National Guard, about the coordination of local, state, and national forces. And it examined their activities during the riots to determine why the National Guard was not ordered in earlier, which it assumed would have ended the rioting sooner.[50] To an observer who considers the Los Angeles riots a problem of black ghettos and not of police strategy the questioning seems wide of the mark. The commission's finding, that Lieutenant Governor Anderson delayed unduly in responding to Chief Parker's request for the National Guard, appears beside the point. And so does its conclusion that local law enforcement agencies and National Guard units should prepare plans for a quicker commitment and better deployment of troops in the event of future emergencies.[51]

Far more serious, the McCone Commission spent little or no time analyzing the ineffectiveness of the internal restraints in the ghetto. It was so concerned about the damage done by the riots that it was oblivious to the risks run by the rioters. To riot with the support of the police, as the Irish did in New York in 1900, is one thing; to riot in the face of the opposition of the police and the military, as the blacks did in Los Angeles in 1965, is quite another.[52] To discount this difference on the grounds that the patrolmen were outnumbered at the initial disturbance, that at first they attempted merely to contain the rioting, and that afterwards they exercised reasonable restraint is to beg the question. However safe the rioters were during the first few days, they were in grave peril during the last few days. By then all available police personnel and over fifteen thousand National Guardsmen were assigned to south-central Los Angeles with orders to fire when fired upon and to take whatever action necessary, short of indiscriminate slaughter, to quell the riotings.[53] Thus for several days the ghetto was so dangerous a place that by the time the authorities restored order thirty-four were dead, over a thousand injured, and nearly four thousand arrested, almost all of whom were black.

Given the grave dangers to life, limb, and liberty at the peak and near the end of the riots, it is not surprising that a majority of ghetto residents sought the safety of their homes. What is surprising is that a large minority, totaling tens of thousands of people, congregated in the streets and participated in the rioting anyway. The McCone Commission implied that their action reflected the growing desperation of the black riffraff. This implication is unacceptable, however, not only because it misconstrues the composition of the rioters and discounts the risks in the rioting but also because the history of native Americans in Appalachia, Puerto Ricans in New York, Mexicans in southern California and other underprivileged groups in the United States reveals that poverty and illiteracy do not necessarily lead to rioting.[54] It is unacceptable, too, because it does not explain why Los Angeles' blacks, however intense their resentment, refused to abide by the time-honored strategy expressed in the aphorism "Cheese it, the cops!" why they, unlike other ethnic minorities, insisted instead on a direct confrontation with the authorities—why, in sum, they disregarded the customary restraints on rioting in the United States.

Among these restraints are the fear of arrest, and possible conviction and imprisonment, which is inconvenient at the time and burdensome later on; the concern for personal safety, the reluctance to risk life and limb, especially when the opposition is much stronger; and the commitment to orderly social change, the conviction that necessary changes can be secured through legitimate channels and that there is no point at which violence is the only recourse.[55] To riot, as the blacks did in Los Angeles, means not only that the grievances provoking them were intolerable but also that the restraints inhibiting them were ineffective. To claim that these circumstances were complementary and equally crucial prerequisites for the riots is not to deny that the grievances generated the resentment which weakened the restraints. Indeed, this is just what happened in south-central Los Angeles. It is rather to insist that there are certain other conditions overlooked by the McCone Commission which have further undermined these restraints in the ghetto. And the reason these conditions were overlooked helps explain the commission's failure.

Why the restraints on rioting were ineffective can be briefly outlined. The fear of arrest did not restrain the rioters because the overwhelming majority of them, or at any rate of the men, had already been arrested, if not convicted and imprisoned. The exact proportion has not been calculated but 70 per cent is a reasonable estimate; and whether it is a trifle too low or too high is not critical because the other 30 per cent presume that they too will be arrested sooner or later and if not for rioting then for something else.[56] The concern for personal safety did not restrain the rioters either because they had been hardened to the point of indifference by the relentless assaults on life and limb in the ghetto. The rioting, tumultuous though it was, did not mark a fundamental discontinuity in their experience, nor pose an extraordinary threat to their security.[57] And the commitment to orderly social change did not restrain the rioters because, whatever their objective circumstances, they were convinced that their trust was misplaced. And according to surveys conducted in the ghetto shortly after the riots, a substantial majority of the residents believed that violence was either necessary or, if not, probable just the same.[58]

The reasons for these conditions can be briefly summarized. The extreme incidence of arrest is due in large part to preventive patrolling in the ghetto, a police practice which, in the name of rigorous law enforcement, often subjects the blacks to intensive surveillance, unwarranted suspicion, and outright harassment. The high level of violence is a consequence of the blacks' tendency to resort to illegitimate enterprises when legitimate channels to success are closed and to express through aggression against blacks resentment which cannot be directed against whites. And the dwindling confidence in orderly change is a reflection of the disparity between the rapid rise in the blacks' expectations and the more gradual advance in their achievements, a disparity more pronounced in the 1960s than at any other time in the twentieth century.[59] From this summary one conclusion emerges: the conditions undermining the restraints and the reasons underlying the conditions are all manifestations of slum life in south-central Los Angeles. For it is only in the slums, though not only in Los Angeles slums, that preventive patrolling is practiced so intensively, illegitimate enterprises operate so openly, and minority groups are frustrated so frequently in their quest for a better life.

To the McCone Commission, however, south-central Los Angeles was not a slum—not an urban gem, it conceded, but not a slum, either.[60] Hence there was no reason for the commission to probe for the conditions which weakened the restraints on rioting there. Commissioner Warren M. Christopher's examination of Judge Loren Miller is illuminating here. Christopher remarked that he returned from a recent visit to other ghettos reassured. "I wouldn't say that this (Watts) is a garden spot of South Los Angeles," he said, "but I see street after street of small well-kept homes and I find the contrast between that and the large tenement structures in New York and Philadelphia . . . quite striking."[61] What about this contrast, he asked? Miller, who was less impressed, answered that Watts did not resemble Harlem, but neither did Los Angeles resemble New York: in any case the south-central ghetto was a slum. Other witnesses agreed, insisting that a close look at the Watts vicinity revealed that one of every three houses was dilapidated or deteriorated. And so did others, who stressed that by any social, economic, or psychological, as opposed to physical, criteria south-central Los Angeles was a slum.[62]

On what, if not the testimony of the witnesses, did the McCone Commission base its conclusion that south-central Los Angeles was not a slum? The commission's observation that the streets were wide, clean, and lined with trees and that the houses were one- and two-family dwellings begs the question. For what the commission observed depended on what it deemed worth observing, which, in turn, depended on how it conceived of a slum. And despite a rash of studies showing that physical condition is only one, and by no means the principal, measure of a slum, the commission's conception was purely environmental.[63] By this conception, which the commission shared with most Americans, a slum is defined by its deviation from a middle-class residential suburb. And on the surface Watts does not deviate very much, a fact which no doubt helps explain why most whites found the 1965 riots beyond belief. This conception of a slum is altogether oblivious to the wide range of social, economic, and psychological indicators of community pathology; and so, accordingly, was the McCone Commission. For this reason it overlooked the extreme incidence of arrest, high level of violence, and dwindling confidence in orderly social change which have undermined the restraints of rioting in south-central Los Angeles.

The McCone Commission also misinterpreted the black leaders' role in the Los Angeles riots. The leaders, the commission argued, incited the ghetto residents by various inflammatory activities. They denounced the disparities between the grandiose promises of the antipoverty program and the patent inadequacy of its provisions and protracted bickering over its implementation. They also encouraged the blacks to feel affronted by the passage of Proposition 14, a statewide referendum which repealed California's fair housing act and precluded future fair housing legislation. The commission's choice of words was perplexing: given the obvious implications of Proposition 14, the blacks needed no encouragement to feel affronted. And inspired by reports of civil disobedience and outright violence elsewhere in the United States, they exhorted blacks to devise extreme and illegal remedies for wrongs in Los Angeles. On the basis of these findings, the McCone Commission recommended that black leaders curb their extremism and—in the phrase of one commissioner, the black pastor, who disagreed with this recommendation—"put the lid on protest."[64]

These findings are not corroborated by the testimony offered at the hearings, however. The moderate black leaders, witnesses pointed out, had attempted to channel the ghetto's discontent into orderly outlets long before the riots.[65] They were middle class in outlook, personally confident in orderly change and professionally committed to nonviolent protest. They also realized that rioting would endanger the rioters and, by alienating their friends and comforting their enemies, undermine the civil rights movement. Once the riots erupted, moreover, the moderate leaders perceived that, their position notwithstanding, they were not leading. They understood that the rioters were challenging their leadership in the black community and subverting their position vis-à-vis the white society. They could and did denounce the conditions responsible for the riots, but the intensity of the outbursts demanded something stronger. Hence, other than to join in the rioting and assume its direction, which they were unwilling to do, the moderate leaders had no alternative but to try to restrain the rioters. And from the very beginning of the riots these leaders roamed the streets of Los Angeles doing precisely that.[66]

Yet none of them was successful.[67] In stressing that local leadership (not to mention national leadership) was incapable of restraining the rioters, I am not implying that the rioters were easily restrained; the excitement was too great, the grievances too strong, and the customary restraints too weak. But I am suggesting that the outbreak of rioting in south-central Los Angeles revealed that the moderate leaders had failed not only to alleviate ghetto conditions but also to confine black resentment to nonviolent channels. I am suggesting, too, that the timing of the riots, which started late in the evening and stopped early in the morning, provided the moderate leaders with an opportunity to meet with the ghetto residents under relatively calm circumstances and that they failed to take advantage of this opportunity. Taken together, these failures highlight the weakness of moderate leadership in south-central Los Angeles, a problem much more serious than the McCone Commission's unfounded allegations about extremism and irresponsibility.

There are several reasons moderate leadership is so weak in the south-central ghetto. There is the intransigence of white Los Angeles, which is responsible for the approval of Proposition 14 and other discriminatory actions which have impaired the moderates' prestige. There is the lower- and working-class blacks' antagonism to the middle-class blacks who alone have the time, money, and energy to organize cohesive groups and fill positions of leadership. There is also the weakness of the ghetto's voluntary associations, which is largely due to the assumption of their traditional functions by public authority, private enterprise, and the mass media. And there are the competition of militant black nationalists and the absence of a distinctive black culture in the United States.[68] These reasons need not be described at any length here. But one other reason is worth discussing in more detail because it has implications for an examination of the McCone Commission as well as for a consideration of black leadership. And that is, the indifference of middle-class blacks to the problems of the residents and institutions of south-central Los Angeles.

Although middle-class blacks have not been unsympathetic to the plight of lower- and working-class blacks in Los Angeles, they have not displayed the same concern for the south-central ghetto that middle-class Italians and Jews in Boston and New York showed for the North End and Lower East Side.[69] Middle-class blacks in Los Angeles have left the ghetto physically and spiritually. They have left it physically not only because social conditions there do not meet middle-class standards, but also because housing there is vastly inferior to housing elsewhere in Los Angeles. According to the U. S. Census of 1965, houses in south-central Los Angeles are the most overcrowded, substandard, and overpriced in the metropolis.[70] Middle-class blacks have also left the Los Angeles ghetto spiritually to dissociate themselves not only from lower and working classes, a common practice of middle-class Americans whatever their color, but from the ghetto itself. It is for them, as the plantation was for their fathers, the embodiment of the blacks' ignominious position in American society, the symbol of their subordination and segregation.[71] Within or without the south-central ghetto, the middle class is not of it, and thus cannot lead it.

What underlies the physical and spiritual flight from the south-central ghetto is the system of residential segregation. Just how widespread the system is has been too well documented elsewhere to require further proof here,[72] but its involuntary character is worth stressing. Unlike Mexicans and other newcomers, blacks did not choose to live as a group in Los Angeles; far from choosing at all, they were compelled to reside together.[73] And the consequences were as unfortunate as they were inevitable. So long as blacks were denied access to the metropolitan real estate market and so long as they were deprived of the chance to move freely if dissatisfied with the quality or cost of their housing, they were confined to overcrowded, substandard, and overpriced dwellings. Also, so long as they lived in south-central Los Angeles only because there were no alternatives and so long as they regarded it as a place of confinement, they perceived the ghetto as the emblem of their subordination and segregation. Under these circumstances middle-class blacks have fled the ghetto whenever they could do so.

The McCone Commission did nothing more than admit that involuntary residential segregation is practiced in metropolitan Los Angeles.[74] It did not consider its consequences or recommend its elimination; nor did it point out the implications of Proposition 14. For this the witnesses were again free of fault. One after another they explained how involuntary residential segregation is implemented in Los Angeles and how the black community is victimized by this practice. The McCone Commission ignored them because their testimony revealed the tremendous stakes that many whites have in perpetuating the black ghetto. Merchants who overcharge customers, manufacturers who underpay laborers, and landlords who exploit tenants are only the most obvious beneficiaries. Less evident but more numerous are the homeowners who spend their lives in all-white suburbs and the parents who send their children to all-white schools. But for the McCone Commission to have investigated involuntary residential segregation would have obliged it to abandon its preconceptions that the Los Angeles riots were manifestations of economic, not racial, problems and individual, not social, deficiencies.

Here as elsewhere the McCone Commission offered inadequate recommendations based on erroneous analyses derived from untenable assumptions. And in so doing it demeaned the rioters, belittled their grievances, misunderstood the ghetto, misconstrued the riots, and thereby discouraged efforts to devise imperative and more drastic reforms. As the official version of the Los Angeles riots, moreover, *Violence in the City* has not only shaped public policy—witness the federal subsidy for the Transit District—but also guided popular opinion. From it the residents of Los Angeles have drawn either the conclusion that the rioting was meaningless or the implication that the blacks somehow lack the qualifications for responsible citizenship. That the McCone Commission provided them no other alternative was not the least of its disservices. Worse still, the commission reflected middle-class, white ideas and values so well that its findings and recommendations, or fascimiles thereof, have appeared in many official comments on other recent riots,[75] and with no more validity. Thus not until white America abandons the preconceptions about rioting, law enforcement, slums, and ghettos which misled the McCone Commission will it recognize the 1960s riots as articulate protests against genuine grievances in the black ghettos.

Notes

CHAPTER 1

VIOLENCE AS PROTEST

1. Fred C. Shapiro and James W. Sullivan, *Race Riot: New York 1964* (New York, 1964).

2. P. W. Homer, City Manager, "Report to the Rochester City Council on the Riots of July 1964," April 27, 1965: Federal Bureau of Investigation, "Report on the 1964 Riots," September 18, 1964, 5–6.

3. Lenora E. Berson, *Case Study of a Riot: The Philadelphia Story* (New York, 1966), 13–22; F.B.I., "Report on the 1964 Riots," 1, 3–15.

4. Oscar Handlin, *Fire-Bell in the Night* (Boston, 1964), 8–22; Anthony Lewis, *Portrait of a Decade* (New York, 1964), 3–15.

5. Martin Luther King, *Stride Toward Freedom* (New York, 1958), chapters 3–9; Louis E. Lomax, *The Negro Revolt* (New York, 1963), 78–222; William Brink and Louis Harris, *The Negro Revolution in America* (New York, 1964), 19–77; Lewis, *Portrait of a Decade*, 15–103.

6. Jerry Cohen and William S. Murphy, *Burn, Baby, Burn! The Los Angeles Race Riot August 1965* (New York, 1966); Governor's Commission on the Los Angeles Riots, *Violence in the City—an End or a Beginning?* (Los Angeles, 1965), 10–25 (hereafter referred to as *McCone Commission Report*).

7. The reports of the Assistant United States Attorneys and files of the Vice-President's Task Force on Youth Opportunity were made available to me by the President's Crime Commission. See also Federal Bureau of Investigation, *Prevention and Control of Mobs and Riots* (Washington, 1965).

8. United States Commission on Civil Rights, "Location of Riots Involving Minority Group Members Chronologically from January 11, 1964 thru June 1966 as reported by the New York *Times*," August 11, 1966.

9. New York *Times*, April 10, 17, May 2, June 3–5, 1967.

10. *Ibid.*, April 19, 27, 30, May 3, 1967.

11. *Report of the National Advisory Commission on Civil Disorders* (New York, 1968), 42–108 (hereafter referred to as *Kerner Commission Report*). See also Tom Hayden, *Rebellion in Newark* (New York, 1967).

217

Violence as Protest

12. Ben W. Gilbert *et al.*, *Ten Blocks from the White House* (New York, 1968), chapters 1–7. See also Arthur T. Waskow, *From Race Riot to Sit-In: 1919 and the 1960s* (Garden City, N.Y., 1964), 1–174.

13. At least this is the implication of the titles of the books on the New York and Los Angeles riots; see Shapiro and Sullivan, *Race Riot*, and Cohen and Murphy, *Burn, Baby, Burn.*

14. Herbert Aptheker, *A Documentary History of the Negro People in the United States* (New York, 1963), I, 102, 220, 501–2, II, 552–59, 788–91, 813–15, 866–68; Waskow, *From Race Riot to Sit-In*, 9–10, 12–104, 219–20; Citizens Protective League, *Story of the Riot* (1900).

15. Chicago Commission on Race Relations, *The Negro in Chicago* (Chicago, 1922), 4–5.

16. Elliot M. Rudwick, *Race Riot at East St. Louis, July 2, 1917* (Carbondale, Ill., 1964), chapters 4 and 5.

17. Waskow, *From Race Riot to Sit-In*, chapter 3.

18. Robert Shogan and Tom Craig, *The Detroit Race Riot* (Philadelphia, 1964), chapters 5 and 6.

19. Chicago Commission on Race Relations, *The Negro in Chicago*, chapter 1; Shogan and Craig, *Detroit Race Riot*, chapter 2; Rudwick, *Race Riot at East St. Louis*, chapters 2–4; Waskow, *From Race Riot to Sit-In*, chapter 3.

20. Waskow, *From Race Riot to Sit-In*, chapters 10 and 11.

21. Charles Abrams, *Forbidden Neighbors* (New York, 1955), chapters 8 and 19.

22. United States Commission on Civil Rights, "Location of Riots"; Assistant United States Attorneys Reports: Chicago, August 5, 1966; New York, August 19, 1966.

23. See "The Colonial War at Home," *Monthly Review*, May 1964, 1–13, "Decolonialization at Home," *ibid.*, October 1965, 1–13; Stokely Carmichael's Chicago, July 28, 1966, speech, in Student Nonviolent Coordinating Committee, *Notes and Comments*, August 1968; and Eldridge Cleaver, *Soul on Ice* (New York, 1968), 128–37.

24. *Report of the Commission of Inquiry into the Disorders in the Eastern Provinces of Nigeria* (London, 1950); *Report of the Commission of Inquiry Into the Disturbances in Uganda during April, 1949* (Entebbe, Uganda, 1950); *Report of the Nyasaland Commission of Inquiry* (London, 1959).

25. Frantz Fanon, *The Wretched of the Earth* (New York, 1966), 27–84. See also G. Balandier, "The Colonial Situation: A Theoretical Approach," in Immanuel Wallerstein, *Social Change: The Colonial Situation* (New York, 1966), 34–61.

26. Harold R. Isaacs, *The New World of Negro Americans* (New York, 1963), 80–96, 288–93; C. Eric Lincoln, *The Black Muslims in America* (Boston, 1961), 9–10.

27. Carl G. Rosberg, Jr., and John Nottingham, *The Myth of "Mau Mau": Nationalism in Kenya* (New York, 1966), chapter 8; Virginia Thompson and Richard Adloff, *The Malagasy Republic* (Stanford, Calif., 1965), chapter 4; James Duffy, *Portugal in Africa* (Baltimore, 1963), chapter 7.

28. *Report on the Disorders in Eastern Nigeria*, 32–46; *Report on the Disturbances in Uganda*, 17–53; *Report of the Nyasaland Commission of Inquiry*, parts 3 and 5.

218

29. Gunnar Myrdal, *An American Dilemma* (New York, 1944).

30. For a scholarly defense of the colonial analogy, see Robert Blauner, "Internal Colonialism and Ghetto Revolt," *Social Problems*, Spring 1969, 393–408.

31. Lomax, *The Negro Revolt*, 88.

32. George Breitman, ed., *Malcolm X Speaks* (New York, 1965), 68, 69, 75, 78, 89, 120–22; Cleaver, *Soul on Ice*, 128–37.

33. See Berson, *Case Study of a Riot*, 18; Cohen and Murphy, *Burn, Baby, Burn*, 133. It should be added, however, that rioters did burn houses in Detroit in 1967 and that demonstrators did attack schools in Boston a year later (New York *Times*, July 24–31, 1967, and Boston *Globe*, September 24–26, 1968).

34. Angus Campbell and Howard Schuman, "Racial Attitudes in Fifteen American Cities," in *Supplemental Studies for the National Advisory Commission on Civil Disorders* (Washington, D.C., 1968), 15–28.

35. New York *Times*, April 16, 1967; Lincoln, *Black Muslims in America*, chapter 5; Stokely Carmichael and Charles V. Hamilton, *Black Power* (New York, 1967), chapter 2; Breitman, ed., *Malcolm X Speaks*, 194–226.

36. New York *Times*, April 24, May 17, 1967. See also Gary Wills, *The Second Civil War* (New York, 1968), chapter 6.

37. *McCone Commission Report*, 4–5. See also New York *Times*, July 22, August 4, 1964; Newark *Evening News*, July 20, 1964; New York *Journal-American*, July 26, 1964; Cohen and Murphy, *Burn, Baby, Burn*, 130.

38. Oscar Handlin, *Boston's Immigrants* (Cambridge, Mass., 1959), 186–90; Edward McGowan, *McGowan vs. California Vigilantes* (Oakland, Calif., 1946); William D. Haywood, *Bill Haywood's Book* (New York, 1929), 352–58.

39. Allan Silver, "The Demand for Order in Civil Society: A Review of Some Themes in the History of Urban Crime, Police, and Riot," in David Bordua, ed., *The Police* (New York, 1967), 23; Louis Hartz, *The Liberal Tradition in America* (New York, 1955), chapter 1.

40. Silver, "The Demand for Public Order," 20–22. See also Daniel Bell, *The End of Ideology* (New York, 1962), 151–74.

41. King, *Stride Toward Freedom*, chapters 5, 7, 9; Lomax, *The Negro Revolt*, chapter 8; Lewis, *Portrait of a Decade*, chapter 5.

42. E. J. Hobsbawm, *Primitive Rebels* (New York, 1959), chapter 8; Silver, "The Demand for Public Order," 15–20.

43. George Rude, *The Crowd in History* (New York, 1964), chapters 3, 13–16; Hobsbawm, *Primitive Rebels*, chapter 8; Silver, "The Demand for Public Order," 15–20.

44. Robert M. Fogelson and Robert B. Hill, "Who Riots? A Study of Participation in the 1967 Riots," in *Supplemental Studies for the National Advisory Commission on Civil Disorders*, 221–43.

45. John F. Kraft, Inc., "Attitudes of Negroes in Various Cities" (1967), 4–7, a report prepared for the U. S. Senate Subcommittee on Executive Reorganization; David O. Sears, "Riot Activity and Evaluation: An Overview of the Negro Survey" (1966), 1–2, an unpublished paper written for the U. S. Office of Economic Opportunity.

46. Shapiro and Sullivan, *Race Riot*, 77–78; Cohen and Murphy, *Burn, Baby, Burn*, 73; Hayden, *Rebellion in Newark*, 32–33.

47. Shapiro and Sullivan, *Race Riot*, 152–54; Berson, *Case Study of a Riot*, 40–42; Cohen and Murphy, *Burn, Baby, Burn*, 132; Bayard Rustin, "The Watts 'Manifesto' and the McCone Report," *Commentary*, March 1966, 29–30.

48. Shapiro and Sullivan, *Race Riot*, 77–78; Rustin, "The Watts 'Manifesto,'" 29–30; Robert Blauner, "Whitewash Over Watts," *Trans-action*, March/April 1966, 54.

49. Campbell and Schuman, "Racial Attitudes in Fifteen American Cities," 47.

50. Ralph Ellison, *The Invisible Man* (New York, 1947), chapters 13–20; Mayor's Commission on Conditions in Harlem, "The Negro in Harlem: A Report on Social and Economic Conditions Responsible for the Outbreak of March 19, 1935," chapters 3–5, New York City Municipal Archives.

51. Walter White, "Behind the Harlem Riot," *The New Republic*, August 16, 1943, 220–22; William C. Hendrick, "Race Riots—Segregated Slums," *Current History*, September 1943, 30–34; Oscar Handlin, *The American People in the Twentieth Century* (Boston, 1963), chapter 9.

52. Claude McKay, "Harlem Runs Wild," *The Nation*, April 3, 1935, 382–83; New York *Times*, March 21, 1935, August 3, 1943; *Time*, August 9, 1943, 19.

53. "This was not a race riot," the Mayor said. "There was no conflict between groups of our citizens. What happened was the thoughtless, criminal acts of hoodlums, reckless, irresponsible people" (*Time*, August 9, 1943, 19). The New York *Times* agreed (August 3, 1943).

54. New York *Times*, March 20, 1935; Mayor's Commission, "The Negro in Harlem," 1–6; Hamilton Basso, "The Riot in Harlem," *The New Republic*, April 3, 1935, 210–11.

55. New York *Times*, August 2, 1943; White, "Behind the Harlem Riot," 221.

56. New York *Times*, March 20–22, 1935; McKay, "Harlem Runs Wild," 382–83; Mayor's Commission, "The Negro in Harlem," 6–12.

57. New York *Times*, August 2–3, 1943; White, "Behind the Harlem Riots," 221.

58. New York *Times*, March 20–22, 1935; McKay, "Harlem Runs Wild," 382.

59. New York *Times*, August 2–3, 1943; White, "Behind the Harlem Riots," 222.

60. New York *Times*, March 21, 1935.

61. New York *Times*, August 2–3, 1943; White, "Behind the Harlem Riots," 222.

62. Gilbert Osofsky, *Harlem: The Making of a Ghetto* (New York, 1966), chapters 5–8.

63. *Ibid.*, 179–89. For fuller treatments of Harlem and the Negro renaissance, see James Weldon Johnson, *Black Manhattan* (New York, 1930), and Alain Locke, ed., *The New Negro: An Interpretation* (New York, 1925).

64. Handlin, *Fire-Bell in the Night*, chapter 2; Brink and Harris, *The Negro Revolution*, chapter 8; Lewis, *Portrait of a Decade*, chapter 13; Abrams, *Forbidden Neighbors*, chapter 21.

65. On the Garvey movement, see E. David Cronon, *Black Moses* (Boston, 1961); and on black nationalism, see E. U. Essien-Udom, *Black Nationalism* (Chicago, 1962).

66. Robert C. Weaver, *The Negro Ghetto* (New York, 1948).

67. Handlin, *Fire-Bell in the Night*, chapter 5.

68. U. S. Commission on Civil Rights, "Location of Riots."

69. Richard C. Wade, *Slavery in the Cities* (New York, 1964), chapter 3.

70. Karl E. Taeuber and Alma F. Taeuber, *Negroes in Cities* (Chicago, 1965), chapter 3.

CHAPTER 2

WHO RIOTS?

1. Detroit Police Chief Ray Girardin was a notable exception.

2. New York *Times*, July 21, 22, 25, 26, 29, August 4, 1964; March 17, July 19, 21, 22, 1966; June 30, July 16, 19, 20, 22, 24, 26, 1967; Governor's Commission on the Los Angeles Riots, *Violence in the City—an End or a Beginning?* (Los Angeles, 1965), 1 (hereafter referred to as *McCone Commission Report*).

3. Robert M. Fogelson, "White on Black: A Critique of the McCone Commission Report on the Los Angeles Riots," *Political Science Quarterly*, September 1967, 342.

4. New York *Times*, July 22, August 4, 1964; July 16, 20, 22, 26, 1967; Newark *Evening News*, July 20, 1964; New York *Journal-American*, July 26, 1964.

5. *McCone Commission Report*, 4–5.

6. New York *Times*, June 30, July 22, 26–28, 1967; Bayard Rustin, "The Watts 'Manifesto' and the McCone Report," *Commentary*, March 1966, 29–35; Robert Blauner, "Whitewash over Watts," *Trans-action*, March/April 1966, 3.

7. David O. Sears, "Riot Activity and Evaluation: An Overview of the Negro Survey" (1966), 1–2, an unpublished paper written for the U. S. Office of Economic Opportunity; Governor's Commission on the Los Angeles Riots, *Archives*, II, in the University of California Library, Los Angeles (hereafter referred to as *McCone Commission Archives*).

8. Allan A. Silver, "Official Interpretation of Racial Riots," in Robert H. Connery, ed., *Urban Riots: Violence and Social Change* (New York, 1969), 151–63; Louis Hartz, *The Liberal Tradition in America* (New York, 1955), chapter 1. The riffraff theory is not of course unique to America. See George Rude, *The Crowd in the French Revolution* (New York, 1959) and *The Crowd in History* (New York, 1964).

9. Sears, "Riot Activity"; Bureau of Criminal Statistics, California Department of Criminal Justice, "Watts Riots Arrests: Los Angeles, August, 1965" (June 30, 1966); Governor's Select Commission on Civil Disorder, *Report for Action* (February 1968) (hereafter referred to as the *N. J. Riot Report*); U. S. Department of Labor, Manpower Administration, "The Detroit Riot" (March 1968); *Report of the National Advisory Commission on Civil Disorders* (New York, 1968), 171–78 (hereafter referred to as *Kerner Commission Report*).

10. *Kerner Commission Report*, chapter 2; California Advisory Committee to the U. S. Commission on Civil Rights, "An Analysis of the McCone Commission

Report" (January 1966); Blauner, "Whitewash over Watts"; Harry Scoble, "The McCone Commission and Social Science" (August 1966), an unpublished paper written for the U. S. Office of Economic Opportunity; Anthony Oberschall, "The Los Angeles Riot of August 1965"; *Social Problems,* Winter 1968, 322–41.

11. *McCone Commission Archives,* III, Testimony of Councilman Thomas Bradley, 29–36; V, Testimony of John A. Buggs, Executive Director of the Los Angeles County Human Relations Commission, 18–23; VI, Testimony of Assemblyman Mervyn M. Dymally, 48–49; VIII, Testimony of Congressman Augustus F. Hawkins, 82–85; X, Testimony of Councilman Billy G. Mills, 9–10.

12. New York *Times,* August 29, 1963; April 16, 1967; May 13, 1968.

13. New York *Times,* July 19–23, 1964; July 4, 5, 1966.

14. Sears, "Riot Activity," table 6; *Kerner Commission Report,* 171.

15. Sears, "Riot Activity," 5; *Kerner Commission Report,* 176.

16. Herbert H. Hyman, *Survey Design and Analysis* (Glencoe, Ill., 1955); Paul F. Lazarsfeld and Morris Rosenberg, eds., *Language of Social Research* (New York, 1955); Patricia Kendall and Paul F. Lazarsfeld, "Problems of Survey Analysis," in *Continuities in Social Research: Studies in the Scope and Method of the American Soldier* (Glencoe, Ill., 1950).

17. Sears, "Riot Activity," 5–8.

18. The extent to which people over- and under-estimate participation in deviant activities has yet to be determined. See F. Ivan Nye, James F. Short, Jr., and Virgil T. Olson, "Socioeconomic Status and Delinquent Behavior," *American Journal of Sociology,* January 1958, 381–89; Lee N. Robbins and George Murphy, "Drug Use in a Normal Population of Young Negro Men," *American Journal of Public Health,* September 1967, 1580–96.

19. "Watts Riots Arrests"; *N. J. Riot Report.*

20. "Watts Riots Arrests," 37; *N. J. Riot Report,* 270–77.

21. Made by Mr. Tom Kneeshaw, who was in charge of tabulating the data for adult arrestees in the Detroit riots.

22. Richard K. Korn and Lloyd W. McCorkle, *Criminology and Penology* (New York, 1959).

23. *Kerner Commission Report,* charts following page 608.

24. For further details on this arrangement, see Fogelson and Hill, "Who Riots?" 227.

25. In Detroit the black arrestees were 1.2 per cent of the nonwhite population; in Newark they were 1.0 per cent of the nonwhite population.

26. *Kerner Commission Report,* 172.

27. See Scoble, "The McCone Commission," 11; and Fogelson, "White on Black," 345.

28. *Kerner Commission Report,* 113.

29. For another definition of potential rioters, see Jay Schulman, "Ghetto Residence, Political Alienation, and Riot Orientation," in L. Masotti, ed., *Urban Disorders, Violence, and Urban Victimization* (Beverly Hills, Calif., 1968), 32.

30. U. S. Bureau of the Census, *U. S. Censuses of Population and Housing: 1960. Census Tracts* (Washington, D.C., 1962).

31. Sears, "Riot Activity"; *Kerner Commission Report*, 171–78.

32. For an attempt to apply this approach to the Washington, D.C., riots of 1968, see Ben W. Gilbert *et al.*, *Ten Blocks from the White House* (New York, 1968), 224–25.

33. See Fogelson and Hill, "Who Riots?" 231.

34. See chapter 5.

35. *McCone Commission Report*, 24–25; *N. J. Riot Report*, 129–33.

36. U. S. Bureau of the Census, *U. S. Censuses of Population and Housing: 1960. Census Tracts;* President's Commission on Law Enforcement and Administration of Justice, *The Challenge of Crime in a Free Society* (Washington, D.C., 1967), 75.

37. Harlem (July 1964), Bedford-Stuyvesant (July 1964), Rochester (July 1964), Philadelphia (August 1964), Los Angeles (August 1965), Cleveland (June 1966), Chicago (July 1966), Atlanta (September 1966), Cincinnati (June 1967), Newark (July 1967), Detroit (July 1967), and New Haven (August 1967).

38. The potential rioters include all the nonwhite residents of the riot areas between the ages of ten and fifty-nine inclusive. Their numbers were obtained from U. S. Bureau of the Census, *U. S. Censuses of Population and Housing: 1960. Census Tracts.*

39. The findings for the Detroit rioters are based on Sheldon Lachman and Benjamin Singer, "The Detroit Riot of 1967" (Detroit, 1968), 19, a study of five hundred male arrestees prepared for the U. S. Department of Labor.

40. The findings for both arrestees and residents are based on males and females fourteen years of age and older.

41. The findings for the arrestees are based on black males eighteen years of age and older. The findings for the Newark arrestees come from *N. J. Riot Report*, 271, and the findings for the Detroit arrestees from Lachman and Singer, "The Detroit Riot of 1967," 14.

42. "Unemployment in 15 Metropolitan Areas," *Monthly Labor Review*, January 1968, 5–6; *N. J. Riot Report*, 271.

43. Especially because the Department only counts people actively seeking employment. See "New Jobless Count Ups the Figure," *Business Week*, December 10, 1966, 160–62, and *Kerner Commission Report*, 257. For further remarks, see Fogelson and Hill, "Who Riots?" 236.

44. The South as defined here includes Alabama, Arkansas, Florida, Georgia, Louisiana, Mississippi, North Carolina, South Carolina, Tennessee, Texas, and Virginia. For obvious reasons I have excluded Atlanta from this survey.

45. See President's Commission on Law Enforcement, *The Challenge of Crime*, 75, and Ronald Christensen, "Projected Percentage of U. S. Population with Criminal Arrest and Conviction Records," in the Commission's *Task Force Report: Science and Technology* (Washington, D.C., 1967), 216–18.

46. See *Report of the President's Commission on Crime in the District of Columbia* (Washington, D.C., 1966), chapter 3.

47. *Kerner Commission Report*, 131.

48. Federal Bureau of Investigation, "Report on the 1964 Riots," September 1964; New York *Times*, August 2, 3, 1967; *Kerner Commission Report*, 201–2.

49. In 1965 the sheets are available only for the Los Angeles riots.

50. I have excluded the Detroit and Los Angeles riots from this analysis because the great number of arrestees there might skew the findings.

51. Gary Marx, *Protest and Prejudice* (New York, 1967), 53–54; Angus Campbell and Howard Schuman, "Racial Attitudes in Fifteen American Cities," in *Supplemental Studies for the National Advisory Commission on Civil Disorders* (Washington, D.C., 1968), 17–19, 55–57.

52. The rioters were arrested mainly for disorderly conduct, curfew violations, and other minor offenses.

53. The assaulters were arrested mainly for throwing stones, obstructing policemen, and carrying weapons.

54. See chapter 4.

55. It should be noted, however, that the arsonists were less than 1 per cent (65 out of about 7600) of the arrestees.

56. I have excluded the Detroit rioters here because the great number of arrestees there might skew the findings.

57. A total of 775 blacks, 95 per cent of whom were born in the South, were arrested in Atlanta.

58. For a brief analysis of the Washington rioters of 1968, see Gilbert *et al.*, *Ten Blocks from the White House*, 226–35.

59. F.B.I., "Report on the 1964 Riots," 5–6. See also chapter 5.

60. New York *Times*, July 27, 1967.

61. See chapter 6.

62. New York *Times*, July 14–18, 26–29, August 1, 2, 7, 10, 11, 16, 1967.

63. William Brink and Louis Harris, *Black and White* (New York, 1967), 184–279: Hazel Erskine, "The Polls: Demonstrations and Race Riots," *Public Opinion Quarterly*, Winter 1967–68, 655–77: Sears, "Riot Activity"; Schulman, "Ghetto Residence."

64. Frank Besag, *The Anatomy of a Riot: Buffalo, 1967* (Buffalo, N.Y., 1967), 138–39, 180–81, 188–90.

65. Sears, "Riot Activity," table 35; Schulman, "Ghetto Residence," 23–24, tables 5, 5.1.

66. Brink and Harris, *Black and White*, 260–66; Erskine, "The Polls," 671.

67. Sears, "Riot Activity," table 17.

68. Brink and Harris, *Black and White*, 264.

69. *McCone Commission Archives*, XV, interview 29; XVI, interview 90; Besag, *Anatomy of a Riot*, 138–39, 188–89.

70. Brink and Harris, *Black and White*, 266. For a more recent survey of black attitudes toward rioting, see Campbell and Schuman, "Racial Attitudes in Fifteen American Cities," 47–57.

CHAPTER 3
FROM RESENTMENT TO CONFRONTATION

1. U. S. Commission on Civil Rights, "Location of Riots Involving Minority Groups Members Chronologically from January 11, 1964, thru June, 1966 as reported by the New York *Times*"; New York *Times*, September 2, 7, 1966; June 12, 1967; April 5, 1968; Federal Bureau of Investigation, "Report on the 1964 Riots," September 18, 1964, 2.

2. U. S. Commission on Civil Rights, "Location of Riots"; F.B.I., "Report on the 1964 Riots," 2, 5–7; Governor's Commission on the Los Angeles Riots, *Violence in the City—an End or a Beginning?* (Los Angeles, 1965), 10–11; New York *Times*, July 4, 13, 1966; July 13, 1967.

3. Fred C. Shapiro and James W. Sullivan, *Race Riot: New York 1964* (New York, 1964), 43–62; Lenora E. Berson, *Case Study of a Riot: The Philadelphia Story* (New York, 1966), 16–17; Tom Hayden, *Rebellion in Newark* (New York, 1967), 13–14.

4. Jerry Cohen and William S. Murphy, *Burn, Baby, Burn! The Los Angeles Race Riot: August 1965* (New York, 1966), 50–59.

5. Assistant U. S. Attorneys' Reports: Indianapolis, August 5, 1966; Los Angeles, August 5, 1966; Kansas City, August 5, 1966; and Philadelphia, August 5, 1966.

6. Two case studies of flagrant misuse of police authority, one involving the Los Angeles Police Department and the other the New Jersey National Guard, are presented in American Civil Liberties Union of Southern California, "Police Malpractice and the Watts Riots" (ca. 1966), and Hayden, *Rebellion in Newark*.

7. Mervyn M. Dymally, "Statement Prepared for the Governor's Commission on the Los Angeles Riots," October 11, 1965, 2. See also U. S. Commission on Civil Rights, *Hearings Held in Cleveland, Ohio, April 1–7, 1966* (Washington, D.C., 1966), 513–19; and U. S. Commission on Civil Rights, *Hearings Held in Detroit, Michigan, December 14–15, 1960* (Washington, D.C., 1961), 379–88.

8. Governor's Commission on the Los Angeles Riots, *Archives*, II, 3–36 (hereafter referred to as *McCone Commission Archives*); U. S. Commission on Civil Rights, *Cleveland Hearings*, 585–602; U. S. Commission on Civil Rights, *Hearings [Held in] Newark, New Jersey, September 11–12, 1962* (Washington, D.C., 1963), 473–83.

9. David G. Monroe and Earle W. Garrett, *Police Conditions in the United States*, in National Commission on Law Observance and Enforcement, *Report on Police* (Washington, D.C., 1931), 13–140; President's Commission on Law Enforcement and Adminstration of Justice, *Task Force Report: The Police* (Washington, D.C., 1967), 13–215.

10. U. S. Commission on Civil Rights, *Hearings Held in Memphis, Tennessee, June 25–26, 1962* (Washington, D.C., 1962), 83–121; U. S. Commission on Civil Rights, *Hearings Held in Jackson, Mississippi, February 16–20, 1965* (Washington, D.C., 1965), II, 1–415; U. S. Commission on Civil Rights,

Law Enforcement: A Report on Equal Protection in the South (Washington, D.C., 1965).

11. Joseph D. Lohman and Gordon E. Misner, *The Police and the Community*, a report prepared for the President's Crime Commission (Washington, D.C., 1966), I, 78–79.

12. New York *Times*, June 23, 25, July 17, 18, 1966. Newark Negroes acted quite differently in 1967, but, according to one firsthand account of the rioting, they did so in self-defense. See Hayden, *Rebellion in Newark*.

13. U. S. Commission on Civil Rights, 1961 *Report. Book 5: Justice* (Washington, D.C., 1961), 5–28; Ed Cray, *The Big Blue Line: Police Power vs. Human Rights* (New York, 1967), 140–52; President's Crime Commission, *The Police*, 181–83.

14. U. S. Commission on Civil Rights, *Justice*, 26.

15. U. S. Commission on Civil Rights, *Jackson Hearings*, 216–22; U. S. Commission on Civil Rights, *Detroit Hearings*, 302–21; U. S. Commission on Civil Rights, *Newark Hearings*, 445–59; U. S. Commission on Civil Rights, *Cleveland Hearings*, 542–48.

16. John F. Kraft, Inc., "Attitudes of Negroes in Various Cities," a report prepared for the U. S. Senate Subcommittee on Executive Reorganization (1966), 13, 24; Albert D. Biderman *et al.*, *Report on a Pilot Study in the District of Columbia on Victimization and Attitudes Toward Law Enforcement*, a report prepared for the President's Crime Commission (Washington, D.C., 1967), 144; Lohman and Misner, *The Police and the Community*, I, 84–85; II, 100–1, 127–30.

17. On police complaint procedures see National Center on Police and Community Relations (School of Police Administration and Public Safety, Michigan State University), *A National Survey of Police and Community Relations*, a report prepared for the President's Crime Commission (Washington, D.C., 1967), 188–257.

18. Walter J. Raine, "The Perception of Police Brutality in South Central Los Angeles Following the Revolt of 1965" (1966), figure 1, an unpublished paper written for the U. S. Office of Economic Opportunity; American Civil Liberties Union, "Police Power vs. Citizens' Rights: The Case for an Independent Police Review Board" (1966), 13; President's Crime Commission, *The Police*, 182.

19. William A. Westley, "Violence and the Police," *American Journal of Sociology*, August 1953, 34–41; National Center on Police and Community Relations, *Police and Community Relations*, 21–24; Albert J. Reiss, Jr., "Career Orientations, Job Satisfaction, and the Assessment of Law Enforcement Problems by Police Officers," in *Studies in Crime and Law Enforcement in Major Metropolitan Areas*, a report prepared for the President's Crime Commission (Washington, D.C., 1967), II, 22, 91, 97–98, 101–2.

20. Arthur Niederhoffer, *Behind the Shield* (Garden City, N.Y., 1967), chapter 3; Michael Banton, *The Policeman in the Community* (London, 1964), 86–126; and David J. Bordua, "Social Organization of the Police," a draft of an article prepared for the *International Encyclopedia of the Social Sciences*, 5–6.

21. Lohman and Misner, *The Police and the Community*, I, 77–79, 98–107; II,

83–85, 97–99; Biderman *et al.*, *Attitudes Toward Law Enforcement*, 135–45. See also Subcommittee on Executive Reorganization of the Committee on Government Operations United States Senate, *Hearings* [on] *Federal Role in Urban Affairs* (Washington, D.C., 1966), part 5, 1097–99.

22. William A. Westley, "The Police: A Sociological Study of Law, Custom, and Morality" (University of Chicago doctoral dissertation, 1951), 174–75; William Kephart, *Racial Factors and Urban Law Enforcement* (Philadelphia, 1957), 75–107; Lohman and Misner, *The Police and the Community*, I, 116–17, 120–31.

23. Westley, "Violence and the Police," 34–41. See also U. S. Commission on Civil Rights, *Detroit Hearings*, 399.

24. National Center on Police and Community Relations, *Police and Community Relations*, 188–257; American Civil Liberties Union, "Police Power vs. Citizens' Rights," 15–23; Lohman and Misner, *The Police and the Community*, I, 168–75; II, 205–12.

25. Zechariah Chaffee, Jr., Walter H. Pollak, and Carl S. Stern, *The Third Degree*, in National Commission on Law Observance and Enforcement, *Report on Lawlessness in Law Enforcement* (Washington D.C., 1931), 13–192; President's Committee on Civil Rights, *To Secure These Rights* (Washington, D.C., 1947), 25–27.

26. Bordua, "Social Organization of the Police," 5–6. See also Walter Gellhorn, "Police Review Board: Hoax or Hope?" *Columbia University Forum*, Summer 1966, 5–7; President's Crime Commission, *The Police*, 181.

27. Biderman *et al.*, *Attitudes Toward Law Enforcement*, 143.

28. *McCone Commission Archives*, X, 9–10; U. S. Commission on Civil Rights, *Detroit Hearings*, 321–43; American Civil Liberties Union, "Police Power vs. Citizens' Rights," 13–15; Cray, *Big Blue Line*, 183–94.

29. See, for example, U. S. Commission on Civil Rights, *Cleveland Hearings*, 537.

30. *McCone Commission Archives*, III, 29–36; VI, 48–49; U. S. Commission on Civil Rights, *Detroit Hearings*, 379–88; Lohman and Misner, *The Police and the Community*, I, 98–107, 138–39; II, 121–27.

31. Biderman *et al.*, *Attitudes Toward Law Enforcement*, 137; Raine, "Police Brutality in South Central Los Angeles," table 9; Phillip H. Ennis, *Criminal Victimization in the United States*, a report prepared for the President's Crime Commission (Washington, D.C., 1967), 54–58.

32. Raine, "Police Brutality in South Central Los Angeles," figure 1; Cray, *Big Blue Line*, 186–91. This is not the case in San Francisco, however. See U. S. Commission on Civil Rights, *Hearings Held in Los Angeles, California, January 25–26, 1960,* [and] *San Francisco, California, January 27–28, 1960* (Washington, D.C., 1960), 771–76.

33. Albert J. Reiss, Jr., *Occupations and Social Status* (Glencoe, Ill., 1961), 56; Robert W. Hodge, Paul M. Siegel, and Peter H. Rossi, "Occupational Prestige in the United States, 1925–1963," *American Journal of Sociology*, November 1964, 290–92; Reiss, "Career Orientations," 84–94.

34. John H. McNamara, "Uncertainties in Police Work: The Relevance of Police Recruits' Backgrounds and Training," in David Bordua, ed., *The Police* (New York, 1967), 191–97.

35. *Ibid.*, 221–22. See also Westley, "The Police," 174–75; Kephart, *Racial Factors and Urban Law Enforcement*, 75–107; James Q. Wilson, "Police Morale, Reform, and Citizen Respect: The Chicago Case," in Bordua, *The Police*, 137–62.

36. Donald J. Black and Albert J. Reiss, Jr., "Patterns of Behavior in Police and Citizen Transactions," in *Studies of Crime and Law Enforcement in Major Metropolitan Areas*, II, 26–27.

37. *McCone Commission Archives*, V, 18–23.

38. *Ibid.*, XIII, 8–9. See also Black and Reiss, "Police and Citizen Transactions," 132–39; U. S. Commission on Civil Rights, *Cleveland Hearings*, 534–39.

39. See Carl Werthman and Irving Piliavin, "Gang Members and the Police," in Bordua, *The Police*, 56–97.

40. On police-community relations programs see National Center on Police and Community Relations, *Police and Community Relations*, 32–127.

41. On preventive patrolling see Diane Fisher, "Police Investigatory Detention Practices" (1966), a report prepared for the President's Crime Commission.

42. Allan Silver, "The Demand for Order in Civil Society: A Review of Some Themes in the History of Urban Crime, Police, and Riot," in Bordua, *The Police*, 6–15. See also Wilson, "The Chicago Case," 162.

43. U. S. Commission on Civil Rights, *Cleveland Hearings*, 522–27; U. S. Commission on Civil Rights, *Detroit Hearings*, 321–30; *McCone Commission Archives*, VIII, 82–93; X, 8–9.

44. Lohman and Misner, *The Police and the Community*, I, 139–40; II, 173–74; John F. Kraft, Inc., "Attitudes of Negroes," 23–29; Ennis, *Criminal Victimization*, 54–55.

45. *Ibid.*, 46–47; Albert J. Reiss, Jr., "Public Perceptions and Recollections About Crime, Law Enforcement, and Criminal Justice," in *Studies in Crime and Law Enforcement in Major Metropolitan Areas*, II, 104.

46. "1965 Crime Rate per 1,000 Population by District," a table compiled for me by the Chicago Police Department; Los Angeles Police Department, "Major Crimes and Attempts—One Year Period July 1, 1964 to June 30, 1965," *McCone Commission Archives*, II.

47. Albert J. Reiss, Jr., "Measurement of the Nature and Amount of Crime," in *Studies in Crime and Law Enforcement in Major Metropolitan Areas*, I, 44.

48. New York State Legislature, *Report and Proceedings of the Senate Committee Appointed to Investigate the Police Department of New York* (Albany, 1895), 5311–84; Herbert Mitgang, *The Man Who Rode the Tiger: The Life and Times of Judge Samuel Seabury* (Philadelphia, 1963), 159–265; St. Clair Drake and Horace R. Cayton, *Black Metropolis: A Study of Negro Life in a Northern City* (New York, 1962), II, chapter 17, Frank Tannenbaum, *Crime and the Community* (New York, 1938), chapters 5, 6.

49. See, for example, U. S. Commission on Civil Rights, *Cleveland Hearings*, 522–28, 578–79.

50. President's Crime Commission, *The Police*, chapter 7; Ralph Lee Smith, *The Tarnished Badge* (New York, 1965).

51. Black and Reiss, "Police and Citizen Transactions," 132–39.

52. *McCone Commission Archives*, XI, 37, 117; O. W. Wilson, "Police Arrest Privileges in a Free Society: A Plea for Modernization," in Claude R. Sowle, ed., *Police Power and Individual Freedom: The Quest for Balance* (Chicago, 1962), 24; Reiss, "Career Orientations," 79–81.

53. See, for example, John F. Kraft, Inc., "Attitudes of Negroes," 23–29, and Biderman *et al.*, *Attitudes Toward Law Enforcement*, 134–45.

54. Richard A. Cloward and Lloyd E. Ohlin, *Delinquency and Opportunity* (Glencoe, Ill., 1960), chapters 1, 4–7; Daniel Bell, *The End of Ideology* (Glencoe, Ill., 1960), 115–36; Thomas E. Pettigrew, *A Profile of the Negro American* (Princeton, N.J., 1964), chapter 6.

55. Carl Werthman, "The Function of Social Definitions in the Development of Delinquent Careers" (1966), a paper prepared for the President's Crime Commission, 39–54.

56. President's Crime Commission, *The Police*, 195.

57. *Ibid.*, 195–97. See also National Center on Police and Community Relations, *Police and Community Relations*, 193–205.

58. U. S. Commission on Civil Rights, *Newark Hearings*, 455; U. S. Commission on Civil Rights, *Detroit Hearings*, 305; U. S. Commission on Civil Rights, *Cleveland Hearings*, 514; Lohman and Misner, *The Police and the Community*, I, 167–75; II, 164–65; American Civil Liberties Union, "Police Power vs. Citizens' Rights," 15–17.

59. President's Crime Commission, *The Police*, 196. See also National Center on Police and Community Relations, *Police and Community Relations*, 186, 201–3.

60. Joseph P. Lyford, *The Airtight Cage* (New York, 1966).

61. American Civil Liberties Union, "Police Power vs. Citizens' Rights," 16–17.

62. *Ibid.*, 17. See also U. S. Commission on Civil Rights, *Cleveland Hearings*, 584–608; National Center on Police and Community Relations, *Police and Community Relations*, 192–93.

63. *Ibid.*, 202–3, 218–29. See also President's Crime Commission, *The Police*, 195–97; American Civil Liberties Union, "Police Power vs. Citizens' Rights," 31.

64. McNamara, "Uncertainties in Police Work," 178–83, 230–36.

65. Reiss, "Career Orientations," 74–79; National Center on Police and Community Relations, *Police and Community Relations*, 216–23.

66. American Civil Liberties Union, "Police Power vs. Citizens' Rights," 27–41. See also *McCone Commission Archives*, XIII, 9–27; Spencer Coxe, "The Philadelphia Police Advisory Board," *Law in Transition Quarterly*, Summer 1965, 179–85; Lohman and Misner, *The Police and the Community*, II, 205–78.

67. U. S. Commission on Civil Rights, *Newark Hearings*, 475–77. See also American Civil Liberties Union, "Police Power vs. Citizens' Rights," 23–27; and Gellhorn, "Police Review Boards," 5–7.

68. New York *Times*, October 23, 1966.

69. Berson, *Case Study of a Riot*, 50–54; Lohman and Misner, *The Police and the Community*, II, 83–85, 105–7, 121–30, 164–65.

70. Ernest Jerome Hopkins, "The Police and the Immigrant," in *Proceedings of the National Conference of Social Work . . . May 15–21, 1932* (Chicago, 1932), 509–19; Chaffee, Pollak, and Stern, *The Third Degree*. See also chapter 5.

71. New York *Times*, June 13–16, 1966; July 23–27, 1967.

72. *Report of the National Advisory Commission on Civil Disorders* (Washington, D.C., 1968), 321–22.

73. Oscar Handlin, *The Uprooted* (Boston, 1951), chapter 8.

74. Chaffee, Pollak, and Stern, *The Third Degree*; Richard Wright, *Native Son* (New York, 1940); Ralph Ellison, *The Invisible Man* (New York, 1952); *McCone Commission Archives*, XI, 86.

75. New York *Times*, September 5, 1966; March 19–25, 1934. For a much less impressive performance, see U. S. Commission on Civil Rights, *Cleveland Hearings*, 568–72.

76. *Ibid.*, 534–35; *McCone Commission Archives*, X, 18–20; Lohman and Misner, *The Police and the Community*, II, 85; Werthman and Piliavin, "Gang Members and the Police," 63–65, 87–89.

77. Inspired by a strong sense of territoriality and the concept of the colonial analogy, Eldridge Cleaver and other militants have concluded that the ghetto police are an occupying army. How deeply this notion has penetrated into the ghetto is hard to tell.

78. Robert Conot, *Rivers of Blood, Years of Darkness* (New York, 1967), 35–36, 51–52, 57–58, 73–74. For the San Diego blacks' interpretation of the Los Angeles riots, which reveals a similar determination to respond in kind to police violence, see Lohman and Misner, *The Police and the Community*, I, 99–100.

79. Of the one hundred persons killed in the three worst riots—namely, the Los Angeles, Newark, and Detroit riots—only four were policemen (and only five were firemen or National Guardsmen). And of the nine victims only two or three were deliberately murdered. See Cohen and Murphy, *Burn, Baby, Burn*, 142–46, 252–53, 317; New York *Times*, July 16–18, 24–31, August 23, 1967.

CHAPTER 4

THE GHETTO'S GRIEVANCES

1. Federal Bureau of Investigation, "Report on the 1964 Riots" (September 18, 1964); Fred C. Shapiro and James W. Sullivan, *Race Riot: New York 1964* (New York, 1964); Robert Conot, *Rivers of Blood, Years of Darkness* (New York, 1967); Tom Hayden, *Rebellion in Newark* (New York, 1967); *Report of the National Advisory Commission on Civil Disorders* (New York, 1968), 35–108 (hereafter referred to as *Kerner Commission Report*).

2. *Kerner Commission Report*, 35–108; *Riots, Civil and Criminal Disorders: Hearings Before the Permanent Subcommittee on Investigations of the Committee on Government Operations*, United States Senate, 90th Congress, 1st Session (Washington, D.C., 1967), part 1, tables following page 15.

3. Harrison Salisbury, *The Shook-Up Generation* (New York, 1958), chapters 2,

5, 6, 11; Louis Yablonsky, *The Violent Gang* (New York, 1966), chapters 1, 2, 5, 6.

4. The observer is Jay Schulman, a sociologist then at Cornell University and now at City College, who has spent several years studying the Rochester ghetto.

5. *Kerner Commission Report*, 116–17, 326–27; Jerry Cohen and William S. Murphy, *Burn, Baby, Burn! The Los Angeles Race Riot: August, 1965* (New York, 1966), 50–59.

6. Russell Dynes and E. L. Quarantelli, "What Looting in Civil Disturbances Really Means," *Trans-action*, May 1968, 9–14. See also Allen H. Barton, *Communities in Disaster* (Garden City, N.Y., 1969).

7. *Kerner Commission Report*, 325. This holds true for the great majority of the race riots too. See Arthur I. Waskow, *From Race Riot to Sit-In: 1919 and the 1960s* (Garden City, N.Y., 1966), chapters 2–4 and 304–7.

8. William Foote Whyte, *Street Corner Society* (Chicago, 1943); Herbert J. Gans, *The Urban Villagers* (Glencoe, Ill., 1962); St. Clair Drake and Horace R. Cayton, *Black Metropolis: A Study of Negro Life in a Northern City* (New York, 1962).

9. Gustave Le Bon, *The Crowd* (New York, 1960), chapters 1–3.

10. Le Bon's ideas have recently been questioned by historians and sociologists, notably George Rude—*The Crowd in History* (New York, 1964)—and Charles Tilly—"À Travers le Chaos des Vivantes Cités," a paper presented to the Sixth World Congress of Sociology, Évian-les-Bains, France, September 1966.

11. See chapter 2.

12. See chapter 1.

13. But, as I mentioned earlier, rioters burned houses in Detroit in 1967 and demonstrators attacked schools in Boston a year later (New York *Times*, July 24–31, 1967, and Boston *Globe*, September 24–26, 1968).

14. See chapter 2.

15. Governor's Commission on the Los Angeles Riots, *Archives*, XVI, Statement of Dr. Harold Jones, 7 (hereafter referred to as *McCone Commission Archives*).

16. New York *Times*, July 15, 1967.

17. Bayard Rustin, "The Watts 'Manifesto' and the McCone Report," *Commentary*, March 1966, 30.

18. Nor, it goes without saying, are they unique to the 1960s riots.

19. James Baldwin, *The Fire Next Time* (New York, 1963); Ralph Ellison, "Harlem is Nowhere," in *Shadow and Act* (New York, 1966), 282–89. See also Abraham Kardiner and Lionel Ovesey, *The Mark of Oppression* (New York, 1962), 82–91.

20. George Breitman, ed., *Malcolm X Speaks* (New York, 1965), 4.

21. William H. Grier and Price M. Cobbs, *Black Rage* (New York, 1968), 71–74.

22. C. Eric Lincoln, *The Black Muslims in America* (Boston, 1961); E. U. Essien-Udom, *Black Nationalism* (New York, 1964).

23. New York *Times*, January 10, 1967; *McCone Commission Archives*, IV, Testi-

mony of the Reverend Hartford Brookins, 24–32; U. S. Commission on Civil Rights, *Hearings Held in Cleveland, Ohio, April 1–7, 1966* (Washington, D.C., 1966), 522–25, 568–72; Harry M. Scoble, "Negro Leadership Study: Tentative Findings" (1966), 9, an unpublished paper written for the U. S. Office of Economic Opportunity.

24. Cohen and Murphy, *Burn, Baby, Burn,* 73. See also *Kerner Commission Report*; Governor's Commission on the Los Angeles Riots, *Violence in the City —an End or a Beginning?* (Los Angeles, 1965); Governor's Select Commission on Civil Disorder, *Report for Action* (February 1968); *Report of the Chicago Riot Study Committee to the Hon. Richard J. Daley* (Chicago, 1968); Mayor's Development Team, "Report to Mayor Jerome P. Cavanagh" (October 1967).

25. See chapter 2.

26. Shapiro and Sullivan, *Race Riot,* 152–54; Rustin, "The Watts 'Manifesto,'" 34; Hayden, *Rebellion in Newark,* 32–33. In Los Angeles, I am told, the looters stopped at the traffic lights, a tribute of sorts to the traffic engineers.

27. Lenora E. Berson, *Case Study of a Riot: The Philadelphia Story* (New York, 1966), 18.

28. U. S. Department of Labor, "A Sharper Look at Unemployment in U.S. Cities and Slums" (1967). The Labor Department has also issued separate reports for ten slum areas where the sub-employment rate varies from a low of 24 per cent (in Boston) to a high of 45 per cent (in New Orleans).

29. Institute of Industrial Relations, University of California, Los Angeles, "Hard-Core Poverty and Unemployment in Los Angeles" (Washington, D.C., 1965), 127–31; Richard A. Cloward and Frances Fox Piven, "A Strategy to End Poverty," *The Nation,* May 2, 1966, 501 ff.

30. Herman P. Miller, *Rich Man, Poor Man* (New York, 1964), chapter 6. See also Alan B. Batchelder, "Decline in the Relative Income of Negro Men," *Quarterly Journal of Economics,* November 1964, 525–48.

31. Miller, *Rich Man, Poor Man,* 90. See also Bernard Levenson and Mary S. McDill, "Employment Experience of Graduates in Automobile Mechanics —Mergenthaler and Carver High Schools Baltimore" (Baltimore, 1964), 8–17; U. S. Department of Labor, *The Negroes in the United States: Their Economic and Social Situation* (Washington, D.C., 1966), 19–31; U. S. Department of Labor and U. S. Department of Commerce, *The Social and Economic Status of Negroes in the United States,* 1969 (Washington, D.C., 1970), 14.

32. Elliot Liebow, *Tally's Corner* (Boston, 1967), chapter 2.

33. Herbert Kohl, *36 Children* (New York, 1967); Jonathan Kozol, *Death at an Early Age* (Boston, 1967); Kenneth A. Martyn, "Report on Education to the Governor's Commission on the Los Angeles Riots" (November 1965), *McCone Commission Archives,* XVII; A. Harry Passow, *Toward Creating a Modern Urban School System: A Study of the Washington, D.C. Public Schools* (New York, 1967).

34. U. S. Department of Labor, *Negroes in the United States,* 24–25.

35. Gunnar Myrdal, *An American Dilemma* (New York, 1964), I, chapter 17; Cayton and Drake, *Black Metropolis,* I, chapter 9.

36. U. S. Commission on Civil Rights, *Cleveland Hearings*, 460–62; U. S. Commission on Civil Rights, *Hearings Held in Detroit, Michigan, December 14–15, 1960* (Washington, D.C., 1961), 95–104. See also New York City Commission on Human Rights, "Bias in the Building Industry: An Updated Report, 1963–1965" (New York, 1967), 8–28.

37. The history of B.E.S.T., a New York City job training program, is particularly illuminating. See Fred C. Shapiro, "A Reporter at Large," *The New Yorker*, October 22, 1966, 181–98. See also U. S. Department of Labor, "A Report on Manpower Requirements, Resources, Utilization, and Training," in *Manpower Report of the President* (Washington, D.C., 1967), 84–85.

38. This conclusion is based upon a brief examination of application forms, investigative manuals, and other records of the New York City and Los Angeles Civil Service commissions, two of the nation's more enlightened commissions.

39. Karl E. Taeuber and Alma F. Taeuber, *Negroes in Cities* (Chicago, 1966), chapter 3.

40. This study was reported on August 22, 1967, at hearings of the Subcommittee on Housing of the U. S. Senate Subcommittee on Banking and Currency and made available to me by Mr. Neil Gold and the National Committee Against Discrimination in Housing.

41. U. S. Department of Labor, *Negroes in the United States*, 83–84.

42. See chapter 2.

43. Shapiro and Sullivan, *Race Riot*, 152–54; Berson, *Case Study of a Riot*, 40–42; Cohen and Murphy, *Burn, Baby, Burn*, 111, 132; Rustin, "The Watts 'Manifesto,'" 29–30; Hayden, *Rebellion in Newark*, 33; *Kerner Commission Report*, 116.

44. Frank Besag, *The Anatomy of a Riot: Buffalo, 1967* (Buffalo, N.Y., 1967), 136–38.

45. *McCone Commission Archives*, IV, Testimony of the Reverend Hartford Brookins, 56.

46. Here I have accepted an estimate by James Heilbrun, an assistant professor of economics at Columbia University, who is supervising a research project on the Harlem economy under the auspices of the Office of Economic Opportunity.

47. David Caplovitz, *The Poor Pay More: Consumer Practices of Low-Income Families* (New York, 1963), 13, 180–81.

48. *Ibid.*, chapters 2–7. See also Berson, *Case Study of Riot*, 40–45; *McCone Commission Archives*, V, Testimony of Harvey Claybrook, 8–13: XIII, Testimony of Helen Nelson, 1–14; *Kerner Commission Report*, 274–77; Federal Trade Commission, *Economic Reports on Installment Credit and Retail Sales Practices of District of Columbia Retailers* (Washington, D.C., 1968), chapters 1 and 3.

49. Caplovitz, *The Poor Pay More*, chapter 10.

50. I know of no systematic study of business costs in the ghetto. But among valuable surveys now available are the Federal Trade Commission's *Installment Credit and Retail Sale Practices*, chapter 2, and the President's National Advisory Panel on Insurance in Riot-Affected Areas, *Meeting the*

Insurance Crisis of Our Cities (Washington, D.C., 1968), chapters 1 and 2 and appendix A.

51. President's Committee on Consumer Interest, *The Most for Their Money: a Report of the Panel on Consumer Education for Persons with Limited Incomes* (Washington, D.C., 1965), 1–16.

52. See chapter 2.

53. Shapiro and Sullivan, *Race Riot*, 77–78; Cohen and Murphy, *Burn, Baby, Burn*, 73. See also chapter 3 above.

54. Including in one case—described by Conot in *Rivers of Blood, Years of Darkness* (74)—a twenty-year-old white, a member of C.O.R.E. who had organized black voters and taught school in Louisiana.

55. Arnold M. Rose, *The Negro's Morale* (Minneapolis, 1949), chapter 3; Harold R. Isaacs, *The New World of Negro Americans* (New York, 1964), part 2, chapter 3; *Kerner Commission Report*, 1–2.

56. Louis Yablonsky, "Negro Youth Gangs and Violence," *New Republic*, 154 (January 1, 1966), 10. See also Essien-Udom, *Black Nationalism*, chapters 4 and 5; Breitman, ed., *Malcolm X Speaks*, 5; Stokely Carmichael and Charles V. Hamilton, *Black Power* (New York, 1967), 37–39.

57. Hayden, *Rebellion in Newark*, 33–34.

58. Shapiro and Sullivan, *Race Riot*, 55; Cohen and Murphy, *Burn, Baby, Burn*, 111. See also Conot, *Rivers of Blood, Years of Darkness*, 74.

59. Myrdal, *An American Dilemma*, II, chapter 29; Robert C. Weaver, *The Negro Ghetto* (New York, 1948), chapters 4–7, 12–14; Charles Abrams, *Forbidden Neighbors* (New York, 1955), chapters 12–14, 16–17.

60. Cf. Carmichael and Hamilton, *Black Power*; E. David Cronon, *Black Moses* (Boston, 1961). See also Essien-Udom, *Black Nationalism*, chapter 2.

61. On the race riots see Elliott M. Rudwick, *Race Riot at East St. Louis July 2, 1917* (Carbondale, Ill., 1964), chapters 4 and 5; Chicago Commission on Race Relations, *The Negro in Chicago* (Chicago, 1922); and Waskow, *From Race Riot to Sit-In*, chapters 3 and 4.

62. See Chapter 1.

63. Quoted in a series of interviews taken shortly after the Los Angeles riots under the auspices of U.C.L.A. and now in the possession of Professor Nat Cohen who kindly allowed me to read them.

64. *Kerner Commission Report*, 56–59, 84–108.

65. Nathan Glazer and Daniel Patrick Moynihan, *Beyond the Melting Pot* (Cambridge, Mass., 1963); Gilbert Osofsky, *Harlem: The Making of a Ghetto* (New York, 1966); Allan H. Spear, *Black Chicago* (Chicago, 1967); Peter M. Blau and Otis Dudley Duncan, *The American Occupational Structure* (New York, 1967).

66. Oscar Handlin, *Boston's Immigrants* (Cambridge, Mass., 1959), chapters 3–5; Moses Rischin, *The Promised City: New York's Jews 1870–1914* (Cambridge, Mass., 1962), chapters 4 and 9; Robert M. Fogelson, *The Fragmented Metropolis: Los Angeles, 1850–1930* (Cambridge, Mass., 1967), chapter 9; Patricia Cayo Sexton, *Spanish Harlem* (New York, 1965), chapters 1–3; Harry M. Caudill, *Night Comes to the Cumberlands* (Boston,

1963), chapters 17–20; Oscar Handlin, *The Uprooted* (Boston, 1951), chapters 3–6.

67. Stanley Elkins, *Slavery* (New York, 1963), chapters 2 and 3; Oscar Handlin, *Fire-Bell in the Night* (Boston, 1964), 20–22; Gary Marx, *Protest and Prejudice* (New York, 1967), 159–67; Louis Wirth, *The Ghetto* (Chicago, 1928), chapter 12; Weaver, *The Negro Ghetto*, chapter 7.

68. Handlin, *Fire-Bell in the Night*, chapter 2; Miller, *Rich Man, Poor Man*, chapter 6; Myrdal, *An American Dilemma*, parts 4, 6, 7; Abrams, *Forbidden Neighbors*, chapters 12, 16, 17. See also Chicago Commission on Race Relations, *The Negro in Chicago*, chapters 5–8; Mayor's Commission on Conditions in Harlem, "The Negro in Harlem: A Report on Social and Economic Conditions Responsible for the Outbreak of March 19, 1935," chapters 3–5, New York City Municipal Archives.

69. Breitman, ed., *Malcolm X Speaks*, 26; Conot, *Rivers of Blood, Years of Darkness*, 35–36, 109–10; Carmichael and Hamilton, *Black Power*, chapter 2; Isaacs, *New World of Negro Americans*, part 2.

70. See chapter 5.

CHAPTER 5

THE EROSION OF RESTRAINT

1. The word "relatively" should be stressed, especially because a recent study suggests this may not be true nowadays. See Ted Gurr, "Urban Disorder: Perspective from the Comparative Study of Civil Strife," in Louis H. Masotti and Don R. Bowen, *Riots and Rebellions: Civil Violence in the Urban Community* (Beverly Hills, Calif., 1968), 51–68. See also Frederick T. Wilson, *Federal Aid in Domestic Disturbances: 1787–1903*, U. S. Congress, *Senate Documents*, 57th Congress, 2nd Session, Number 209.

2. Oscar Handlin, *The Uprooted* (Boston, 1951), chapter 3; Oscar Lewis, *La Vida* (New York, 1966), parts 2 and 4; Broadus Mitchell, *Depression Decade* (New York, 1962), chapter 3; Harry M. Caudill, *Night Comes to the Cumberlands* (Boston, 1963), chapters 13, 17, and 18.

3. William H. Grier and Price M. Cobbs, *Black Rage* (New York, 1968), 69–70.

4. Fred C. Shapiro and James W. Sullivan, *Race Riot: New York 1964* (New York, 1964), chapter 3; Lenora E. Berson, *Case Study of a Riot: The Philadelphia Story* (New York, 1966), 16–18; Jerry Cohen and William S. Murphy, *Burn, Baby, Burn! The Los Angeles Race Riot August 1965* (New York, 1966), 93; *Report of the National Advisory Commission on Civil Disorders* (New York, 1968), 64–65, 86–89 (hereafter referred to as *Kerner Commission Report*).

5. Arthur T. Waskow, *From Race Riot to Sit-In: 1919 and the 1960s* (Garden City, N.Y., 1966), chapters 9 and 10; Gary Marx, "Civil Disorder and the Agents of Social Control," 12–26, a paper delivered at the 1968 American Sociological Association meeting in Boston.

6. Shapiro and Sullivan, *Race Riot*, chapter 5; Berson, *Case Study of a Riot*, 20; Governor's Commission on the Los Angeles Riots, *Violence in the City—*

an End or a Beginning? (Los Angeles, 1965), 17–20 (hereafter referred to as *McCone Commission Report*); *Kerner Commission Report*, 67–69, 93–107; *Riots, Civil and Criminal Disorders: Hearings Before the Permanent Subcommittee on Investigations of the Committee on Government Operations,* United States Senate, 90th Congress, 1st Session (Washington, D.C., 1967), part 1, tables following page 15.

7. Shapiro and Sullivan, *Race Riot,* 76; Berson, *Case Study of a Riot,* 17–18; Cohen and Murphy, *Burn, Baby, Burn,* 119–20; Tom Hayden, *Rebellion in Newark* (New York, 1967), 37–44; *Kerner Commission Report,* 93; New York *Times,* August 10, 1966; May 29, July 24, 28, 29, 1968.

8. I spoke with the Los Angeles teen-ager in the summer of 1966. The other examples are drawn from John Hersey, *The Algiers Motel Incident* (New York, 1968), 61–62, and Shapiro and Sullivan, *Race Riot,* 80.

9. William Brink and Louis Harris, *Black and White* (New York, 1967), 266.

10. Angus Campbell and Howard Schuman, "Racial Attitudes in Fifteen American Cities," in *Supplemental Studies for the National Advisory Commission on Civil Disorders* (Washington, D.C., 1968), 55 and 62.

11. *McCone Commission Report,* 1–5.

12. *Kerner Commission Report,* 1–2.

13. See chapter 4.

14. Robert Conot, *Rivers of Blood, Years of Darkness* (New York, 1967), 250, 279, 285–86, 317–18; Hayden, *Rebellion in Newark,* 45–61; *Kerner Commission Report,* 97–99, 115–16.

15. *Ibid.,* 42, 61, 326.

16. Nothing documents this point more vividly than the unedited film clips of the riots, to which, as a consultant to the President's Crime Commission, I was granted access by N.B.C. News in 1966.

17. Walter B. Miller, "Lower Class Culture as a Generating Milieu of Gang Delinquency," *Journal of Social Issues,* July 1958, 5–19. See also Herbert J. Gans, *The Urban Villagers* (Glencoe, Ill., 1962), 63–71, 230–42.

18. Cf. Norman Mailer, *Miami and the Siege of Chicago* (New York, 1968), 131–74, and Patrick Seale and Maureen McConville, *Red Flag/Black Flag* (New York, 1968), 71–94. See also Kenneth Keniston, *Young Radicals* (New York, 1968), chapter 7.

19. Albert J. Reiss, Jr., "Measurement of the Nature and Amount of Crime," in *Studies in Crime and Law Enforcement in Major Metropolitan Areas* (Washington, D.C., 1967), I, 44, a report prepared for the President's Crime Commission.

20. Jacob Riis, *How the Other Half Lives* (New York, 1890); Frederic M. Thrasher, *The Gang* (Chicago, 1927); Arthur Aryeh Goren, "The New York Kehillah: 1908–1922" (Columbia University doctoral dissertation, 1966); Daniel Bell, *The End of Ideology* (Glencoe, Ill., 1960); Kenneth B. Clark, *Dark Ghetto* (New York, 1965); Claude Brown, *Manchild in the Promised Land* (New York, 1965); Dan Wakefield, ed., *The Addict* (New York, 1963); Malcolm X, *The Autobiography of Malcolm X* (New York, 1966).

21. I have probably underestimated the discontinuity somewhat, but if an article by Roldo S. Bartimole and Murray Gruber—"Cleveland: Recipe for Vio-

lence," *The Nation*, June 26, 1967, 814–17–is indicative, only somewhat.

22. Brown, *Manchild in the Promised Land*; Malcolm X, *Autobiography*; Clark, *Dark Ghetto*; James Baldwin, *The Fire Next Time* (New York, 1963); Richard Wright, *White Man, Listen!* (Garden City, N.Y., 1964). See also Robert K. Merton, *Social Theory and Social Structure* (Glencoe, Ill., 1957), 131–60, and Richard A. Cloward and Lloyd E. Ohlin, *Delinquency and Opportunity* (New York, 1960), 77–107.

23. See chapter 3.

24. Harold R. Isaacs, *The New World of Negro Americans* (Cambridge, Mass., 1963).

25. Cohen and Murphy, *Burn, Baby, Burn*, 209. See also Robert F. Williams, *Negroes with Guns* (New York, 1962), 42–124; George Breitman, ed., *Malcolm X Speaks* (New York, 1965), 43–44; Stokely Carmichael and Charles V. Hamilton, *Black Power* (New York, 1967), 52–53.

26. Carl Werthman, "The Function of Social Definitions in the Development of Delinquent Careers," August 1968, 39–54, a paper prepared for the President's Crime Commission; U. S. Department of Labor, "A Report on Manpower Requirements, Resources, Utilization, and Training," in *Manpower Report to the President* (Washington, D.C., 1967), 84–85.

27. Brown, *Manchild in the Promised Land*.

28. *Riots, Civil and Criminal Disorders*, part 1, tables following page 15.

29. See chapter 2.

30. William Foote Whyte, *Street Corner Society* (Chicago, 1955), chapters 3 and 5; Gans, *The Urban Villagers*, chapters 3 and 4.

31. Howard Zinn, *SNCC: The New Abolitionists* (Boston, 1964); Seymour Martin Lipset and Sheldon S. Wolin, eds., *The Berkeley Student Revolt* (Garden City, N.Y., 1965); *Crisis at Columbia: Report of the Fact-finding Commission Appointed to Investigate the Disturbances at Columbia University in April and May 1968* (New York, 1968); Keniston, *Young Radicals*.

32. See chapter 2. See also Harry W. Reynolds, "Black Power, Community Power, and Jobs," in Masotti and Bowen, *Riots and Rebellions*, 247.

33. President's Commission on Law Enforcement and Administration of Justice, *The Challenge of Crime in a Free Society* (Washington, D.C., 1967), 75. See also Ronald Christensen, "Projected Percentage of U. S. Population with Criminal Arrest and Conviction Records," in the commission's *Task Force Report: Science and Technology* (Washington, D.C., 1967), 216–28.

34. Though James Q. Wilson–in *Varieties of Police Behavior* (Cambridge, Mass., 1968), 114–15–has raised questions about this point.

35. Cohen and Murphy, *Burn, Baby, Burn*, 208. See also Reynolds, "Black Power, Community Power, and Jobs," 247–48; Gerald D. Suttles, *The Social Order of the Slum* (Chicago, 1968), 1–23; chapter 3.

36. Albert G. Hess and Fre Le Poole, "The Use of Arrest Records: an International Survey," August 1966, 1–23, an unpublished paper prepared for the New York Chapter of the American Liberties Union.

37. *Kerner Commission Report*, 337–57. See also the forthcoming doctoral dissertation by Isaac D. Balbus of the University of Chicago, "Urban Violence and the Criminal Courts: A Study of the Allocation of Mass Justice."

38. Except, of course, when they are ignored. See Roger Lane, *Policing the City* (Cambridge, Mass., 1967), 30–31.

39. Louis Hartz, *The Liberal Tradition in America* (New York, 1955), chapters 2 and 3. See also Abe Fortas, *Concerning Dissent and Civil Disobedience* (New York, 1968).

40. Herbert Aptheker, A *Documentary History of the Negro People in the United States* (New York, 1963), I, 102, 220, 501–2: II, 552–59, 788–91, 813–15, 866–68; Waskow, *From Race Riot to Sit-In*, 12–104; Arthur Raper, *The Tragedy of Lynching* (Chapel Hill, N.C., 1933); "The Colonial War at Home," *Monthly Review*, October 1965, 2–3.

41. *McCone Commission Report*, 6–7; Governor's Select Commission on Civil Disorder, *Report for Action*, February 1968, xii; *Report of the Chicago Riot Study Committee to the Hon. Richard J. Daley*, August 1968, 3–4; *Kerner Commission Report*, 1–2. See also Allan A. Silver, "Official Interpretations of Race Riots," in Robert Connery, ed., *Urban Riots: Violence and Social Change* (New York, 1969), 151–63.

42. J. T. Headley, *The Great Riots of New York* (New York, 1873); Ray Allan Billington, *The Protestant Crusade 1800–1860* (New York, 1938); John Higham, *Strangers in the Land* (New Brunswick, N.J., 1955).

43. *New York Times*, January 1, 1966; February 2, September 9, October 18, 1968.

44. Campbell and Schuman, "Racial Attitudes in Fifteen American Cities," 22 and 52. See also *Kerner Commission Report*, 78.

45. Gary Wills, *The Second Civil War* (New York, 1968).

46. Oscar Handlin, *Fire-Bell in the Night* (Boston, 1964), 8–22; Anthony Lewis, *Portrait of a Decade* (New York, 1964), 3–15. See also Edmund David Cronon, *Black Moses* (Madison, Wisc., 1955); E. U. Essien-Udom, *Black Nationalism* (Chicago, 1962); and Isaacs, *New World of Negro Americans*.

47. Martin Luther King, Jr., *Stride Toward Freedom* (New York, 1958), 28–157; Louis B. Lomax, *The Negro Revolt* (New York, 1963), 78–222; Zinn, *The New Abolitionists*, 16–166; and Lewis, *Portrait of a Decade*, 15–103.

48. Harry Scoble, "Negro Leadership Study: Tentative Findings," August 1966, 9, an unpublished paper prepared for the U. S. Office of Economic Opportunity.

49. *New York Times*, January 10, 1967; Governor's Commission on the Los Angeles Riots, *Archives*, 4, Testimony of the Reverend Hartford Brookins, 24–32; U. S. Commission on Civil Rights, *Hearings Held in Cleveland, Ohio, April 1–7, 1966* (Washington, D.C., 1966), 522–25, 568–72.

50. There is some evidence that things were even worse in some ghettos in 1965 than in 1960. See U. S. Bureau of the Census, *Current Population Reports*, series P-23, No. 21, "Characteristics of Selected Neighborhoods in Cleveland, Ohio: April 1965" (Washington, D.C., 1967).

51. See note 41.

52. Lillian Smith, *Strange Fruit* (New York, 1944), 87–88; John Dollard, *Caste and Class in a Southern Town* (New York, 1957), 267–68; U. S. Commission on Civil Rights, *Hearings Held in Boston, Massachusetts October 4–5, 1966* (Washington, D.C., 1966), 64–65.

53. Stanley Elkins, *Slavery* (Chicago, 1959), part 3.

54. Rayford W. Logan, *The Negro in American Life and Thought: The Nadir, 1877–1901* (New York, 1954), chapters 9–13; Gunnar Myrdal, *An American Dilemma* (New York, 1964), II, 763–64; Arnold M. Rose, *The Negro's Morale* (Minneapolis, 1949), 57–67, 85–95.

55. Kenneth M. Stampp, *The Peculiar Institution* (New York, 1956), chapter 3. See also Herbert Aptheker, *American Negro Slave Revolts* (New York, 1943).

56. Hortense Powdermaker, "The Channeling of Negro Aggression by the Cultural Process," *American Journal of Sociology*, May 1943, 750–58. See also Dollard, *Caste and Class in a Southern Town*, chapter 14.

57. Powdermaker, "The Channeling of Negro Aggression," 755–56. See also Carl Werthman and Irving Piliavin, "Gang Members and the Police," in David Bordua, ed., *The Police* (New York, 1967), 63–65, 87–89.

58. Cf., for example, U. S. Commission on Civil Rights, *Hearings Held in Jackson, Miss. February 16–20, 1965* (Washington, D.C., 1965), II, and U. S. Commission on Civil Rights, *Hearings Held in Detroit, Michigan December 14–15, 1960* (Washington, D.C., 1961), 302–427.

59. *Kerner Commission Report*, chapters 6, 7, 8, and 11.

60. Oscar Handlin, *Race and Nationality in American Life* (Garden City, N.Y., 1957), chapter 7; David M. Reimers, *White Protestantism and the Negro* (New York, 1965), chapter 5.

61. Breitman, ed., *Malcolm X Speaks*, 39–40; Carmichael and Hamilton, *Black Power*, 34–55; Isaacs, *New World of Negro Americans*, 80–96; Eldridge Cleaver, *Soul on Ice* (New York, 1968), 65–83; Julius Lester, *Look Out Whitey! Black Power's Gon' Get Your Mama* (New York, 1968), 137–43.

62. But there has been a resurgence of viligante groups in the wake of rioting in Newark and other cities with large ethnic blocks.

63. See Stephan Thernstrom, "Up from Slavery," in *Perspectives in American History*, 1967, 434–39.

64. On the difficulties in computing crime rates see Bell, *End of Ideology*, chapter 8; Marvin Wolfgang, "Crimes of Violence" (1967), 31–36, a report prepared for the President's Crime Commission; and the commission's *Challenge of Crime*, 20–27.

65. Clifford R. Shaw and Henry D. McKay, *Social Factors in Juvenile Delinquency*, in National Commission on Law Observance and Enforcement, *Report on the Causes of Crime* (Washington, D.C., 1931), II, parts 2 and 5; Ernest Jerome Hopkins, "The Police and the Immigrant," in *Proceedings of the National Conference of Social Work . . . May 15–21, 1932* (Chicago, 1932), 509–19.

66. Here television has had a profound, if not easily measurable, impact. See John Horn's comments in *The Nation*, December 11, 1967, 638. On the aspirations and achievements of the other immigrants see Handlin, *The Uprooted*, chapters 4, 6, 12, and Nathan Glazer and Daniel Patrick Moynihan, *Beyond the Melting Pot* (Cambridge, Mass., 1963), 86–288.

67. Cf. Kenneth B. Clark, *Dark Ghetto* (New York, 1965), chapter 5, and St. Clair Drake and Horace R. Cayton, *Black Metropolis* (New York 1962), II, chapter 17. How much this difference is a reflection of the blacks'

growing demands for public order is hard to measure. See John F. Kraft, Inc., "Attitudes of Negroes in Various Cities" (1966), 23–29, a report prepared for the U. S. Senate Subcommittee on Executive Reorganization.

68. Allan H. Spear, *Black Chicago* (Chicago, 1967), chapters 2 and 11; Gilbert Osofsky, *Harlem: The Making of a Ghetto* (New York, 1966), 146–47; Chicago Commission on Race Relations, *The Negro in Chicago* (Chicago, 1922), chapter 7; W. E. B. DuBois, *The Philadelphia Negro* (New York, 1967), chapter 13.

69. Myrdal, *An American Dilemma*, II, chapters 35 and 45; Handlin, *Fire-Bell in the Night*, chapters 2 and 4–6; Lomax, *The Negro Revolt*, chapters 5 and 6; Campbell and Schuman, "Racial Attitudes in Fifteen American Cities," 22–23; Everett F. Cataldo, Richard M. Johnson, and Lyman A. Kellstadt, "Social Strain and Urban Violence," in Masotti and Bowen, *Riots and Rebellion*, 285–98.

70. August Meier, *Negro Thought in America, 1880–1915* (Ann Arbor, Mich., 1966), chapters 5, 8, 10, and 14; Gary Marx, *Protest and Prejudice* (New York, 1967), chapter 2; Campbell and Schuman, "Racial Attitudes in Fifteen American Cities," chapter 2.

CHAPTER 6

THE MODERATES' DILEMMA

1. Jerry Cohen and William S. Murphy, *Burn, Baby, Burn! The Los Angeles Race Riot August 1965* (New York, 1966), 119.

2. Fred C. Shapiro and James W. Sullivan, *Race Riot: New York 1964* (New York, 1964), 119–20. See also Benjamin Muse, *The American Negro Revolution* (Bloomington, Ind., 1968), 297–98.

3. Federal Bureau of Investigation, "Report on the 1964 Riots," September 18, 1964, 9; New York *Times*, August 2–3, 1967.

4. *Report of the National Advisory Commission on Civil Disorders* (Washington, D.C., 1968), 61–62, 88–89, 483 (hereafter referred to as *Kerner Commission Report*); Cohen and Murphy, *Burn, Baby, Burn*, 91–92; Muse, *American Negro Revolution*, 296–97; Tom Hayden, *Rebellion in Newark* (New York, 1967), 23–24.

5. F.B.I., "Report on the 1964 Riots," 3; Governor's Commission on the Los Angeles Riots, *Violence in the City—an End or a Beginning?* (Los Angeles, 1965), 85–88.

6. Shapiro and Sullivan, *Race Riot*, 80.

7. *Ibid.*, 76; Thomas H. Allen to Gloster B. Current, August 9, 1964, a memo on the Rochester riots in the N.A.A.C.P.'s files in New York City; Lenora E. Berson, *Case Study of a Riot: The Philadelphia Story* (New York, 1966), 17–18.

8. Robert Conot, *Rivers of Blood, Years of Darkness* (New York, 1967), 144–54.

9. New York *Times*, July 15, 1966; Omaha *World-Herald*, July 5, 1966.

10. *Kerner Commission Report*, 61–62, 88–89.

11. Muse, *American Negro Revolution*, 297–98.

12. New York *Times*, April 5–9, 1968. See also Ben W. Gilbert *et al.*, *Ten Blocks from the White House* (New York, 1968), chapters 1–6; and *Report of the Chicago Riot Study Committee to the Hon. Richard Daley* (Chicago, 1968), chapters 1 and 2.

13. No doubt the moderates succeeded occasionally. But success (or, in other words, order) is not considered particularly newsworthy. And I have not found many references to it.

14. *Kerner Commission Report*, charts following page 608. See also New York *Times*, June 15–16, 1967; Nora Sayre, "A Riot Prevented," *New Statesman*, September 22, 1967, 349–50.

15. Daniel C. Thompson, *The Negro Leadership Class* (Englewood Cliffs, N.J., 1963), 2–4.

16. Gunnar Myrdal, *An American Dilemma* (New York, 1964), II, chapter 39. See also Clement E. Vose, *Caucasians Only* (Berkeley, Calif., 1959); Herbert Garfinkel, *When Negroes March* (Glencoe, Ill., 1959); and Louis B. Lomax, *The Negro Revolt* (New York, 1962).

17. Oscar Handlin, *Fire-Bell in the Night* (Boston, 1964), 8–22.

18. Governor's Commission on the Los Angeles Riots, *Archives*, 4, Testimony of the Reverend Hartford Brookins, 24–32 (hereafter referred to as *McCone Commission Archives*); David Rogers, *110 Livingston Street* (New York, 1968), chapter 1; U .S. Commission on Civil Rights, *Civil Rights '63* (Washington, D.C., 1963), 157–58.

19. *Kerner Commission Report*, chapters 6–8. See chapter 4.

20. "What is needed," Mr. Young said, "is to give to those of us who remain with a faith and a hope in America and a belief in nonviolence the tangible, concrete victories—in jobs, housing, education, opportunities—that will enable us to go into the ghetto and say to people: 'Look—be patient; be nonviolent, because here we now have job opportunities, we now have assurances that your kids will have quality education, here we have assurances that there will be access to better housing and more decent housing, that the codes will be enforced.' If we get this," he concluded, "we can stop riots." (*U. S. News & World Report*, April 22, 1968, 45)

21. Arnold Schucter, *White Power/Black Freedom* (Boston, 1968), 64–65.

22. Edward C. Banfield and James Q. Wilson, *City Politics* (Cambridge, Mass., 1963), 293–303.

23. Angus Campbell and Howard Schuman, "Racial Attitudes in Fifteen American Cities," in *Supplemental Studies for the National Advisory Commission on Civil Disorders* (Washington, D.C., 1968), 39–41.

24. New York *Times*, November 4, 1964; November 10, 1966. See also Winthrop D. Jordan, *White Over Black: American Attitudes Toward the Negro 1550–1812* (Chapel Hill, N.C., 1968), parts 4 and 5; Myrdal, *An American Dilemma*, parts 1 and 2; Oscar Handlin, *Race and Nationality in American Life* (Garden City, N.Y., 1957), chapters 2 and 4.

25. Banfield and Wilson, *City Politics*, chapter 15. See also Jason Epstein, "The New York School Revolt," *The New York Review of Books*, October 10, 1968, 37–41; Jason Epstein, "The Issue at Ocean Hill," *ibid.*, November 21,

1968, 3 ff.; and Martin Mayer, *The Teachers Strike: New York, 1968* (New York, 1969).

26. Oscar Handlin, *The Newcomers* (Garden City, N.Y., 1959), chapter 4. See also chapters 4 and 5.

27. Harry Scoble, "Negro Leadership Study: Tentative Findings" (1966), 14–15, an unpublished paper prepared for the U. S. Office of Economic Opportunity. There is, I know, only impressionistic evidence, and not much of it, either, to support this generalization.

28. From a statement by Gloster B. Current, in "Community Unrest: Causes, Effects, Prevention, Cure," 18, a special seminar held by the N.A.A.C.P. in Columbus, Ohio, April 2, 1966. See also Cohen and Murphy, *Burn, Baby, Burn*, 118; Myrdal, *An American Dilemma*, II, chapters 32, 36, and 37; and Gary Marx, *Protest and Prejudice* (New York, 1967), 25–28.

29. E. Franklin Frazier, *Black Bourgeoisie* (Chicago, 1957), part 2; Kenneth B. Clark, *Dark Ghetto* (New York, 1965), 55–62; Harold Cruse, *Rebellion or Revolution?* (New York, 1968), 89–90.

30. Arthur Aryeh Goren, "The New York Kehillah: 1908–1922" (Columbia University doctoral dissertation, 1966).

31. James Q. Wilson, *Negro Politics: The Search for Leadership* (Glencoe, Ill., 1960), chapter 8.

32. Martin Meyerson and Edward C. Banfield, *Politics, Planning, and the Public Interest* (Glencoe, Ill., 1955), chapter 4.

33. Moses Rischin, *The Promised City* (Cambridge, Mass., 1962), chapter 6; Herbert J. Gans, *The Urban Villagers* (Glencoe, Ill., 1962), chapters 1 and 2; Nathan Glazer and Daniel Patrick Moynihan, *Beyond the Melting Pot* (Cambridge, Mass., 1964), parts 3 and 4.

34. Gilbert Osofsky, *Harlem: The Making of a Ghetto* (New York, 1966), chapters 5–8; Allan H. Spear, *Black Chicago* (Chicago, 1967), chapters 1 and 8; Robert M. Fogelson, *The Fragmented Metropolis: Los Angeles, 1850–1930* (Cambridge, Mass., 1967), chapter 9; U. S. Commission on Civil Rights, *1959 Report* (Washington, D.C., 1959), part 4; U. S. Department of Labor, *The Negroes in the United States* (Washington, D.C., 1966), 37; U. S. Bureau of the Census, *Census of Housing: 1960*, volume II, *Metropolitan Housing* (Washington, D.C., 1963), parts 2, 4, and 5.

35. Davis McEntire, *Residence and Race* (New York, 1960), 155.

36. Clark, *Dark Ghetto*, 55–62.

37. But see *Life*, August 27, 1965, 18.

38. Karl E. Taeuber and Alma F. Taeuber, *Negroes in Cities* (Chicago, 1965), chapter 3.

39. Clark, *Dark Ghetto*, chapter 4.

40. Fogelson, *Fragmented Metropolis*, chapters 7 and 9; Charles Abrams, *Forbidden Neighbors* (New York, 1955), chapter 12; Sam B. Warner, Jr., *Streetcar Suburbs* (Cambridge, Mass., 1962), chapters 1 and 6.

41. Myrdal, *An American Dilemma*, II, 622–24; Abrams, *Forbidden Neighbors*, chapters 12–14, 16–17; Robert C. Weaver, *The Negro Ghetto* (New York, 1948), chapters 4, 7, 10, 12, 13; Commission on Race and Housing, *Where*

Shall We Live? (Berkeley and Los Angeles, 1958), 23–30; Scott Greer, *Urban Renewal and American Cities* (New York, 1965), chapter 6.

42. Wilson, *Negro Politics*, chapter 1.

43. Oscar Handlin, *The Dimensions of Liberty* (Cambridge, Mass., 1961), chapter 5.

44. Handlin, *The Uprooted*, chapter 7; Oscar Handlin, *Boston's Immigrants* (Cambridge, Mass., 1941), chapter 6; W. I. Thomas and Florian Znaniecki, *Polish Peasant in Europe and America* (New York, 1958), II, part 3, chapters 2 and 3; Goren, "The Kehillah."

45. Commenting on the voluntary associations' problems in south-central Los Angeles, one middle-class black told the McCone Commission: "We couldn't keep these organizations going, because the people just didn't know how to organize. And we got—we seemed to have more of the type of people who were just struggling so hard to keep body and soul together that they had no time for community activities." (*McCone Commission Archives*, III, Testimony of Herb Atkinson, 25)

46. *Kerner Commission Report*, 430. On the political implications of residential mobility see *McCone Commission Archives*, VII, Testimony of Kenneth Hahn, 51–52.

47. James Baldwin, *The Fire Next Time* (New York, 1963), 17–24; Stanley Elkins, *Slavery* (Chicago, 1958), parts 2 and 3. See also the essays of Erik H. Erikson ("The Concept of Identity in Race Relations: Notes and Queries," 145–71) and Oscar Handlin ("The Goals of Integration," 268–86) in *Daedalus*, Winter 1966, *The Negro American*, volume II.

48. Handlin, "The Goals of Integration," 283; Fogelson, *Fragmented Metropolis*, 192–94, 202–4.

49. Handlin, *The Uprooted*, chapter 8; William L. Riordon, ed., *Plunkett of Tammany Hall* (New York, 1963), 91–98; Robert K. Merton, *Social Theory and Social Structure* (Glencoe, Ill., 1957), 71–81.

50. Meyerson and Banfield, *Politics, Planning, and the Public Interest*, 65–79, 229–33. See also Harold F. Gosnell, *Negro Politicians* (Chicago, 1966), chapters 1, 2, 5, 7, and 16.

51. Wallace S. Sayre and Herbert Kaufmann, *Governing New York* (New York, 1965), chapters 3 and 11. See also Robert H. Wiebe, *The Search for Order 1877–1920* (New York, 1967), chapters 5–7.

52. Banfield and Wilson, *City Politics*, chapter 11 and conclusion. See also Richard Hofstadter, *The Age of Reform* (New York, 1955), chapter 4.

53. Frazier, *Black Bourgeoisie*, chapter 4; Myrdal, *An American Dilemma*, II, chapter 39.

54. Edmund David Cronon, *Black Moses* (Madison, Wisc., 1955); C. Eric Lincoln, *The Black Muslims in America* (Boston, 1961); and E. U. Essien-Udom, *Black Nationalism* (Chicago, 1962).

55. See George Breitman, ed., *Malcolm X Speaks* (New York, 1965); George Breitman, ed., *The Last Year of Malcolm X* (New York, 1967); Stokely Carmichael and Charles V. Hamilton, *Black Power* (New York, 1967); Harold Cruse, *The Crisis of the Negro Intellectual* (New York, 1967), 544–65.

56. *New York Times*, July 7, 1968.

57. Breitman, ed., *Malcolm X Speaks*, 4.

58. Martin Luther King, Jr., *Why We Can't Wait* (New York, 1964), 77–100.

59. Marx, *Protest and Prejudice*, 53–54, 78–79, 185–86; Campbell and Schuman, "Racial Attitudes in Fifteen American Cities," 17–19, 55–57.

60. Breitman, ed., *Malcolm X Speaks*, 68–69.

61. Robert MacNeil, *The People Machine* (New York, 1969), 49–50.

62. New York *Times*, August 3, 9, 1968.

63. *Ibid.*, January 14, 1969.

64. *Kerner Commission Report*, 248.

65. *U. S. News & World Report*, February 21, 1966, 72.

66. Unless of course the militants manage to reverse the trends toward centralization, professionalization, and bureaucratization. About which see chapter 7.

67. Frances Fox Piven and Richard A. Cloward, "Black Control of Cities: Heading It Off by Metropolitan Government," *The New Republic*, September 30, 1967, 19–21; Richard A. Cloward and Frances Fox Piven, "Ghetto Redevelopment: Corporate Imperialism for the Poor," *The Nation*, October 16, 1967, 365–67.

68. H. Paul Friesma, "Black Control of Central Cities: The Hollow Prize," *Journal of the American Institute of Planners*, March 1969, 75–79.

69. Marx, *Protest and Prejudice*, 78–79.

70. Richard A. Cloward and Frances Fox Piven, "The Urban Crises and the Consolidation of National Power," in Robert H. Connery, ed., *Urban Riots: Violence and Social Change* (New York, 1969), 164–73.

CHAPTER 7

LIBERALISM AT AN IMPASSE

1. Besides Governor Kerner, the commission included Mayor John V. Lindsay of New York City (its vice-chairman), Senators Fred R. Harris of Oklahoma (Democrat) and Edward W. Brooke of Massachusetts (Republican), Congressmen James W. Corman of California (Democrat) and William M. McCulloch of Ohio (Republican), I. W. Abel, President of the United Steelworkers, Charles B. Thornton, President and Chairman of the Board of Litton Industries, Roy Wilkins, Executive Director of the N.A.A.C.P., Katherine Graham Peden, Kentucky Commerce Commissioner, and Herbert Jenkins, Atlanta Police Chief (New York *Times*, July 28, 1967).

2. *Ibid.*, July 30, 1967.

3. *Ibid.*, July 29, 1967. See also Chicago Commission on Race Relations, *The Negro in Chicago* (Chicago, 1922); Mayor's Commission on Conditions in Harlem, "The Negro in Harlem: A Report on Social and Economic Conditions Responsible for the Outbreak of March 19, 1935," New York City Municipal Archives; Governor's Commission on the Los Angeles Riots, *Violence in the City—an End or a Beginning?* (Los Angeles, 1965); and Arthur Waskow, *From Race Riot to Sit-In: 1919 and the 1960s* (Garden City, N.Y., 1966).

4. Michael Lipsky and David J. Olson, "On the Politics of Riot Commissions," a paper presented at the 1968 Annual Meeting of the American Political Science Association, Washington, D.C., September 3–7, 1968. See also New York *Times*, August 1, 2, 17, October 6, 25, 31, November 12, 19, 24, 1967; February 25, March 1, 1968.

5. *Report of the National Advisory Commission on Civil Disorders* (New York, 1968), 1–2 (hereafter referred to as *Kerner Commission Report*). All citations herein are from the paperback edition, which was published by Bantam Books.

6. *Ibid.*, 1–2, 31–34, 201–2, 410–13.

7. *Ibid.*, 413–82. See also Chicago Commission on Race Relations, *The Negro in Chicago*; and Gunnar Myrdal, *An American Dilemma* (New York, 1944).

8. New York *Times*, March 2, 4, 6, 11, April 24, 1968.

9. In his introduction to the paperback edition (*Kerner Commission Report*, IX).

10. New York *Times*, March 2, 5, 6, 7, 10, 23, 25, 1968; Frank S. Meyers, "Principles & Heresies," and Ernest Van Den Haag, "How Not to Prevent Civil Disorders," in *National Review*, March 26, 1968, 283–87.

11. See the reviews by Gary Marx in *Trans-action*, September 1968, 56–58; Jeffery K. Hadden in *Commonweal*, March 29, 1968, 39; and Richard Light and Robert L. Green in *Harvard Educational Review*, Fall 1968, 756–71.

12. Governor's Select Commission on Civil Disorder, *Report for Action* (February 1968): Governor's Commission on the Los Angeles Riots, *Violence in the City*.

13. Federal Bureau of Investigation, "Report on the 1964 Riots," September 18, 1964, 9; New York *Times*, August 2, 3, 1967; Robert M. Fogelson, "White on Black: A Critique of the McCone Commission Report on the Los Angeles Riots," *Political Science Quarterly*, September 1967, 342–47; *Kerner Commission Report*, 201–2.

14. Robert M. Fogelson and Robert B. Hill, "Who Riots? A Study of Participation in the 1967 Riots," in *Supplemental Studies for the National Advisory Commission on Civil Disorders* (Washington, D.C., 1968), 217–48.

15. Allan A. Silver, "Official Interpretations of Racial Riots," in Robert H. Connery, ed., *Urban Riots: Violence and Social Change* (New York, 1969), 151–63.

16. *Kerner Commission Report*, chapters 4, 6, 7, 10, and 11.

17. Governor's Commission on the Los Angeles Riots, *Violence in the City*; Cuyahoga County Grand Jury, "Special Grand Jury Report Relating to the Hough Riots" (August 9, 1966); Governor's Select Commission on Civil Disorder, *Report for Action: Report of the Chicago Riot Study Committee to the Hon. Richard J. Daley* (Chicago, 1968).

18. *Kerner Commission Report*, chapters 6–8. See also chapter 4.

19. Gary Marx, "Two Cheers for the Riot Commission Report," in J. Szwed, ed., *Black America* (New York, 1970), 78–96.

20. *Kerner Commission Report*, 143–50.

21. *Ibid.*, 283–88.

22. The commission pointed out in the introduction: "What white Americans

have never fully understood—but what the Negro can never forget—is that white society is deeply implicated in the ghetto. White institutions created it, white institutions maintain it, and white society condones it" (*Kerner Commission Report*, 2). But it did not pursue this idea in the report.

23. Hannah Arendt, "Reflections on Violence," *The New York Review of Books*, February 27, 1969, 28. See also Gordon W. Allport, *The Nature of Prejudice* (Garden City, N.Y., 1958), chapter 5.

24. Paul B. Sheatsley, "White Attitudes Toward the Negro," *Daedalus*, Winter 1966, *The Negro American*, II, 217–38; Paul Jacobs, *Prelude to Riot* (New York, 1966); Joseph P. Lyford, *The Airtight Cage* (New York, 1966); Richard M. Elman, *The Poorhouse State* (New York, 1966); David Rogers, *110 Livingston Street* (New York, 1968).

25. *Kerner Commission Report*, 395–483.

26. Though not as specific as the legislative action recommended by some of the local commissions. See, for example, the Mayor's Development Team's "Report to Mayor Jerome P. Cavanagh" (October 1967).

27. *Kerner Commission Report*, 413–82.

28. Whether, as Gary Marx suggested in his *Trans-action* review, cited in note 11 above, there is a causal relation between the Vietnam War and the ghetto riots is open to debate. But there is no question that the nation cannot resolve ghetto problems without revising national priorities (and, above all, current defense and military policies). The commissioners completely overlooked this issue.

29. On income distribution in the United States see Gabriel Kolko, *Wealth and Power in America* (New York, 1962), and Herman P. Miller, *Income Distribution in the United States* (Washington, D.C., 1966). And on income distribution among blacks see Herman P. Miller, *Rich Man, Poor Man* (New York, 1964), chapter 6, and Alan B. Batchelder, "Decline in the Relative Income of Negro Man," *Quarterly Journal of Economics*, November 1964, 525–48.

30. *Kerner Commission Report*, 288–98.

31. Jacobs, *Prelude to Riot*, chapters 1–6; Lyford, *Airtight Cage*, chapter 14; Elman, *Poorhouse State*, chapters 1–3; Rogers, *110 Livingston Street*, chapters 7 and 8.

32. Frances Fox Piven and Richard A. Cloward, "Black Control of Cities: Heading It Off by Metropolitan Government," *The New Republic*, September 30, 1967, 19–21; and the authors' "Black Control of Cities—II: How the Negroes Will Lose," *ibid.*, October 7, 1967, 15–19.

33. *Kerner Commission Report*, 419–20, 440–44, 481–82.

34. Equal Employment Opportunity Commission, *Equal Employment Opportunity Report No. 1: Job Patterns for Minorities and Women in Private Industry*, 1966 (Washington, D.C., 1968), part 1; U. S. Commission on Civil Rights, *Racial Isolation in the Public Schools* (Washington, D.C., 1967), volume I; Karl E. Taeuber and Alma F. Taeuber, *Negroes in Cities* (Chicago, 1965).

35. To make matters worse, individual prejudice and institutional rigidity often complement one another. For a discussion of this relationship see chapter 3.

36. See Stokely Carmichael's Chicago, July 28, 1966, speech, in Student Non-violent Coordinating Committee, *Notes and Comments* (August 1968); and Eldridge Cleaver, *Soul on Ice* (New York, 1968), 128–37.

37. See chapter 1.

38. *Kerner Commission Report*, 230–36.

39. August Meier, *Negro Thought in America, 1880–1915* (Ann Arbor, Mich., 1966); Edmund David Cronon, *Black Moses* (Madison, Wisc., 1955); E. U. Essien-Udom, *Black Nationalism* (Chicago, 1962); Harold Cruse, *The Crisis of the Negro Intellectual* (New York, 1967).

40. Stokely Carmichael and Charles V. Hamilton, *Black Power* (New York, 1967), chapters 2 and 3. For an incisive review of this and other books on black power, see Christopher Lasch, *The Agony of the American Left* (New York, 1969), chapter 4.

41. Carmichael and Hamilton, *Black Power*, chapter 2; Cruse, *Crisis of the Negro Intellectual*, 3–10. See also Oscar Handlin, *Fire-Bell in the Night* (Boston, 1964), chapter 1.

42. Whether it is politically feasible is another matter. Cf. Bayard Rustin, " 'Black Power' and Coalition Politics," *Commentary*, September 1966, 35–40, and David Danzig, "In Defense of 'Black Power,' " *ibid.*, 41–46.

43. Except for a brief critical analysis of its economic implications (*Kerner Commission Report*, 404–6).

44. For the differences between this generation and its predecessor, see Gary Marx, *Protest and Prejudice* (New York, 1967), 53–55, 77–79, 185–86, and Angus Campbell and Howard Schuman, "Racial Attitudes in Fifteen American Cities," in *Supplemental Studies for the National Advisory Commission on Civil Disorders*, 17–19, 55–57.

45. Cruse, *Crisis of the Negro Intellectual*, 141–42; George Breitman, ed., *Malcolm X Speaks* (New York, 1965), 45–58; Carmichael and Hamilton, *Black Power*, chapter 1; Eldridge Cleaver, *Post-Prison Writings and Speeches* (New York, 1969), 57–72; Kenneth B. Clark, *Dark Ghetto* (New York, 1965), chapter 2. See also Jerome H. Skolnick, *The Politics of Protest*, a report submitted to the National Commission on the Causes and Prevention of Violence (New York, 1969), 137–43.

46. See chapter 1 above. For a scholarly defense of the colonial analogy, see Robert Blauner, "Internal Colonialism and Ghetto Revolt," *Social Problems*, Spring 1969, 393–408.

47. *Kerner Commission Report*, 248–50; *U. S. News & World Report*, February 21, 1966, 72.

48. Breitman, ed., *Malcolm X Speaks*, 38–42; Carmichael and Hamilton, *Black Power*, chapters 2 and 8; Skolnick, *The Politics of Protest*, 158–62; Roy Innis and Victor Solomon, "Harlem Must Control Its Schools," *New Generation*, Fall 1967, 2; New York *Times*, November 16, 1968.

49. Breitman, ed., *Malcolm X Speaks*, 38–39; Carmichael and Hamilton, *Black Power*, 18–23; Cleaver, *Soul on Ice*, 135–36. For the Black Muslim's diagnosis of the ghetto's economic problems, which foreshadowed the other militants' interpretation, see C. Eric Lincoln, *The Black Muslims in America* (Boston, 1964), 90–93.

50. Floyd McKissick, ⅗ *of a Man* (London, 1969), 151–59.

51. See Rhea Wilson, "Guerrilla War on Poverty" (April 1969), an unpublished paper prepared for the Laboratory for Environmental Studies, M.I.T.

52. On the profits of commercial enterprise in the ghettos see Federal Trade Commission, *Economic Reports on Installment Credit and Retail Sales Practices of District of Columbia Retailers* (Washington, D.C., 1968), chapters 1 and 3.

53. New York *Times*, June 4, 1968.

54. Frederick D. Sturdivant, "The Limits of Black Capitalism," *Harvard Business Review*, January/February 1969, 122–28.

55. Breitman, ed., *Malcolm X Speaks*, 41–42; Carmichael and Hamilton, *Black Power*, 40–44, 166–72; McKissick, ⅗ *of a Man*, 88–95. For an attempt to place the demand for community control in a broader (and nonracial) context, see Nathan Glazer, "For White and Black, Community Control Is the Issue," *New York Times Magazine*, April 27, 1969, 35 ff.

56. Carmichael and Hamilton, *Black Power*, 166–67.

57. David K. Cohen, "The Price of Community Control," *Commentary*, July 1969, 21–32. See also Wallace S. Sayre and Herbert Kaufman, *Governing New York* (New York, 1965), chapter 11.

58. Which is sorely lacking, especially in the schools and welfare departments. See Jacobs, *Prelude to Riot*, chapters 2 and 6; Rogers, *110 Livingston Street*, chapters 8 and 9; Elman, *Poorhouse State*, chapters 1 and 3.

59. But only so long as what the blacks do does not raise their taxes or otherwise inconvenience them.

60. On the struggle over community control of the New York City schools see Maurice R. Berube and Marilyn Gittell, eds., *Confrontation at Ocean Hill-Brownsville* (New York, 1969).

61. For an indication of the impact community control might have on the highway program (and the business and labor interests served by it), see A. Q. Mowbray, *Road to Ruin* (Philadelphia, 1969), chapter 11. And for an indication of the concern community control aroused among liberal groups during the recent New York City teachers' strike, see Milton Himmelfarb, "Is American Jewry in Crisis," *Commentary*, March 1969, 33–42.

62. According to the New York *Times* (March 3, 1968), the liberals included Governor Kerner, Mayor Lindsay, Senator Harris, Senator Brooke, Mr. Wilkins, and Chief Jenkins; and the conservatives included Congressman Corman, Congressman McCulloch, Mr. Abel, Mr. Thornton, and Mrs. Peden.

63. A few of these questions are discussed in Cruse, *The Crisis of the Negro Intellectual*.

64. New York *Times*, March 3, 1968.

65. Chicago Commission on Race Relations, *The Negro in Chicago*; Myrdal, *An American Dilemma*. See also Gary Marx, "Report of the National Commission: The Analysis of Disorder or Disorderly Analysis?" a paper presented at the 1968 Annual Meeting of the American Political Science Association, Washington, D.C., September 3–7, 1968.

66. Hazel Erskine, "The Polls: Demonstrations and Race Riots," *Public Opinion*

Quarterly, Winter 1967, 654–77; Campbell and Schuman, "Racial Attitudes in Fifteen American Cities," 29–38.

67. *Congressional Quarterly*, September 8, 1967, 1737–39.

68. *Ibid.*, 1739–42.

69. New York *Times*, August 17, 1967; March 12, May 14, June 20, 1968; May 1, 18, 29, June 11, 19, July 4, 1969.

70. C. Vann Woodward, "What Happened to the Civil Rights Movement?" *Harper's*, January 1967, 29–37.

EPILOGUE

1. Urban America, Inc., and The Urban Coalition, *One Year Later* (1969), 4–62.

2. New York *Times*, June 5, August 9, 1969.

3. For an attempt to place their problem in a national perspective, see James Q. Wilson and Harold R. Wilde, "The Urban Mood," *Commentary*, October 1969, 52–61.

4. Urban America, Inc., and The Urban Coalition, *One Year Later*, 66–118.

5. "Report from Black America," *Newsweek*, June 30, 1969, 17–35.

6. "The Troubled American," *ibid.*, October 6, 1969, 29–73.

7. Morris Janowitz, "Patterns of Collective Racial Violence," in Hugh Davis Graham and Ted Robert Gurr, *Violence in America*, a report to the National Commission on the Causes and Prevention of Violence (New York, 1969), 408–11.

8. Professional Standards Division, International Association of Chiefs of Police, *Civil Disorders: After-Action Reports Spring 1968*, a report to the Attorney General of the United States, chapters 1–4.

9. Angus Campbell and Howard Schuman, "Racial Attitudes in Fifteen American Cities," in *Supplemental Studies for the National Advisory Commission on Civil Disorders* (Washington, D.C., 1968), chapter 5.

10. For a sample of these warnings, see *Hearings Before the Permanent Subcommittee on Investigations of the Committee on Government Operations: United States Senate, Ninety-First Congress, First Session* (Washington, D.C., 1969), part 20, 4175–4498.

11. "Sniping Incidents—a New Pattern of Violence," in Lemberg Center for the Study of Violence, Brandeis University, *Riot Data Review*, February 1969. See also Louis H. Masotti and Jerome R. Corsi, *Shoot-out in Cleveland*, a report to the National Commission on the Causes and Prevention of Violence (New York, 1969).

12. Barrington Moore, Jr., "Revolution in America," *The New York Review of Books*, January 30, 1969, 6–12. See also Martin Oppenheimer, *The Urban Guerrilla* (Chicago, 1969), chapters 4 and 5.

13. Gary Wills, *The Second Civil War* (New York, 1968). The Federal Bureau of Investigation's *Prevention and Control of Mobs and Riots* (Washington,

Violence as Protest

D.C., 1965) and the Department of the Army's *Civil Disturbances and Disasters* (Washington, D.C., 1968) are quite revealing too.

14. Tom Hayden, *Rebellion in Newark* (New York, 1967), chapter 4; *Hearings Before Special Subcommittee to Inquire into the Capability of the National Guard to Cope with Civil Disturbances: Committee on Armed Services, House of Representatives, Ninetieth Congress, First Session* (Washington, D.C., 1967), 6122–33; Urban America, Inc., and The Urban Coalition, *One Year Later*, 68–70.

15. *Report of the National Advisory Commission on Civil Disorders* (New York, 1968), 484–527; Urban America, Inc., and The Urban Coalition, *One Year Later*, 67–68.

APPENDIX

WHITE ON BLACK

1. Jerry Cohen and William S. Murphy, *Burn, Baby, Burn! The Los Angeles Race Riot August, 1965* (New York, 1966), 78–222; Governor's Commission on the Los Angeles Riots, *Archives*, II, in the University of California Library, Los Angeles (hereafter referred to as MCA).

2. Governor's Commission on the Los Angeles Riots, *Violence in the City—an End or a Beginning?* (Los Angeles, 1965) (hereafter referred to as MCR). For Governor Brown's charge see *ibid.*, i–iii.

3. *Ibid.*, 2–9.

4. California Advisory Committee to the United States Commission on Civil Rights, "An Analysis of the McCone Commission Report" (January 1966); Bayard Rustin, "The Watts 'Manifesto' and the McCone Report," *Commentary*, March 1966, 29–35; Robert Blauner, "Whitewash Over Watts," *Trans-action*, III, March/April 1966, 3 ff.; Harry Scoble, "The McCone Commission and Social Science" (August 1966), an unpublished paper written for the U. S. Office of Economic Opportunity.

5. Robert M. Fogelson, "The 1960s Riots: Interpretations and Recommendations" (1966), a report prepared for the President's Commission on Law Enforcement and Administration of Justice. The Institute's study was prepared under the supervision of Professor Nat Cohen who kindly allowed me to read the findings.

6. Blauner, "Whitewash Over Watts," 2.

7. Chicago Commission on Race Relations, *The Negro in Chicago* (Chicago, 1922); Mayor's Commission on Conditions in Harlem, "The Negro in Harlem: A Report on Social and Economic Conditions Responsible for the Outbreak of March 19, 1935," New York City Municipal Archives.

8. Rustin, "The Watts 'Manifesto,'" 33–34; Blauner, "Whitewash Over Watts," 2–3.

9. Charles J. Hanser, *Guide to Decision: The Royal Commission* (Tottowa, N.J., 1965), chapter 10.

10. MCA, III, Testimony of Lieutenant Governor Glenn M. Anderson, 22; MCR, 1, 3, 5, 24.

11. New York *Times,* July 22, August 4, 1964; Newark *Evening News,* July 20, 1964; New York *Journal-American,* July 26, 1964.

12. MCR, 4–5.

13. MCA, III, Testimony of Lieutenant Governor Glenn M. Anderson, 22–23; XI, Testimony of Police Chief William H. Parker, 87–89; XIV, Testimony of Mayor Samuel W. Yorty, 58–61.

14. Bureau of Criminal Statistics, California Department of Justice, "Summary of a Preliminary Report of Persons Arrested in the Los Angeles Riots" (November 1965), *ibid.,* II; MCR, 24; U. S. Bureau of the Census, *Current Population Reports,* Series P-23, No. 18, "Characteristics of the South and East Los Angeles Areas: November 1965" (Washington, D.C., 1966), 38; *idem, United States Census of Population: 1960. Detailed Characteristics. California. Final Report* (Washington, D.C., 1962), 478, 485; President's Commission on Law Enforcement and Administration of Justice, *The Challenge of Crime in a Free Society* (Washington, D.C., 1967), 75.

15. MCA, XV, interview 29; XVI, interview 90.

16. MCR, 6–7. See also Louis Hartz, *The Liberal Tradition in America* (New York, 1955), chapter 1; Gresham M. Sykes, *Crime and Society* (New York, 1966), 79.

17. Scoble, "The McCone Commission," 11.

18. John F. Kraft, Inc., "Attitudes of Negroes in Various Cities," a report prepared for the U. S. Senate Subcommittee on Executive Reorganization (1966), 5–6; David O. Sears, "Riot Activity and Evaluation: An Overview of the Negro Survey" (1966), 1–2, an unpublished paper written for the U. S. Office of Economic Opportunity.

19. U. S. Bureau of the Census, "Characteristics of the South and East Los Angeles Areas," 38.

20. Institute of Industrial Relations, University of California, Los Angeles, "Hard-Core Unemployment and Poverty in Los Angeles" (Washington, D.C., 1965), 143–45.

21. Sears, "Riot Activity and Evaluation," 1–13; Los Angeles County Probation Department, "Riot Participation Study: Juvenile Offenders" (November 1965); Bureau of Criminal Statistics, California Department of Criminal Justice, "Watts Riots Arrests: Los Angeles August 1965" (June 30, 1966).

22. MCA, XVI, interview 90.

23. John F. Kraft, Inc., "Attitudes of Negroes," 4, 6, 7; Sears, "Riot Activity and Evaluation," 5–6.

24. MCR, 10–12; MCA, XII, Testimony of Benjamin Peery, a longtime Watts resident, 5–6; Cohen and Murphy, *Burn, Baby, Burn,* 50–59.

25. MCA, III, Testimony of Councilman Thomas Bradley, 29–36; V, Testimony of John A. Buggs, Executive Director of the Los Angeles County Human Relations Commission, 18–23; VI, Testimony of Assemblyman Mervyn M. Dymally, 48–49; VIII, Testimony of Congressman Augustus F. Hawkins, 82–85; X, Testimony of Councilman Billy G. Mills, 9–10.

26. Mervyn M. Dymally, "Statement Prepared for the Governor's Commission on the Los Angeles Riots" (October 11, 1965), 2.

27. MCA, VI, Testimony of John Ferraro, President of the Los Angeles Board of Police Commissioners, 5–8; XI, Testimony of Police Chief William H. Parker, 3–36; XIV, Testimony of Mayor Samuel W. Yorty, 58–61.

28. MCR, 27–28.

29. *Ibid.*, 29–37.

30. MCA, XIII, Testimony of Richard Simon, Los Angeles Police Department, 8–9; XIII, Testimony of George Slaff, American Civil Liberties Union, 9–12.

31. For indications of Parker's paranoia, see *ibid.*, XI, Testimony of Police Chief William H. Parker, 16, 37–38, 119, and especially 121, where he claimed that black leaders, "seem to think that if Parker can be destroyed officially, then they will have no more trouble in imposing their will upon the police of America, and that's about what it amounts to, because nobody else will dare stand up."

32. *Ibid.*, XIII, Testimony of George Slaff, American Civil Liberties Union, 9–11.

33. See McCone's statement in *ibid.*, 26–27, and the commission's position in MCR, 28–29.

34. John F. Kraft, Inc., "Attitudes of Negroes," 12–14, 23–25; Walter J. Raine, "The Perception of Police Brutality in South Central Los Angeles Following the Revolt of August 1965" (1966), 2–12, an unpublished paper written for the U. S. Office of Economic Opportunity; California Advisory Committee to the United States Commission on Civil Rights, "Report on California: Police-Minority Group Relations" (August 1963), 7–31.

35. MCR, 12–20; MCA, II; XVI, interview 29; Cohen and Murphy, *Burn, Baby, Burn*, 85–175.

36. Harrison Salisbury, *The Shook-up Generation* (New York, 1958), chapters 2, 5, 6, 11.

37. Rustin, "The Watts 'Manifesto,'" 29–30; Alex Rosen, "The Riots in Watts, Los Angeles," 7, a paper presented at the 13th National Institute on Crime and Delinquency, Atlantic City, New Jersey, June 14, 1966; Fogelson, "The 1960s' Riots," chapter 3.

38. Michael E. DePrano and Jeffrey B. Nugent, "Economic Aspects of the L.A. Riots and Proposed Solutions," MCA, XVII.

39. *Ibid.*, XII, Testimony of Paul Schrade, United Automobile Workers, 42–44.

40. *Ibid.*, Testimony of Thomas Reddin, Los Angeles Police Department, 21.

41. MCR, 38–47, 49–60, 65–67.

42. *Ibid.*, 47–48, 60–61, 67–68.

43. New York *Times*, May 28, 1966.

44. U. S. Department of Labor, "Sub-Employment in the Slums of Los Angeles" (Washington, D.C., 1966). For the commission's remarks on criminal records and employment opportunities, see MCR, 47.

45. Kenneth A. Martyn, "Report on Education to the Governor's Commission on the Los Angeles Riots" (November 1965), 2–30, MCA, XVIII; U. S. Department of Labor, *The Negroes in the United States: Their Social and Economic Situation* (Washington, D.C., 1966), 24–25.

46. U. S. Bureau of the Census, *Current Population Reports*, Series P-23, No.

17, "Special Census Survey of the South and East Los Angeles Areas: November 1965" (Washington, D.C., 1966), 13.

47. MCR, 62–65.

48. MCA, V, Testimony of Harvey Claybrook, an accountant formerly employed in Watts, 8–13; XII, Testimony of Thomas Reddin, Los Angeles Police Department, 21–22; XIII, Testimony of Helen Nelson, Consumer Counsel, State of California, 1–14. See also Rustin, "The Watts 'Manifesto,'" 29–30; Cohen and Murphy, Burn, Baby, Burn, 111, 132; David Caplovitz, The Poor Pay More: Consumer Practices of Low-Income Families (New York, 1963).

49. Loren Miller, "Relationship of Racial Residential Segregation to Los Angeles Riots," MCA, X; ibid., XIV, Testimony of Sue Welch, a junior high school teacher in Watts, 17–22, 47–48.

50. Ibid., III, Testimony of Lieutenant Governor Glenn M. Anderson; VIII, Testimony of Lieutenant General Roderic L. Hill; XI, Testimony of Police Chief William H. Parker.

51. MCR, 17, 19.

52. Citizens Protective League, Story of the Riot (1900): Gilbert Osofsky, Harlem: The Making of a Ghetto (New York, 1966), 46–52.

53. MCR, 17–20; MCA, II; Cohen and Murphy, Burn, Baby, Burn, chapters 15–21.

54. The McCone Commission lumped the Mexicans and blacks together just the same. See MCR, 5.

55. For a fuller discussion of these restraints, see chapter 5.

56. For nationwide estimates see President's Crime Commission, The Challenge of Crime, 75. See also Cohen and Murphy, Burn, Baby, Burn, 208.

57. President's Crime Commission, The Challenge of Crime, 62; Marvin E. Wolfgang, Crime and Race: Conceptions and Misconceptions (New York, 1964), 38–44.

58. MCA, II, 32; Cohen and Murphy, Burn, Baby, Burn, 207; John F. Kraft, Inc., "Attitudes of Negroes," 7.

59. Diane Fisher, "Police Investigatory Practices" (1966), a report prepared for the President's Crime Commission; Richard A. Cloward and Lloyd E. Ohlin, Delinquency and Opportunity (Glencoe, Ill., 1960), chapters 1, 2, 4; Abraham Kardiner and Lionel Ovesey, The Mark of Oppression (Cleveland, 1962), chapter 5; William Brink and Louis Harris, The Negro Revolution in America (New York, 1964), chapters 1 and 2.

60. MCR, 3.

61. MCA, X, Testimony of Judge Loren Miller, 17–18.

62. Ibid., III, Testimony of Herb Atkinson, Vice-President, South Los Angeles Transportation Company, 25; X, Testimony of John C. Monning, Superintendent, Los Angeles Department of Building and Safety, 5–8; XIII, Testimony of Winston Slaughter, Compton Junior College student, 5–29; XIV, Testimony of Edward Warren, Watts real estate broker, 9–11.

63. MCR, 3, 75–80; MCA, X, Testimony of Judge Loren Miller, 17–18. See also Herbert J. Gans, The Urban Villagers (Glencoe, Ill., 1962), chapters 1, 14.

64. MCR, 2, 85–88.

65. MCA, IV, Testimony of the Reverend Hartford Brookins, 24–32; Harry M. Scoble, "Negro Leadership Study: Tentative Findings" (1966), 9, an unpublished paper written for the U. S. Office of Economic Opportunity.

66. MCA, V, Testimony of Wendell Collins, First Vice-Chairman of C.O.R.E., 6–25; Dymally, "Statement"; Cohen and Murphy, *Burn, Baby, Burn*, 119–20.

67. *Ibid.*, 130–31. Nor were moderate black leaders in other cities; see Federal Bureau of Investigation, "Report on the 1964 Riots," September 18, 1964, 3.

68. MCA, III, Testimony of Herb Atkinson, 25; statement by Gloster B. Current in "Community Unrest: Causes, Effects, Prevention, Cure," transcript of N.A.A.C.P. seminar, Columbus, Ohio, April 2, 1966, 27–28.

69. Gans, *Urban Villagers*, 298; Arthur Aryeh Goren, "The New York Kehillah: 1908–1922" (Columbia University doctoral dissertation, 1966); Moses Rischin, *The Promised City* (Cambridge, Mass., 1962), chapter 6.

70. U. S. Bureau of the Census, "Characteristics of the South and East Los Angeles Areas," 34–37. See also Fred E. Case, "Housing in the Los Angeles Riot Area," MCA, XVII.

71. MCA, III, Testimony of Herb Atkinson, 25. See also E. Franklin Frazier, *Black Bourgeoisie* (Chicago, 1957), part 2; Louis E. Lomax, *The Negro Revolt* (New York, 1962), 202.

72. Karl E. Taeuber ad Alma F. Taeuber, *Negroes in Cities* (Chicago, 1965).

73. Robert M. Fogelson, *The Fragmented Metropolis: Los Angeles, 1850–1930* (Cambridge, Mass., 1967), chapter 9. See also Charles Abrams, *Forbidden Neighbors* (New York, 1955), chapters 12–14, 16–18; Commission on Race and Housing, *Where Shall We Live* (Berkeley and Los Angeles, 1958), 36.

74. MCR, 75–80.

75. See P. W. Homer, City Manager, "Report to the Rochester City Council on the Riots of July 1964" (April 27, 1965); New York *Times*, July 22, August 4, 1964.

Index

Abrams, Charles, 141
Accomplishment, sense of, 83, 85
Addonizio, Hugh J., 158
Africa, 9, 10–11, 123, 171; Garveyites and, 146, 170; lack of commerce and industry, 173
Age, and statistics on rioters, 35 ff., 44 ff., 50, 196
Algeria, 127, 187
American Civil Liberties Union, 58, 70; and Los Angeles riots, 201, 202
American Dilemma, An, 157, 178
Anderson, Glenn, 191, 208
Angola, 10
Appalachian area, 94, 209
Arendt, Hannah, 163
Army. *See* Federal troops
Arrests and arrestees, 33–35 ff., 125, 126, 196 ff., 210, 211 (*See also* Police; specific crimes); fear of, as restraint, 105, 112–16, 124 ff., 209–10
Arson (burning), 17, 45, 46, 79 ff., 90–94, 99, 102 (*See also* specific places); survey on shooting of arsonists, 179
Asia, 9, 173
Assault, 45, 50, 79 ff., 94–99, 102. *See also* specific places
Assistant United States Attorneys, 3–4
Atlanta, Georgia, 4, 24, 25; earlier riots, 5; immediate cause of riot-

ing, 53; percentage of blacks, 150; and police complaint procedures, 70; statistics on rioters, 37, 38, 40, 41, 46, 114
Attorney General's Office, xii
Automobiles (cars), 205–6, 207

"Bait-ads," 92–93
Baltimore, Maryland, 26; employment in, 89; and King's assassination, 5, 132, 188; pay for mechanics, 87; possibility of black majority in, 150
Bedford-Stuyvesant (Brooklyn), 1, 25, 95, 119, 196; Abe Stark on riots, 27; statistics on rioters, 37, 38, 40
Birmingham, Alabama, 24
Black Legion, 7
Black Muslims, 13, 146, 170
Black Panthers, 12
Black Power, 13, 146, 168–69 ff. *See also* Community control; Militants; Nationalism and nationalists; specific persons
Blauner, Robert, 193
Bolivia, 187
Bonding, 89
Boston, Massachusetts, 4, 15, 25, 27, 214; Irish in, 99; police, 58, 66, 70; Protestant-Catholic rioting, 14; schools, 88; urban renewal, 139
Brandeis University, 149, 187

255